Library of
Davidson College

Economic Policy Coordination

Moderator
Wilfried Guth

International Monetary Fund
HWWA-Institut für Wirtschaftsforschung-Hamburg

Economic Policy Coordination

Economic Policy Coordination

Moderator
Wilfried Guth

Proceedings of an international seminar held in Hamburg

International Monetary Fund
HWWA-Institut für Wirtschaftsforschung-Hamburg

Library of Congress Cataloging-in-Publication Data

Economic policy coordination : conference organized by the International Monetary Fund in co-sponsorship with the HWWA–Institut für Wirtschaftsforschung-Hamburg in memory of Armin Gutowski / moderator, Wilfried Guth.
   p.   cm.
ISBN 1-557-75025-4
   1. Economic policy—Congresses. 2. International finance—Congresses. I. Guth, Wilfried, 1919-   . II. Gutowski, Armin. III. International Monetary Fund. IV. HWWA-Institut für Wirtschaftsforschung-Hamburg.
HD73.E255   1988
332'.042—dc19   88-23010
                                                              CIP

Price: U.S.$15.00

ISBN 1-55775-025-4
© 1988 International Monetary Fund
INTERNATIONAL MONETARY FUND
Washington, D.C. 20431

Contents

	Foreword	vii
	Introductory Remarks **Wilfried Guth**	ix
1	Economic Policy Objectives and Policymaking in the Major Industrial Countries **Jacques J. Polak**	1
	Comments	
	Helmut Schlesinger	26
	Martin Feldstein	33
	Tyoo Gyohten	37
	Erik Hoffmeyer	40
2	International Adjustment and the Dollar: Policy Illusions and Economic Constraints **William H. Branson**	44
	Comments	
	Niels Thygesen	84
	Alexander K. Swoboda	93
	Hans-Eckart Scharrer	105
3	Empirical Evidence of Effects of Policy Coordination Among Major Industrial Countries Since Rambouillet Summit of 1975 **Günter Großer**	110
	Comments	
	Hans Tietmeyer	135
	Manuel Guitian	142
4	International Coordination of Economic Policies: Scope, Methods, and Effects **Jacob A. Frenkel, Morris Goldstein, and Paul R. Masson**	149
	Comments	
	Jürg Niehans	192
	John Flemming	197

CONTENTS

5   Summary and Conclusions
Wilfried Guth   201

    Appendix   217

The following symbols have been used throughout this paper:

...   to indicate that data are not available;

—   to indicate that the figure is zero or less than half the final digit shown, or that the item does not exist;

–   between years or months (e.g., 1984–85 or January–June) to indicate the years or months covered, including the beginning and ending years or months;

/   between years (e.g., 1985/86) to indicate a crop or fiscal (financial) year.

"Billion" means a thousand million.

Minor discrepancies between constituent figures and totals are due to rounding.

Foreword

The recognition that international policy coordination is crucial for globally balanced economic growth has always been fundamental for the Fund's work. The need for such coordination has assumed new prominence since the major industrial countries met in Paris in February 1987, and, in the Louvre Accord, agreed to intensify coordination to promote more balanced economic growth and to reduce existing imbalances. Since then, the heads of state or government of the major countries have agreed, in the Venice Economic Declaration in June 1987, to strengthen existing arrangements for multilateral surveillance and economic cooperation, and the need for these stronger arrangements has been confirmed by a number of subsequent statements by the ministers and central bank governors of the Group of Seven industrial countries.

With a little over a year's experience with such intensified coordination among the major countries, and against the background of the Fund's continuing involvement in this area, we thought it appropriate to step back and invite a number of practitioners and experts to give their views. The result was a seminar organized by the Fund and cosponsored by the HWWA-Institute in Hamburg in commemoration of the distinguished economist, Armin Gutowski, who was the President of the HWWA-Institute and Professor of Economics at the University of Hamburg until his death in 1988. The papers and comments that are brought together in this volume represent the current thinking of those who have been intimately involved in how coordination has worked, and in how it can be expected to work in the future. Although these views are personal, they are expert, and represent a substantial practical and theoretical contribution to an important debate. My thanks go to all who have contributed to this conference, in particular to my friend Wilfried Guth who has conducted the proceedings of the seminar in an admirable and most productive manner.

MICHEL CAMDESSUS
Managing Director
International Monetary Fund

Introductory Remarks

Wilfried Guth

Ladies and gentlemen:

It is a privilege and a pleasure for me to serve as moderator of this conference with its distinguished authors, panelists, and participants. My pleasure was even greater when I saw the high quality of the prepared papers.

I gladly accepted the invitation to act as moderator because it was our dear and sadly missed friend Armin Gutowski who, together with the International Monetary Fund, initiated the concept for this conference and asked me to take on this task. In addition, I have had close ties with the Fund, where I served as Executive Director from 1959 to 1961 under the inspiring leadership of Per Jacobsson.

I think it is fitting for me to thank the Fund and the HWWA-Institut für Wirtschaftsforschung on behalf of the participants for arranging this high-level seminar in advance of the Annual Meetings of the Fund and the World Bank, which are to take place for the first time in Germay, in Berlin, in September.

The subject of our conference is very topical indeed. Even though the chosen title is more narrowly defined, the central issue of our deliberations is, to my mind economic policy coordination, its virtues, possible pitfalls, and limitations. It is clearly a question of *political* economy and, as the prepared papers show, an extremely complex one in its factual and methodological aspects. Not surprisingly, therefore, the attitudes toward coordination as well as the prescriptions for actual policy issues are highly controversial—although, it seems to me, more so among academics than politicians. Among the latter, the need for international policy coordination or cooperation is today largely uncontested, at least in words if not sufficiently in deeds. The *academic* controversies are highly valuable for our discussion, as they help to bring the real problems into much sharper focus than polished summit statements or Louvre Accords.

Needless to say, international policy coordination is not an entirely new concern. In the past decades we always had a degree of such cooperation, although concerted action was more or less limited to relatively short periods of crisis management rather than crisis prevention. However, in the 1980s the issue of ongoing policy coordination has attracted increasing attention and assumed new dimensions owing to structural changes and some deeply rooted problems in our global environment:

- The interdependence of national economies and policies has greatly increased (a fact that is implied in the title of our conference);
- the former hegemonic role of the U.S. economy (*l'économie dominante*) has to a great extent vanished, although it has retained a special position in important respects;
- in the process of financial deregulation and liberalization, international capital flows have gained overwhelming importance;
- there have been large exchange rate fluctuations and misalignments, especially of the dollar, accompanied by greatly disturbing balance of payments disequilibria and protectionist tendencies; and
- the business and banking communities have responded to these far-reaching changes by developing global or multinational corporate strategies, for example, by replacing trade with international production.

All this implies new challenges to the major trading nations' governments and central banks. And although they have fully recognized that they cannot adequately cope with these challenges individually, their collective effort still leaves much to be desired. As I see it, the basic tasks and questions before them are threefold:

- how to achieve a more satisfactory rate of world economic growth without renewed inflation;
- how to arrive at more stable exchange rates and sustainable external payments balances of the main industrial countries without recourse to protectionism; and
- how to ease the debt problem of the Third World.

I am sure the first two issues will be at the center of our discussions and we should never lose sight of the third one as it is closely interrelated with the others.

I stress these actual world economic problems as we should, in my opinion, always be aware that international cooperation is not an end in itself. The question which must occupy our minds is mainly whether it can help to solve these basic problems. Or, to put the same question differently: why is it that in spite of good intentions on the part of all partners, international cooperation has not produced better results thus far, and how could it be improved? Or, to bring in a more sceptical note which is reflected in a number of the papers presented here: does it make sense to talk about, conceive models for, and try to enact international cooperation as long as the principal partners agree neither on priorities of economic policy objectives nor on the underlying theoretical models or philosophies? Could one not merely rely on the assumption that every country is well aware of its "enlightened self interest" which must take into account the repercussions of its policy actions on its partner countries and their likely reactions?

These might be questions which will arise in the course of our debates and I am sure there will be many others. I am confident that we will all greatly benefit from an exchange of views on these pressing issues among the eminent academics and practitioners who are gathered around this table.

CHAPTER 1
Economic Policy Objectives and Policymaking in the Major Industrial Countries

Jacques J. Polak[1]

Chart A in the 41st *OECD Economic Outlook* (June 1987), which is reproduced as Chart 1, reflects the traditional approach to the judgment of the quality of economic performance. What are called "the usual objectives of real growth, unemployment, inflation and current account equilibrium" are measured along the four axes of a diamond. The judgment is to be read in terms of this diamond. The note at the bottom of the chart tells us that "the more symmetric the diamond, the better balanced the macroeconomic performance" and "within limits set by the current account equilibrium goal, the bigger the diamond, the 'better' the projected performance."[2]

This OECD presentation provides a good starting point for our discussion of the objectives of economic policy in the main industrial countries and the process by which policies are set in these countries to pursue these objectives.[3] (The OECD is the Organization for Economic Cooperation and Development.) It is a good starting point in the negative sense that it shows the traditional framework of economic policymaking that prevailed in the 1960s and 1970s—a framework from which the mode of the 1980s diverges in important respects.

---

[1]The author wants to acknowledge with thanks the assistance he has received from staff members in the European, Asian, and Western Hemisphere Departments of the Fund in the description and analysis of the policies of major countries, as well as from staff members in the Research Department. However, the facts and interpretations as presented in this paper are solely the author's responsibility.
[2]*OECD Economic Outlook* 41 (June 1987), p. 4. As the note to the chart shows, the quotation marks around the second "better" are in the original. They presumably serve to convey the notion that "better" does not necessarily mean better.
[3]Throughout this paper the analysis is restricted to the five largest countries (the United States, Japan, the Federal Republic of Germany, France, and the United Kingdom).

Chart 1. Revisions to the 1987 Projections

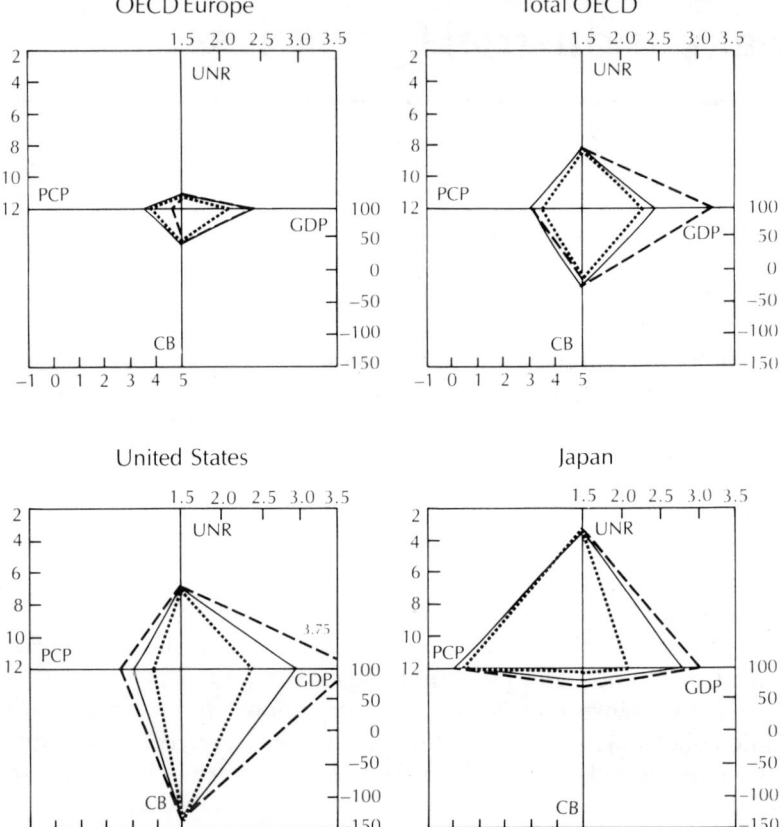

Source: *OECD Economic Outlook* (June 1987).
Note: The more symmetric the "diamond," the better balanced the projected macroeconomic performance in terms of the usual objectives of real growth, unemployment, inflation and current account equilibrium. Within the limits set by the current account equilibrium goal, the bigger the diamond, the "better" the projected performance.

Economic Policies in 1960s and 1970s

Under the earlier mode of policy setting, governments in the main countries—and in the smaller countries as well—did typically have the four objectives for economic policy indicated on Chart 1, as well as some other objectives relating to income distribution, regional development, the support of agriculture, and so on. To achieve the four central objectives, they needed, according to the well-known Tinbergen rule about instruments and targets, at least four policy instruments.[4] These traditionally included fiscal policy, monetary policy, incomes policy, and exchange rate policy. As long as the par value system lasted, the fourth instrument could be used only in rather extreme situations, namely to correct a "fundamental disequilibrium."[5] If this constraint on the use of the exchange rate implies some shortfall of instruments compared with targets, there were many occasions in the 1960s and 1970s where additional instruments were used. Some of these were aimed at holding down inflation—such as price controls—which were used throughout the postwar period in France, and, for example, as late as in 1971–72 in the United States. Other policies involved direct controls to affect the current account of the balance of payments, including advance deposits and temporary surcharges to reduce imports (both used on and off in the United Kingdom), travel restrictions (in Japan, France, and the United Kingdom), export promotion activities, as well as, in the case of the Federal Republic of Germany in 1968, tax measures to restrain exports.

Thus, with a wide variety of policies at their disposal, governments in the 1960s and 1970s pursued an activist line designed to keep their economies as close to the track of the announced policy objectives as was possible. The annual budget process in the United Kingdom, for

---

[4] The formal requirement of equality in numbers of targets and instruments should not be pushed too far in this case: neither the targets nor the instruments mentioned are fully independent *inter se*.

[5] Among the main industrial countries there was indeed a strong tendency not to consider adjustment of the exchange rate as an available policy option at all. A very carefully drafted 1964 statement by the Deputies of the Group of Ten listed six categories of instruments of economic policy (not including exchange rate policy) to counteract a tendency toward a sustained deficit or surplus in the balance of payments, namely "budgetary and fiscal policies, incomes policies, monetary policies, other measures relating to international capital transactions, commercial policies, and selective policies directed to particular sectors of the economy." Then, in the next paragraph, the possibility of use of the exchange rate was allowed, but only as a constraint: "Such instruments must be employed with proper regard for obligations in the field of international trade and for the IMF obligation to maintain stable exchange parities which are subject to change only in cases of fundamental disequilibrium." (Group of Ten Deputies, 1964, p. 5).

example, provided the occasion for a careful weighing of the amount of slack in the economy and the consequent need for corrective fiscal action; in many years, this process was repeated in an autumn budget. In between budgets, the duties on tobacco, alcoholic drinks, and so on, could be raised or lowered by up to 10 percent by means of the "Regulator"; this instrument was invoked in July 1961, July 1966, and November 1968 to raise taxes. In the United States, the Report of the Council of Economic Advisers, brought out each January at about the same time as the Administration's budget proposals, served the purpose of tracing the likely performance of the economy against the objectives as set out by the Employment Act of 1946. In Germany too, after the demise of the "ordo-liberal" school with the formation of the SPD-CDU government in 1966, economic policy activism took over. The "stability law" of 1967 ordered that fiscal policy at all levels of government should be directed toward the objectives of: price stability, a high level of employment, external balance, and appropriate economic growth. But beyond the setting of annual budget policy, a wide array of policy instruments was readied to fine tune the economy in the course of each fiscal year, including freezes on government expenditures, ceilings on public borrowings, additions to government expenditures, and investment premiums to stimulate, and cuts in depreciation allowances to dampen, investment demand. The most powerful instrument established by the "stability law" was the "tax regulator" which could be used to raise or lower both personal and corporate tax rates by up to 10 percent; under that provision, temporary tax increases were introduced in 1971 and again in 1973. Japan often enacted supplementary budgets to provide demand stimulus or to restrain the current account deficit.

At the same time, monetary policy in most countries was expected to play its part in keeping the economy close to its high employment path; however, the Bundesbank has always placed the objective of medium-term price stability above that of full employment.

During this period of policy activism the authorities were, on the whole, successful in keeping two of their economic policy objectives, growth and employment, on track although it should be noted that with respect to the latter, policy had already become less ambitious than it had been in the immediate postwar years, under the aegis of the full employment pledge of Article 55 of the U.N. Charter.[6] The authorities were less successful in dealing with the balance of payments and, from the early 1970s onward, inflation. To keep the indicators of their domestic policy objectives within a narrow range, governments were quite prepared to make frequent adjustments in

---

[6]On this phase of economic policy modification, see Polak (1962), pp. 165–67.

their policy instruments. (As mentioned earlier, they were, however, quite hesitant to use the exchange rate to remedy wide divergences in the current account of the balance of payments from its target of approximate balance.) The sharp distinction between objectives (or targets) as variables about which we care, and instruments as variables about which we do not care, was still *grosso modo* true at that time, although there were indications even then that this distinction began to lose its power in a period when objectives were very nearly attained and the cost of permitting wide swings in instrument variables received increasing notice.[7]

The broad comment to be made about economic policymaking in the main industrial countries in the 1980s is that the activist period highlighted in the preceding paragraphs has passed. To some extent the change in focus may be related to the coming into power of conservative governments, in Britain in 1979, in the United States in 1981, in the Federal Republic of Germany in 1983, and in France in 1986. But this may be a questionable reading of the causal process. In Britain, the Labor Party government shifted policy significantly in 1976. In both Germany and in France, the change in policy preceded the change in governments: Chancellor Schmidt in 1981 and President Mitterrand in 1982 presided over the transition to a more conservative financial policy. Note, also, that in both Australia and New Zealand it fell to the newly elected Labor governments to reverse the previous interventionist policies.

Change in Policy Priorities in the 1980s

The current decade has seen two fundamental changes in the approach to economic policymaking. The first of these has been a radical reordering in the priorities that governments implicitly or explicitly apply to the various objectives of economic policy. The second can perhaps best be described as a weakening distinction between targets (objectives) and instruments; in this process the clear difference in emotional content referred to above between targets and instruments prevalent in the earlier period has been reduced to the vanishing point; it may indeed in some cases have been reversed.

The two major changes mentioned—the reordering among objectives and the reordering between objectives and instruments—are obviously interrelated. Most strikingly, the downgrading of unemployment as a primary concern of economic policy reflects at the same time the disenchantment with incomes policy as an instrument to reduce the price component, and raise the output component, of a

---

[7]Polak (1962), pp. 151–53.

specified increase in money GDP. Nevertheless, the two changes are, to an important degree, separable. The present section will cover the first change, the change in priorities among objectives. The next section, on the changing role of policy instruments, will discuss the new relationship between what, in the past, were the clearly distinguishable concepts of targets and instruments.

Inflation Versus Unemployment

The first switch in priorities among the policy objectives of the major countries is the relative weight attached to the control of inflation on the one hand and the avoidance of more-than-frictional unemployment on the other hand. The received wisdom of the 1960s and early 1970s was that there was a trade-off between these two objectives; the Phillips curve for each country indicated the locus of the trade-off points that the government could choose, and it was seen as one of the advantages of exchange rate flexibility that this regime permitted each country to choose its preferred trade-off.

To be sure, the outbreak of double-digit inflation in all industrial countries in 1973–74, while unemployment rates were still generally low, could explain an increasing relative emphasis on price stability versus employment even without a change in the governments' trade-off scale; and the same comment might still be applicable to the 1979–80 constellation, with the resurgence of inflation throughout the industrial countries in response to the second oil shock. But this interpretation is clearly not applicable to the current scene, where high unemployment rates—in most European countries—coexist with low-to-zero inflation rates. The persistent concern about actual or potential inflation, in conjunction with the limited action against unemployment rates of 10 percent or more, is an obvious indication of a shift in priorities.

The reordering of priorities has probably been most explicit in the United Kingdom. Under the "medium-term financial strategy," first presented in the budget for 1980/81, it was stated that "the Government's objectives for the medium term are to bring down the rate of inflation and to create conditions for a sustainable growth of output and employment" (H.M. Treasury (1980), p.16). In pursuit of this objective, an extremely tight monetary policy was introduced in 1980,[8] which led to a sharp appreciation of sterling and a severe recession, in part because the government's policy engendered credibility in financial markets, but not in labor markets where wage-push inflation continued unabated. Ultimately, credibility for the anti-inflation pol-

---

[8] Matthews and Minford (1987), p. 62.

icy was established not by the achievement of its monetary targets (they were, in fact, exceeded) but by the refusal of the government to react to a recession which proved deeper than had been anticipated.[9]

In the United States, drastic action against inflation had been inhibited during most of the 1970s by the expectation that the cost in terms of loss in output would be prohibitive. Writing in 1978, Arthur Okun had estimated that cost at 10:1, meaning that a loss of 10 percent of real GNP would be required to bring the annual inflation rate down to 1 percent.[10] Throughout much of the 1970s, the prevailing rate of inflation was decried as "unacceptably high" (a term often used in the Fund's *Annual Report*); yet it was, in fact, accepted. A radical attack on inflation did not begin until the autumn of 1979, when the Federal Reserve changed its operating procedures as the only available method to put a stop to its previous, accommodating, monetary policy. The measure produced a sharp recession, with unemployment approaching 11 percent in late 1982. In contrast to earlier recessions, this situation was not met by recourse to a reflationary policy.[11] Subsequently, however, an expansionary fiscal policy, a relaxation of monetary policy, and greater wage flexibility in the United States than in Europe made for a gradual decline in the unemployment rate, toward a level close to that of the mid-1970s. The relatively quick improvement in the employment and unemployment figures in the United States while inflation remained low did not raise the issue of the priority of alternative policy objectives as sharply as in the United Kingdom, or elsewhere in Europe.

In the Federal Republic of Germany, unemployment has been about 8 percent since 1983, twice as high as in the late 1970s; even with inflation near zero, this situation has not led to the adoption of general policies to expand demand. In France, the Mitterrand government came to power in 1981 on a strong platform to reduce unemployment;[12] nevertheless, the unemployment rate in France has increased every year to reach about 11 percent in 1987 as against 6.6 percent in

---

[9]Buiter and Miller (1983), p. 362.

[10]Cagan (1986b), p. 256. Ex post estimates arrive at much lower figures of this "sacrifice ratio," ranging from 2 to 4 or 6, depending essentially on the assumptions made regarding the potential of the economy (p. 258).

[11]In his *Economic Report* of February 1982, the President stated: "The Administration views the current recession with concern. However, it is of the greatest importance that we avoid a return to stop-and-go policies of the past. The private sector works the best when the Government intervenes the least. The Government's task is to construct a sound, stable, long-term framework in which the private sector is the key engine to growth."

[12]"Une volonté: l'emploi. Une méthode: la relance. Un moyen: la solidarité." Projet de loi de finances pour 1982, Rapport économique et financier.

1980. The priorities were clearly switched in 1982. Having decided to stay in the exchange rate mechanism of the European Monetary System (EMS), the government's immediate objective became to reduce the inflation differential with other participating countries and to achieve equilibrium in the current account. Growth and employment were thus temporarily removed from the forefront of policy objectives. In the process, the approach to incomes policies was reversed. In support first of the devaluation in March 1983 and then of policies aimed at enhancing competitiveness and profitability, a policy of wage restraint was adopted. As a result, the long succession of years during which wages had risen in real terms at the expense of profitability was broken. Fiscal policy became focused toward achieving small, gradual reductions in the budget deficit expressed as a percentage of GDP by means of expenditure reductions. Emphasis was given to strengthening the financial position of newly nationalized enterprises. Over time, the authorities also initiated a major shift toward the deregulation of financial markets and reduced reliance on quantitative controls.

In Japan, unemployment had always been lower than in the other industrial countries and it rose marginally (from 1.4 percent to 2 percent) in the period 1974 to 1978 when inflation was brought down sharply. Even that modest rise may at least in part have been due to a noncyclical rise in Japanese unemployment, which continued throughout the 1980s to a rate of about 3 percent at present.

Output Targeting

With a varying degree of precision depending on the country, policy in the 1960s and 1970s had been formulated in terms of achieving a specified level of output, or, planning ahead from the current level, a specified growth rate for output. Specifically, the concept behind this policy was to approximate as closely as possible the full employment output trend. The pursuit of this concept (even if it was not directly operational) was particularly explicit in the United Kingdom, as well as in the United States, where it was mandated by the Employment Act of 1946. Targeting of a physical level of output was judged to be compatible with the containment of inflation, provided "full" employment was not defined in an excessively ambitious manner and other policy instruments, such as incomes policy and the control over installment sales (hire purchase), were brought in as needed.

In the 1980s, by contrast, output targeting has largely disappeared from economic policymaking in the major industrial countries. To be sure, official "targets" or "projections" for the growth rate of real GNP are still being released in these countries, with the notable exception of the United Kingdom. But these numbers have little if any operational content. They are forecasts or projections of a conditional character, saying essentially that if exogenous factors—such as the exchange rate of the country's currency against the U.S. dollar, or the upcoming wage round—develop as expected, GNP is expected to grow by – percent over the next year. Since there is room for differences of view with respect to the conditions imposed on the model, there is also room for introducing a certain degree of optimism in the forecasts for real GNP, without doing violence to the model itself. It is not surprising, then, that in some countries official growth "targets" have shown an optimistic bias.

But, whatever the accuracy of these numbers, these targets do not act as policy triggers if the outcome differs from the targets. If performance is reasonably in line with the announced figures, governments congratulate themselves. But if the outcome falls short of the "target," there is no presumption that policy action will be taken to correct the situation. Instead, there may be explanations: the dollar depreciated more than expected, the winter was excessively severe, etc.; and there may be the announcement of more pleasing "targets" for the next year or the next quarter. Two recent instances of this "jam tomorrow" approach, both relating to the United States, may be recalled.[13] Early in 1986, a disappointing growth rate for the last quarter of 1985 was reported (1.2 percent, about half of the earlier estimate); the administration announced at the same time a robust 4 percent growth target for 1986.[14] Half a year later, this target was acknowledged as unrealistic (the outcome proved to be 2.2 percent), but again the pill was sweetened by a simultaneous release of an estimate for 1987 growth at 4.5 percent.[15]

The abandonment of operationally meaningful growth targets for the economy should not be seen—as it probably would have been seen 10 or 15 years ago—as a dereliction by governments of their responsibilities. It reflects, rather, a new and chastened view on how growth can be promoted over the long term. The new philosophy was clearly expressed in a December 1985 programmatic paper by the German Federal Ministry of Finance: "In an economic system based on free enterprise, economic growth is not so much the aim as the result of market processes. The task of the public sector is not to realize the highest possible growth rates at the cost of unwarrantable

---

[13] . . . the Queen said: "The rule is, jam tomorrow and jam yesterday — but never jam today." Carroll (1871).

[14] *New York Times*, February 21, 1986.

[15] *New York Times*, July 25, 1986. The outcome for 1987 was 4.0 percent.

fiscal policy measures, but to ensure that economic activity can develop unhindered and is provided with sufficient incentive. The price signals transmitted by the market must reach the recipients . . . with as little distortion as possible. Sound public finances will increase the confidence of markets in the dependability of policies. Well-ordered public budgets are thus an important basis for long-term decisions . . . and part of the foundation of an efficient free-market system."[16]

Similar views on the issue of the most effective policy for economic growth can be found in other industrial countries.[17] Indeed, the extent to which official opinion in general has moved away from the growth activism of earlier decades can be inferred from the radical change in evaluation of the concept of "fine tuning" of the economy: in the 1960s and 1970s, it conveyed the notion of the consummate skill of economic policymakers; in the 1980s, "fine tuning" stands for a new taboo which (like any generally respected taboo) needs no further explanation.

Nominal Targeting

While governments stepped away from attempts to regulate output, they have tended to show more confidence in their ability to keep nominal demand (for example, nominal GNP) on track. Thus, they approach demand management as an exercise of achieving a desired growth rate for nominal demand, without the ambition to determine the split of the growth in nominal GNP between a price component and a quantity component. The authorities in the United Kingdom, a country where policymaking in the past had perhaps suffered more than elsewhere from excessive concern with "real" variables, have been particularly clear on the fundamental difference in approach that is implied in nominal versus real targeting. The medium-term financial strategy, which (it should be recalled) was introduced at a time of double-digit inflation, was addressed to a gradual reduction of the rate of growth in nominal GDP. Since 1985/86, the annual outlook figures at budget time include tentative target ranges for the growth in nominal GDP. In the same context, numbers are also provided for the

---

[16]Federal Ministry of Finance (1985), p. 19. This view of the role of economic policy can be seen as a reversion to ideas expressed 40 years earlier by Ludwig Erhard, the guiding spirit behind the "miracle" of Germany's postwar recovery.

[17]In France, for example, Minister Balladur (Economy, Finance and Privatization) stressed the change from short-run to medium-term policies and gave as an example of this change in focus: "Rather than introduce measures to give investment an artificial and transitory fillip by direct fiscal stimuli, we have preferred supporting investment by improving company profitability by lowering the burden of company taxation . . . ." (Budget presentation, October 13, 1987).

possible price and quantity components of GDP, but these numbers are described as "assumptions," not "targets," to underline the authorities' position that the distribution of the growth in nominal GDP would be determined entirely by market forces. (Although the distinction between "targets" and "assumptions" establishes a clear hierarchy in the degree of official commitment, the tentative target ranges suggest only a limited commitment even at the top of the hierarchy.)

The switch to nominal GDP or GNP as the target variable for economic policy coincided, not surprisingly, with increased attention to monetary aggregates as intermediate control variables. If the assumption is valid that income velocity in terms of one or another of the wide array of monetary aggregates is stable, then, of course, control of that aggregate will at the same time ensure control over nominal GDP. This is not the place to review in detail the (remarkably short!) story of the rise and decline of monetary targeting in the 1980s. Suffice it to state that the rapid deregulation of the financial system—itself a reflection of the same market-oriented policy stance that lay behind the movement away from fine tuning demand—had the effect of undermining the assumption of stable velocity that would have to be fulfilled to make monetary control effective. Thus both the United States (between 1979 and 1983) and the United Kingdom (over a somewhat longer period), went through a succession of monetary aggregates and finished by not paying a great deal of attention to any of them. The Federal Republic of Germany was more successful in adopting from the start (for the year 1975) a monetary aggregate, namely central bank money, that could be controlled in most years within a relatively narrow band. The central value for the growth rate for money was based on the growth of potential output, a minimum tolerable rate of inflation, and any estimated change in velocity (Deutsche Bundesbank (1985)). Since early 1987, however, certain weaknesses have transpired with central bank money as the monetary target, in particular that its growth might be biased upward, from the the point of view of controlling nominal GDP, by the demand for deutsche mark notes in the grey economy and, in Eastern European countries, as a substitute for the dollar as a parallel currency. In the light of this evidence, the Bundesbank has switched to M3, which in recent years has been growing more slowly than central bank money. One may perhaps wonder how long it will take before it is discovered that the income velocity of M3 is subject to certain quirks too, and the Bundesbank may have to follow the Federal Reserve and the Bank of England in the direction of a more judgmental basis for its monetary policy.

France joined the practice of other central banks in the 1980s of announcing money supply targets. This approach to monetary policy in a country that was struggling with recurrent balance of payments difficulties was open to question, since it tended to invalidate the auto-corrective mechanism by which payments deficits would tighten domestic liquidity. As the smaller members of the EMS had recognized from the start, money supply targeting is not compatible with exchange rate pegging. The same comment would also be of some relevance to monetary policy in the United Kingdom since the time that it has—de facto and approximately—pegged sterling to the deutsche mark.

Of all the major countries, only Japan has not made a radical change in its monetary policy in the 1980s. This is in line with the greater continuity of economic policy in Japan generally, to be discussed presently. Monetary policy, whose main operational target is the level of short-term interest rates, continues to be made on a judgmental basis, in the light of both domestic demand conditions and the exchange rate for the yen. The Bank of Japan does follow the practice of other major countries of announcing each quarter a projection for the growth of broad money (M2 + certificates of deposit), but the operational significance of this projection is minimal, since it is made from the same quarter of the preceding year—that is to say, it covers a year of which nine months have already passed into history.

The distinction made in this section between targeting real growth and nominal GDP was of great importance in countries such as the United Kingdom where the rate of inflation was high. It should be noted, however, that the distinction loses its significance as the inflation rate drops to zero. Of the five countries considered, this observation carries the greatest relevance for Japan, where inflation (as measured by the consumer price index) has been at about 2 percent or less for the last five years (1983–87). This success of Japan in bringing inflation under control may explain why Japan has found it less necessary to abandon the judgmental approach to demand management, in the execution of which it has used both monetary and fiscal policy in a flexible way (see the subsection on fiscal policy in the next section).

Balance of Payments

The balance of payments could not but remain an important objective of policy where (1) the imbalance to be avoided was a deficit, not a surplus, and (2) this deficit posed financing problems. At some stages in the past decade, this applied to France. Large surpluses of Japan and the Federal Republic of Germany could be viewed as a problem from a world point of view; it is less clear that these surpluses were seen as incompatible with the economic objectives of the countries concerned, except in an indirect way as they could lead to protectionist policies abroad. The huge current account deficits of the United States in the 1980s initially provoked a quite different response from that caused by the small payments deficits of the 1960s. In the 1960s, U.S. policy was quite clearly directed toward reducing balance of payments deficits in the framework of the par value system, including the use of such rather unattractive instruments as the Interest Equalization Tax to influence the capital account. In the 1980s, on the other hand, up to September 1985, the current account deficit and the accompanying heavy inflow of capital into the United States were officially regarded as evidence of the strength of the U.S. economy.

Changing Role of Policy Instruments

The willingness of the authorities to change some economic variables (instruments) in order to change or to stabilize other economic variables presupposes a clear distinction of the welfare effects of the former compared with the latter. The lesson of the 1960s and 1970s is that this distinction may, after all, not be clear and that there may well be a point beyond which the manipulation of instruments may be more costly in terms of welfare than the welfare gain that could be derived from greater stability of what are traditionally considered as target variables.

Incomes Policy

The clearest case of re-evaluation of an instrument is presented by the virtual disappearance of incomes policies from the policy armory of the main industrial countries, except, as mentioned, France. In the 1970s, when incomes policy was still treated as a respectable instrument, it used to be stressed that that policy should be used "as a supplement to sound fiscal and monetary policies, but not as a substitute for them."[18] Experience showed, however, that this was a counsel of perfection: countries that relied on incomes policy typically failed to adopt demand policies of sufficient strength or relaxed them in the light of the apparent anti-inflationary success of the incomes policies (see, for example, the United States from late 1971 to 1972). Most countries have drawn the lesson from this that even though incomes policies might assist in the containment of inflation in the very short

---

[18]International Monetary Fund (1976), p. 18. Suitable incomes policies were described as "useful adjuncts" to other policies in the Fund's 1979, 1980, and 1981 *Annual Reports*, after which references to incomes policies ceased.

run, reliance on such policies tends to increase inflation over the longer run. Indeed, the remarkable reduction in the inflation rate in most industrial countries has been brought about without the help of—one could fairly say, thanks to the abandonment of—incomes policies.

The disappearance of incomes policy has, of course, had an immediate effect on the ability (or the presumed ability) of governments to regulate the short-run distribution of the growth in nominal demand between price increases and output increases. Thus, strictly speaking, governments can no longer have objectives for these two variables separately, only for their sum. This is explicitly recognized in the U.K. approach, mentioned above, which recognizes only "assumptions" for these variables. Again, the contrast is less stark in Japan and Germany, where the rate of inflation is both very low and (perhaps therefore) predictable within narrow margins.[19] The implication of this loss of an instrument on the issue of international policy coordination will be taken up in the next section, which deals with the broad implications of coordination.

Fiscal Policy

With respect to fiscal policy as practiced in the 1960s and 1970s, the general experience has also been less than satisfactory. First, the promise of Keynesian anticyclical fiscal policy that the authorities would promptly offset any shortfall in private demand by fiscal stimulus became increasingly regarded as an invitation to inflationary price and wage setting by all groups in the private sector; without some effective nominal constraint, inflationary action by the private sector was virtually risk free. Second, the authorities experienced great difficulties in finding the correct timing for their fiscal action; policies designed to be anticyclical all too often worked out to be procyclical.[20] Third, the reverse component of the anticyclical policy, fiscal contraction to offset excessive strength in private demand, often tended to be even less prompt. More generally, the all-pervasive belief that government expenditure was "good for the economy" produced over time an increase in the ratio of this expenditure to GNP that *had* to be brought

---

[19]Switzerland, now that it has essentially a zero rate of inflation, goes one step further; it sets its monetary targets on the basis of the growth potential of its economy. (Russo and Tullio (1987), p. 41.)

[20]A typical example was the stimulative fiscal package introduced in the Federal Republic of Germany with the budget for 1979, pursuant to Germany's undertaking at the 1978 Bonn Summit. By the time the public works under this package added to demand in 1979–80, a private construction boom was also underway, and the official construction program was phased out at the same time as private building activity subsided.

to a halt for a number of well-known reasons: the economic cost, in terms of incentives, of attempting to match even in part the growth in official expenditure by raising taxes; the increasing government deficits, and hence the rise in the government debt, as taxes could not be raised as fast as expenditure; and, finally, the risk that the service of the enlarged government debt could itself become the flywheel of ever-increasing deficits.

For all these reasons it became necessary in country after country to take a radically different view of government finance. The variable which, in the hey-day of Keynesianism, had been regarded as an instrument that could be manipulated to achieve the stabilization of the economy, now needed itself the urgent attention of policymakers. In particular, policymakers had to establish credibility for their new approach to fiscal policy, based on the principle that they were no longer prepared to validate any excesses of the private sector. For this purpose, official commitment to a medium-term program of fiscal policy was a particularly important step, and measures of this general intent were most explicitly taken in Japan and the United Kingdom: in the former country by the adoption of the fiscal consolidation plan in 1980, and in the latter by the announcement of a path for the contraction of the public sector borrowing requirement as part of the medium-term financial strategy introduced in 1980. The three-year path for the borrowing requirement in the United Kingdom was raised somewhat in 1981 and 1982, as the recession turned out to be deeper than the authorities had expected, but in fact only part of the automatic stabilizers was accommodated; and between 1983 and 1986, no further significant changes in the path for public borrowing were made, even though there were temporary disturbances such as the coal strike. Changes in fiscal policy in mid-year are no longer made. In the Federal Republic of Germany as well, the process of reducing the government deficit has received high policy priority, which has acted as an obvious constraint to the adoption of more expansionary fiscal action that might bring about a reduction in the current account surplus.

In the United States, too, the concept of adjusting fiscal policy to indicators of the short-term cyclical position has lost a great deal of weight. But the main reason why fiscal policy has become less available as a policy instrument has been the extreme difficulty of introducing any major measures to correct the large deficit that was created by the income tax reductions and the increases in defense spending introduced at the beginning of the Reagan Administration.[21] Unlike in

---

[21] Action to correct the deficit was, moreover, stymied by (1) the officially voiced expectations that the tax cuts would result in large increases in tax receipts and (2) the

other countries, fiscal policy in the United States has not been set on a course that is considered desirable and which therefore should not be subjected to needless short-run adjustments; more nearly, in the United States, fiscal policy is immobilized on a course that continues to produce "unacceptable" fiscal deficits. Though to a large extent political, the fiscal immobilism in the United States also reflects an increasing awareness of the economic limitations on the use of fiscal instruments for the control of aggregate demand, in particular, the fear that a reversal of income tax reductions would have undesirable incentive effects on supply.

The change in policy emphasis appears somewhat less pronounced in Japan. Since 1980, the main objective of fiscal policy in Japan has been to strengthen the fiscal position of the central government which had deteriorated in the second half of the 1970s. The medium-term goal of fiscal consolidation was to eliminate deficits on current account of the central government by fiscal year 1984/85. But the announced purpose of the plan was to restore flexibility to fiscal policy, and the pace of consolidation has been adjusted in response to short-term developments in the economy.

Thus, when confronted with weak growth in the early 1980s, the government pushed back the target date for external payments balance to 1990/91. Substantial progress toward the goal had been made by 1986/87, when the deficit on current account had been approximately halved, to 1½ percent of GNP. Capital spending was also reduced and with the improvements in the position of the social security funds and the local governments, the deficit of the general government declined from 4½ percent of GNP in 1979/80 to ½ of 1 percent of GNP in 1986/87.

With the slowdown in growth in 1986, the focus of budgetary policy for 1987/88 shifted again to support economic activity, although fiscal consolidation continued to be pursued. A package of measures was introduced in May 1987 to support domestic demand, but this package consisted mostly of public works expenditure by the central government and local authorities, which does not affect the target of fiscal consolidation. In spite of some tax reduction, the government's current deficit is expected to decline, but there will be some increase in the deficit of the general government. But that deficit too is expected to resume its downward course in 1988/89 as the economy continues its recovery, in response to a major improvement in the terms of trade as well as the (relatively mild) fiscal stimulus.

---

theory espoused for some time by the U.S. Treasury that fiscal deficits could not be held responsible for high real interest rates.

Pressure from abroad as well as the need to respond to domestic political factors may well have played a role in the frequent instances in recent years where Japan's fiscal and monetary policies were adjusted in the light of changing demand conditions; moreover, the adjustments did not always achieve the desired (stimulative or contractionary) effects. Nevertheless, it would appear that Japan has preserved a greater degree of policy flexibility than most of its major trading partners.

In general, concern for the long-run efficiency of fiscal policy in the industrial countries has turned that policy into a much less flexible instrument for the control of aggregate demand than was assumed only a decade ago.[22] Fiscal policy does get used to influence aggregate demand—but only when the case for action (domestically or as urged by trading partners) has become overwhelming.

Structural Policy

This is the place to devote some attention to "structural policy," or "micro-policy," that did not rank in the major league of economic (macro) policies before the 1980s, but that has since acquired that status.[23] Under optimistic assumptions, structural policy could (operating from the supply side) be expected to fill, in part, the voids left by the disappearance of incomes policy and the retreat of fiscal policy on the demand side.

When conservative governments came into power in Britain, the United States, the Federal Republic of Germany, and France, each announced as a major component of its platform a reduction of the role of the government in the private economy of the country, through such measures as deregulation and privatization.

In principle, such policies could have had a major impact on the performance of the major economies—by increasing competition, lowering costs, reducing the share of government in GNP, and raising efficiency and thus economic growth. Indeed, "structural reform" (or action against Eurosclerosis) has often been put forward as the pre-

---

[22]The following observations are pertinent in this connection: "The experience of many countries, both industrial and developing, indicates that fiscal policy is not like a faucet that can be turned on and off. It is relatively easy to create a large deficit, as the United States proved in 1981. It is very difficult to reduce a large deficit, as the United States has been proving since 1982. There is a clear asymmetry in fiscal policy. Most spending programs once in place cannot be easily removed. Taxes are easier to reduce than to increase. These facts should bias the attitude of policymakers toward caution." (Tanzi (1988), p. 38.)

[23]This was not true for the Federal Republic of Germany, where structural policy was seen as very important in the 1950s and 1960s.

ferred alternative to fiscal stimulation to bring about higher growth rates in Europe. In Germany in particular, where fiscal and monetary conditions have become less stringent in the last year and real incomes have benefited from improvements of the terms of trade, the scope for increased consumption and investment as inhibiting restrictions are relaxed could be substantial.

In practice, however, the results of the new policy stance have generally been unimpressive. In the United States, the zeal for regulatory reform soon faded as reform of social regulations in particular met too many political impediments.[24] Financial deregulation, which had started under the Carter Administration, is still in an uncertain state.[25]

In the Federal Republic of Germany, too, only little progress was made on deregulation and, contrary to the authorities' announced intentions, subsidy payments continue to increase. Some progress was, however, made in labor market legislation in 1984–86, which reduced the trade unions' bargaining power in labor disputes, facilitated the hiring of youths and part-time workers, and increased the flexibility of labor contracts. In France, the new approach is perhaps still too young to permit any assessment. Only in the United Kingdom has there been a sharp change in the business climate. The power of trade unions, which exceeded that in most other countries, has been radically curbed; this has facilitated large-scale labor shedding and raised unemployment, but it has not put an end to the upward pressure of wages of the employed. Privatization of large state-owned enterprises has significantly reduced the government's role in business, and continues to help the public sector borrowing requirement. The elimination of exchange control and the Big Bang recasting of the London financial markets have been instrumental in consolidating London's position as the major European financial center.

Monetary Policy

Monetary policy has become the preferred instrument in many countries since 1979, in the hope that the prescription of a certain growth rate for some monetary aggregate would bring about the same growth rate for nominal GDP. (A weaker version of the same hope was that control over a suitable monetary aggregate would provide

---

[24]Cagan (1986a), Introduction, p. 2. Similarly, Boskin (1987): "The consensus is that progress has been slow on general deregulation," (p. 68).

[25]"Despite a philosophical commitment to fewer regulations and more competition in financial services, the Reagan administration has little to show in the way of concrete financial deregulation. The elimination of ceilings on deposit interest rates is the major achievement in the deregulation of depository institutions." (Pyle (1986), p. 186.)

the much-needed "nominal anchor" that would keep inflation down to a few percentage points below the growth of that aggregate.) Note that under this approach monetary policy was being assigned to a domestic task, the control over GDP, no doubt in recognition of the fact that the earlier expectations for the performance of this task by fiscal policy had been disappointed. However, one instrument cannot serve two purposes; the consequence was that monetary policy was not available to regulate the balance of payments. Thus, the only exchange rate regime compatible with this approach was free floating. This fitted the mood of the major countries at the time.

We can perhaps leave it as a moot point whether this approach to monetary policy fell out of favor because it proved inefficient to its assigned task (owing to unpredictable changes in velocity) or because of disenchantment with leaving the exchange market as the residual of policies in other areas. Thus, without much fanfare, monetary policy in recent years has, to an important extent, been reassigned to the international task of keeping exchange rate movements within acceptable (or unavoidable) limits; that is to say, it has become, to a smaller or larger degree, depending on the country, the instrument to achieve the objectives of exchange rate policy.

There is little doubt that this is a task that monetary policy can normally perform. Moreover, if considerable freedom is allowed to exchange rates (as, for example, under the target zone system with wide bands), monetary policy should frequently be able to take time off from its exchange rate assignment and thus become available to help out with the management of domestic demand.[26]

Exchange Rate Policy

These observations on monetary policy lead to a comment on the role of the exchange rate as a policy instrument. That role needs to be differentiated in accordance with the exchange rate regime under which countries conduct their international economic policies. In a stable rate regime, such as the EMS, changes in the peg are available as a policy instrument. They have been used by France (as well as by other EMS members) to remove the pressure arising from higher rates of inflation than in the Federal Republic of Germany, when that pressure began to affect market expectations. But care has been taken, especially in the more recent years of the EMS (say, since 1983), not to use the exchange rate as too easy an escape valve for inflation by not treating the EMS regime as an automatic crawling peg, but instead to take advantage of every realignment to bring the aim of convergence

---

[26]Williamson and Miller (1987), p. 48.

on a low inflation rate for the European Community closer to reality.

In contrast with France, the exchange rate policies of the other major countries operated within the parameters of a floating rate regime.[27] But within this regime, the policies of other countries were constrained by the choice made by the United States.[28] As long as the United States followed a hands-off policy on the exchange rate for the dollar, there was little that Germany or Japan could do for the dollar/DM and the dollar/yen rate respectively—unless they had been prepared to take the risk of pegging on the dollar. Like the dollar in 1980–85, sterling in 1980–82 was allowed to be priced on the basis of "market forces" (read in this case: U.K. monetary policy), without government intervention in the exchange markets. As the damage done by the uncontrolled appreciations of their respective currencies sank in, first in the United Kingdom and then, in the second half of 1985, in the United States, exchange rate policy again became an option, and this also provided new opportunities for exchange rate management in Germany and Japan. Of course, still in a floating rate regime, exchange rate management meant management of the exchange rate by means of another policy instrument, primarily monetary policy. Since expectations on the medium-term strength of the dollar hinged importantly on the outlook for control of the budget deficit, fiscal policy also acquired a (mostly psychological) role in relation to the short-term management of the exchange rate. During 1987, the exchange rate policy of other countries vis-à-vis the U.S. dollar has increasingly begun to resemble the practices in the latter years of the par value system, where exchange rate stability became a policy objective by itself, supported more strongly by intervention and exhortation than by changes in underlying policies. This has led to the expansion of monetary aggregates in some other countries beyond what would be found desirable from the point of view of domestic demand—leading, of course, to some adjustment via this route.

Some Implications for International Policy Coordination

It is not the purpose of this paper to enter into the issues that coordination of macroeconomic policies among major countries presents. This final section serves merely to highlight certain implications from our findings that may be relevant to the subject of policy coordination.

---

[27]For the United Kingdom, up to early 1987, when stability of the £/DM rate became a dominant objective.

[28]This shows that the Fund's Article IV, Section 2(b), to the effect that each member may select the exchange arrangement of its choice, is only true within limits.

As a framework for this discussion, I refer to the "blueprint" set out by Williamson and Miller (1987) as a version of what would be widely accepted as a model of cooperative interaction of national economic policies.[29] The design of the blueprint can, in essence, be summarized in a few sentences.

(1) In each country, fiscal policies should be adjusted from time to time to achieve national target rates of growth in nominal domestic demand. These target rates should be set in such a way as to steer the economy over time toward a real growth rate determined by capacity growth and price stability (assuming the compatibility of these two targets).[30]

(2) Monetary policy in industrial countries should be aimed at achieving differences in short-term interest rates which, together with exchange market intervention, assure the exchange rate objectives of the system.

(3) With n fiscal policies and (n–1) interest rate differentials lined up to perform the adjustment tasks of the system, there remains one more variable, the average level of world (real) short-term interest rates, which can be adjusted to keep world growth ("the sum of the target growth of nominal demand for the participating countries") on the desired path.

If we compare the public discussion on policy coordination with this blueprint and with the findings in the preceding pages, we discover that some rather glaring discrepancies emerge.

GNP Growth Rates

There is no publicly available information on the use made of various possible indicators of the Group of Seven discussions. However, insofar as the debate with regard to growth rates is conducted in public, it would appear to proceed without taking adequately into account (1) policy practices as they have developed in the last decade

---

[29] The blueprint is designed to show how a target zone system of exchange rates can be made to work; this question is not considered here, and the applicability of the blueprint is wider than that particular exchange rate regime.

[30] The concept of approaching desired targets over time would presumably imply that supply shocks would, to a considerable extent, be accommodated in the short run, with their effects being squeezed out over time. The target for nominal domestic demand would always *aim* at a steady state equilibrium, but it would most likely never get there.

A closely related question is the proper definition of the price level for purposes of this exercise. As suggested by Tobin (1987), p. 67, in a slightly different context, "price targets should be for indexes of domestic value added . . . . A country should not contract demand just because depreciation of its currency has raised the local price of oil products . . . .If and when these price changes feed into domestic factor costs, they will become relevant to macroeconomic policy."

and (2) rules for policy setting that are essential to achieve the adjustment and growth objectives of the system.

As to (1), public debate seems to focus predominantly on real growth rates, with inflation rates kept in the background as a potential constraint, but one that in present circumstances is considered as virtually negligible in importance. The clear implication is that countries should seek to achieve certain real growth rates and that they fail in their obligations to their partners, as well as in their duties in the context of the debt problem, if they allow their economies to underperform on this score.

Yet, as we have seen, governments do not wield policy instruments that are directly aimed at real variables. Their instruments influence ("control" would be too strong a term) nominal demand, with the distribution between the real component and the price component no better than an informed guess ("assumption," the term used in the U.K. approach, should perhaps be qualified as an understatement).

Next to the real/nominal discrepancy, there is the question how output is defined from the point of view of international cooperation. There is no evidence that the indicator for growth endorsed at the Tokyo meeting of the Group of Seven was anything else than the growth rate for total GNP. This overlooks the fundamental point that total demand equals domestic demand plus or minus the foreign balance, with the latter co-determined by the exchange rate and demand policy abroad. In an international context, the proper distribution of responsibilities in terms of demand management is for each country to look after its own domestic demand, and to make that variable grow above or below the growth rate of potential output, depending on the amount of slack or overheating in the economy and the state of the current account of the balance of payments. Any other assignment of responsibilities creates a "free-rider" conflict: countries with an undervalued currency can, without having to face fiscal conflicts, maintain their growth rates thanks to export surpluses, while their trading partners appear to fail in their duties in terms of GNP, even though they maintain domestic demand at an appropriate level.[31]

The importance of the distinction between total and domestic demand for purposes of policy coordination is by no means a new one. It

---

[31]Polak (1981), pp. 14–15. In theory (as discussed there) the free-rider problem could also be overcome by expressing the requirement for demand management in terms of GNP and relying for the distribution between the domestic and the net foreign component on exchange rate surveillance. Experience to date with surveillance would suggest that it might be a more promising approach to concentrate on domestic demand directly.

was, indeed, incorporated in the Declaration issued by the 1978 Bonn Summit.[32] In a recent statement Helmut Schlesinger notes that "it is uncontested, in particular, that in deficit countries domestic demand must grow more slowly than overall output, while in surplus countries the growth rate of domestic demand should exceed the pace of expansion of GNP."[33] With this theoretical point so thoroughly established, it seems surprising that the coordination effort has paid it so little attention.

Is Fiscal Policy up to its Task?

In any system in which exchange rates are not entirely left to market forces—including such wide variations of regime from leaning against the wind, reference rates, target zones in any of the many versions, and "stable but adjustable rates," up to the gold standard—monetary policy must remain available to help achieve or maintain the exchange rate objectives of the system. Monetary policy may sometimes be available to help out in demand policy; but in some of the most difficult moments of an adjustment program its setting may be determined by the demands of its exchange rate task. Sometimes, this may be helpful to achieve the objectives of demand management, as when the exchange rate needs to be defended and demand disinflated. But in "conflict situations," such as may be brought about by a recession abroad, the performance of its primary duty by monetary policy may add to the burdens of fiscal policy to regulate demand.

As indicated in the earlier subsection on fiscal policy, such policy in most of the main industrial countries can no longer be treated as the patient workhorse of economic management, ready to move in one direction or the other at a tug at the reins. On the contrary, governments have learned the hard lesson that fiscal policy itself needs to be treated with a considerable dose of Tender Loving Care in the present in order to keep it in good enough health for the uncertain tasks of the future.

While fiscal policy can be assigned the task of influencing nominal domestic demand in the desired direction, governments can no longer credibly promise (or expect credible promises from their trading partners) that moves in the fiscal stance can quickly change the demand situation. Also, with short-run changes in fiscal policy now

---

[32]Paragraph 3 of this Declaration stated: "A program of different actions by countries that face different conditions is needed to assure steady non-inflationary growth. In countries whose balance-of-payments situation and inflation rate does (sic) not impose special restrictions, this requires a faster rise in domestic demand." Cited in Polak (1981), p. 20.

[33]Schlesinger (1988), p. 1.

seen as costly in themselves, governments will want to see relatively large and/or persistent indications of the need for adjustment before changing fiscal course.

These changes in attitude toward the fiscal instrument could well explain at least part of the slowness of the international adjustment process in recent years; and to the extent that the attitude reflects inherent structural limitations of fiscal policy, intensified attempts at international coordination of policy may be more productive in terms of understanding of each others' problems than in removing imbalances.

Two further considerations need, however, to be adduced to put this finding into proper perspective. The first is that the reduced flexibility of fiscal policy may in part be temporary. This would be the case to the extent that some period of fiscal rigidity may be needed to convince the public that the days of fiscal pliancy (upward pliancy, of course) are over. The experience of the Federal Reserve with a rigid monetary policy after October 1979 is instructive in this connection; once the Federal Reserve had for three years running established a clear track record of resisting inflationary pressures with whatever degree of tightness of the money supply was required, it could relax that tightness to meet deflationary pressures in the U.S. (and the world) economy without provoking a new outbreak of inflation. Over time, a government that has established its fiscal conservatism may thereby have gained a useful degree of flexibility in its use of fiscal policy for the future. As indicated in the previous subsection on fiscal policy, Japan may already have succeeded in overcoming the cycle from excessive flexibility via excessive rigidity to workable flexibility.

The second consideration is that it is very difficult, on the basis of a small number of country cases (each of which has, of course, its own peculiarities) to determine in an objective way the degree of fiscal inflexibility that is needed, first to stamp out the overly optimistic expectations of the past and then, on a permanent basis, to preserve the integrity of the fiscal tool. Inevitably, the operationally relevant opinion presented on this subject—both to the electorate at home and to interested governments and institutions abroad—is that of the authorities in power in the country concerned. That opinion may well represent an inseparable mixture of economic judgment concerning the usability of the instrument and political judgment concerning the desirability of using it. If the lady does not want to tango, she is nicer if she blames a hurting ankle than just says "no." The outsider may find it difficult to discern the true reason; nor would it help him much if he could. Even if the potential usability of the instrument could be established in an objective way, this might not facilitate much the process of international policy coordination: that process requires not only the availability of instruments to achieve desired objectives, but just as much a unity of view as to what these objectives are.

REFERENCES

Boskin, Michael J., *Reagan and the U.S. Economy* (San Francisco: Institute for Contemporary Studies, 1987).

Buiter, Willem, and Marcus Miller, "Changing the Rules: Economic Consequences of the Thatcher Regime," *Brookings Papers on Economic Activity:2* (1983), The Brookings Institution (Washington).

Cagan, Phillip, ed. (1986a), *Essays in Contemporary Economic Problems, 1986. The Impact of the Reagan Program* (Washington: American Enterprise Institute).

———, (1986b), "Containing Inflation," in Cagan (1986a).

Carroll, Lewis, *Through the Looking Glass*, 1871.

Deutsche Bundesbank, "The Longer-Term Trend and Control of the Money Stock," *Monthly Report*, January 1985, p. 19.

Federal Ministry of Finance, *Tasks and Objectives of a New Fiscal Policy: The Limits to Public Indebtedness* (Bonn: Bundesministerium der Finanzen, 1985).

Group of Ten Deputies, *Report to Ministers and Governors by the Group of Ten Deputies* (Paris: Group of Ten, 1964).

H.M. Treasury, *Financial Statement and Budget Report, 1980/81* (London, March 1980).

International Monetary Fund, *Annual Report* (Washington: I.M.F., various issues).

Matthews, Kent, and Patrick Minford, "Mrs. Thatcher's Economic Policies, 1979–87," *Economic Policy*, No. 5 (1987).

Polak, Jacques J., "International Coordination of Economic Policy,"*Staff Papers*, International Monetary Fund (Washington), Vol. 9 (July 1962), pp. 149–81.

———, *Coordination of National Economic Policies*, Group of Thirty Occasional Paper No. 7 (New York: Group of Thirty, 1981).

Pyle, David H., "Financial Deregulation," in Cagan (1986a).

Russo, Massimo, and Giuseppe Tullio, "Monetary Policy Coordination Within the EMS: Is There a Rule?" Conference on the EMS, Perugia, 1987 (unpublished).

Schlesinger, Helmut, "Will We Ever Achieve World-Wide Coordination of Economic Policies?" Deutsche Bundesbank, *Monthly Report*, No. 8, February 1, 1988.

Tanzi, Vito, "Fiscal Policy and International Coordination: Current and Future Issues," Conference on Fiscal Policy, Economic Adjustment, and Financial Markets, Milan, 1988 (unpublished).

Tobin, James, "Agenda for International Coordination of Macroeconomic Policies," in Peter B. Kenen, ed., *International Monetary Cooperation: Essays in Honor of Henry C. Wallich*, Essays in International Finance No. 169 (Princeton, New Jersey: Princeton University, December 1987).

Williamson, John, and Marcus Miller, *Targets and Indicators: A Blueprint for the International Coordination of Economic Policy* (Washington: Institute for International Economics, 1987).

Comment

Helmut Schlesinger

Jacques Polak's paper provides a stimulating introduction to the national and international economic policy problems currently facing the major industrial countries. Polak's encyclopedic knowledge of the details of the historical development enables him to analyze penetratingly the profound change of style that has taken place in general economic policy as well as in the monetary policies of many industrial countries. Happily, he does not abstain from economic policy assessments, which bear his own unmistakable stamp. Since I myself belong to a generation whose economic outlook was shaped by the conditions of the tempestuous 1950s and the "golden" 1960s, and no less of course by the disappointments of the turbulent 1970s, I find Polak's paper very attractive in this respect, too. But although I was exposed to, and influenced by, the pendulum swings in economic policy objectives and philosophies, in retrospect my verdict would perhaps differ slightly in some particulars.

Up to the beginning of the 1970s it was possible to speak of a "post-Keynesian basic consensus" among the leading economic policymakers in the major industrial countries, albeit with national modifications. The thinking behind this consensus reached the Federal Republic of Germany with a distinct time lag. During the successful 1950s the influential economists who built up the intellectual framework of the "social market economy" were no close admirers of Keynes. But then, under the strong influence of Karl Schiller, the ideas of Keynes and Walter Eucken, the architect of "German neoliberalism," were amalgamated. Anticyclical behavior was chosen as the guiding principle of German fiscal policy.

This to a large extent common platform, which (as Polak rightly notes) from the outset met with a rather skeptical response from the Bundesbank, seems to have quite disappeared. Today, any comments on fundamental or current questions of national and international economic policy first require the discussants to define where they stand. Polak's remarks on the special features of "activist" and "nonactivist" economic and monetary policies avoid any oversimplified categorization, but if his comments were to be ascribed to an "enlightened neo-Keynesian" rather than to a "pragmatic monetarist," to use Lamfalussy's categories, I hope that this would not be unjust.

On the basis of my own experience, I look back on the 1960s and early 1970s with less nostalgia than Polak does. I am also less optimistic than he is that, given the successes achieved to date in the field of stabilization and consolidation policy, monetary and fiscal policy can now be set to work efficiently again in the cause of demand and exchange rate management of the traditional type, even though the number of advocates of such a policy is growing. While I agree with Polak's overall assessment in many respects, let me take up a few of the points he touched upon in which I detect certain disparities which presumably derive above all from differences in our economic and monetary policy starting points.

In assessing conditions during the 1960s and 1970s, which some advocates of an "activist" budgetary and monetary policy stance today look back upon in rather a favorable light, I would sometimes put the emphases in slightly different places. I have no wish to deny that, during the period when economic policy action was dominated by the use of economic policy tools to achieve the "magic quadrangle," some industrial countries scored considerable successes in the field of growth and employment policies. The question which arises in this connection is, however, to what extent the economic growth that was achieved is attributable to these policies or to other factors.

Specifically, I have two comments on this question:
(1) The highly satisfactory growth and employment figures recorded in many industrial countries from the mid-1950s to the second half of the 1960s were due in substantial measure to distinctly favorable supply-side conditions. The fact that real GNP in the OECD countries was expanding during that time at an annual trend rate of 4½–5 percent was due, among other things, to the very low level of commodity and energy prices over a long period, the rapid spreading of comparative cost advantages, technology transfer in the wake of the intensification of cross-border trade and capital transactions, the release of labor from shrinking sectors with low labor productivity (such as agriculture), immigration into the more developed industrial countries, and the spreading of cost-curbing mass production to up-market consumer goods. Against this background, an OECD growth study compiled in 1970 for the period up to 1980 concluded with an optimism that is almost unthinkable today: "The risk for modern industrial countries is not that of not achieving growth."[1]

(2) It appears to me—also in the light of German experience—to be certain that the discretionary use of fiscal and monetary policy (with an expansionary "bias") and the "fine tuning" of aggregate demand at the limits of full employment and beyond, especially in the five to seven years up to the eruption of the first oil crisis in 1973, paved the

---

[1]*The Growth of Output, 1960–1980* (Paris: Organization for Economic Cooperation and Development, 1970), p. 8.

way for the later emergence of stabilization crises and impediments to growth. Inflationary expectations grew seemingly irresistibly and took on more concrete shape, struggles over income distribution increasingly affected wage and price formation, and the ballooning of public expenditure and tax ratios, the spreading of government intervention in the market, and growing market rigidities lessened the efficiency of the free market system. These signs of crisis were clearly discernible even before the two oil shocks exposed the industrial countries to quite exceptional additional pressures, and these oil price hikes themselves were not solely an exogenous factor but—apart from the hectic movements—a successful endeavor to prevent the real price from falling more sharply, as it had done until 1973.

Against this macroeconomic background, unlike Polak, I would not say so unambiguously that in the late 1970s and early 1980s the economic policy priorities had been shifted deliberately in favor of combating inflation and of "conservative" structural and supply-side policies. The governments in office at that time, regardless of which political party they belonged to, had no choice but to try to protect the market-economy conditions prevailing in the industrial economies from further serious erosion. In the words of a leading U.S. Keynesian (A.M. Okun), during the 1970s the "Phillips curve" became an "unidentified flying object"; administrative price and wage controls foundered either on the lack of a social consensus or because "incomes policy" very often only amounted to an attempt to stop the consequences of fundamental factors, especially inflationary influences, which was bound to fail. In particular countries (such as the United States) the system of fixed exchange rates permitted pent-up inflation to develop at times. However, in the countries where price movements had been relatively moderate at first, massive buying of the U.S. dollar had become necessary, with the result that control over domestic monetary trends was being lost.

In the view of some major central banks there was, therefore, no real alternative to the abandonment of the fixed rate system and hence to a transition to a more nationally orientated monetary policy. However, the strategy pursued from the mid-1970s onward—in fact, from as early as 1975 in a few major countries, if I may add this in amplification of Polak's paper—of adopting pragmatically handled "monetary growth rate rules" likewise pursued the objective of persuading the general public as well as management and labor that monetary policy would not be accommodating again and that it would be important to keep the cost of fighting inflation as low as possible. At all events, the Bundesbank, which was the first central bank to announce an annual monetary target (at the end of 1974), interpreted its "experiment" along these lines from the very beginning.

As far as the currently pressing issues of international economic policy or monetary and economic policy cooperation are concerned, Polak has generally placed the focal points where I would put them too: in the eyes of world public opinion, the achievement of appropriate noninflationary economic growth has become a key economic policy problem in the industrial countries (unlike the situation as recently as the early 1970s). The outlook in this area can be lastingly improved only if the disturbing disequilibria among the industrial countries can be eliminated and, moreover, the debt problems of the Third World progressively resolved. To this end, cooperative monetary and economic policy strategies appear to be essential, although—as Polak to my mind quite rightly points out—approaches of this kind must not overlook the fact that the style of economic policy has changed during the 1980s. Unless I am much mistaken, the major countries are not on the threshold of a return to old-time religion demand management policies, to fine tuning in monetary policy, to anticyclical fiscal policy, or to a Bretton Woods system in a new guise. (But I may indeed be mistaken; swings of this kind can never be ruled out entirely.) The following points corroborate this view.

A main point of effort in economic policy today is generally deemed to be the improvement of supply-side conditions in the broadest sense. In the international arena, this should first be a matter of lessening the substantial risks which the global economic disequilibria present to investment propensity and the operation of the financial markets. Second, the fight to prevent new restrictions from being imposed on international trade and capital movements, the circumvention of the formal GATT regulations and the like must be continued. (GATT is the General Agreement on Tariffs and Trade.) Similarly, all industrial countries must strive to contain the misdirection by agricultural policy. The ambitious project of the common European internal market planned for 1992, which is being strongly promoted by Germany, might well be instrumental in reducing the numerous international impediments to competition in the shape of regulations, government-owned firms, and subsidized firms. It may be rather an overstatement for the EEC Commission to claim that the planned project might yield a growth gain equivalent to over 4–6½ percent of Community GNP for the European Community countries by the end of the 1990s, but there should be no doubt at all about the economic usefulness of this European initiative, even if particular intractable problems (such as those posed by agricultural, transportation, and communication policy), which have rarely diminished but often actually increased in the last 30 years, set bounds to enthusiasm.

Such efforts, which have an international bias from the start, must be accompanied by stronger national endeavors to put "one's own house" in order (microeconomically speaking) in the area of structural policy. The OECD in Paris, which relied rather one-sidedly on traditional demand management for a long time, has demonstrated in a recent report the extent to which production and adjustment conditions in many sectors in the industrial countries have deteriorated, primarily as a consequence of undue government intervention.[2] The moves concerned are not simply distorting and conserving measures but also include the disproportionately rapid expansion of the public sector and social budgets, the increase in taxes and social security contributions, and—not least in Germany—the system of subsidies. However, Germany's modest successes in the field of deregulation, in the consolidation of the public sector and social budgets, and in the promising reform schemes which are due to be implemented in 1989 and 1990 show clearly that this is an arduous path with limited room for maneuver, since social groups' and other pressure groups' thinking in terms of vested interests and inertia may make radical reform packages appear to be politically unattainable. In this connection, the way in which a government is formed (whether it is a coalition government or government by a majority party) is also of some significance.

In this situation, with respect to longer-range global growth prospects, I think we have to admit without illusions that the growth successes of the first decades after the war, which were achieved under exceptionally favorable supply-side conditions, are unrepeatable today in the industrial countries. Nor do they need to be repeated. After all, economic growth is not a final goal. National prosperity is a goal; high employment is a goal; peace between the social groups of a society is a goal; and social fairness is desirable. Preservation of nature as a basis for human existence is a goal which is increasingly being recognized as a duty in the old, densely populated but still fairly prosperous industrial countries. And the figures of the real gross national product, which are often invested with almost mystical properties, reflect this at best highly imperfectly.

This is not to say that there is no reason or room for an active shaping of shorter-term economic activity. The Federal Republic of Germany, for instance, has shown in the last two years that it remains prepared to respond flexibly to unusual internal and external economic policy challenges. Monetary and fiscal policies have been

---

[2]*Structural Adjustment and Economic Performance* (Paris: Organization for Economic Cooperation and Development, 1987).

steered onto an expansionary course in consideration of Germany's surplus position, the steep appreciation of the deutsche mark, and temporary signs of cooling off in domestic business activity. In the process, we have achieved respectable economic growth rates in Germany, with rises in GNP of 2½ percent in 1986 and 1¾ percent in 1987, and are anticipating an increase of 2 percent and more in 1988. Needless to say, the short-term growth prospects for a country that is running down its real external surplus position are not particularly good. In 1986 and 1987 alike, the real foreign surplus declined by an amount equivalent to 1¼ percent of GNP, and this tendency will persist in 1988, albeit less rapidly. These trends gave rise to substantial frictional adjustment burdens for German industry, which is much more dependent on foreign trade and exposed to international competition than is, say, Japanese or U.S. industry; moreover, these burdens cannot be offset at will by domestic stimulatory measures. To be sure, in order to foster the adjustment process and promote orderly exchange rate movements, we have tolerated a marked overshooting of the annual monetary targets more than once; moreover, the medium-term deficit estimates for the public sector budget in Germany have been substantially overshot. Hence it can hardly be maintained that monetary and fiscal policy in Germany have completely forfeited their traditional instrument role.[3]

By thus departing temporarily from the steadying course of its monetary and budgetary policy over the medium term, Germany is deliberately contributing to a globally coordinated adjustment strategy which Polak, if I understand him rightly, endorses: in the major surplus countries the growth rate of domestic demand should be above that of GNP, while in the deficit countries domestic demand should expand more slowly than total output. Political and institutional obstacles naturally set limits to globally coordinated adjustment strategies of this kind; it would be unrealistic to disregard them. In addition, care must be taken to ensure that the flexible, discretionary use of monetary and fiscal policy instruments does not in the longer run trigger developments which are clearly incompatible with the medium-term stabilization and consolidation goals of the countries concerned.

---

[3] A well-known "enlightened Keynesian" even drew the following conclusion from a description of German monetary policy that I gave on another occasion: "It is hard to imagine a clearer description of a purely discretionary regime . . ." (A.S. Blinder, "The Rules-Versus-Discretion Debate in the Light of Recent Experience," Paper prepared for the Kiel Conference, Institute of World Economics, Kiel, June 1987, published in: *Weltwirtschaftliches Archiv*, Vol. 123, No. 3 (1987), p. 409). This characterization is of course not quite in keeping with my intentions, but it does show how little the Bundesbank's reputation of being a "bastion of monetarism" seems to be warranted.

In this connection I should like to make an—open—remark on the comments which Polak's paper contains about the relationship between exchange rate management and national monetary policy: for the central banks of the major industrial countries, the stabilization of nominal exchange rates has not of late been a goal "in its own right," as it was toward the end of the Bretton Woods system; nor can it in the future become the central banks' main function, regardless of the prevailing circumstances, to try to implement fixed targets for exchange rate movements. It is true that central banks have recently been willing to maintain orderly conditions in the foreign exchange markets, as far as possible, by means of coordinated interest rate measures and interventions, and to foster the real adjustment process; indeed, no central bank outside the United States has the option of adopting an attitude of "benign neglect" vis-à-vis exchange rates. Central banks' most important function, however, resides in the fact that they collectively bear the ultimate responsibility for the "global rate of inflation" and that each individual major central bank is responsible for the stability of the purchasing power of its own currency. In the long run, these functions inevitably fall to the lot of monetary policy, since they cannot seriously be assigned to government incomes policy without endangering the foundations of free-market systems. This is why the monetary policies of the major industrial countries must provide a nominal anchor for economic policy decisions and thus facilitate the attainment of medium-term stabilization goals. Where the major countries are concerned, however, nominal exchange rate goals cannot form such an "anchor"; indeed, as past experience has shown, they may provide the instrument for synchronized national monetary policies which may expose the world economy to a cycle of unduly expansionary or unduly contractionary monetary influences.

A final remark should not be suppressed either: a forward-looking monetary policy, geared to stable prices over the long term, is possible in principle both with and without pre-announced monetary targets. Indeed, good monetary policy is conceivable without them, and bad monetary policy with them, as I said when they were first introduced 13 years ago. Hence, monetary targets, the benefits of which Polak seemingly rates rather low at present, have never been treated by the Bundesbank as targets in their own right, but have always been regarded literally as "intermediate targets"; however, we thought and still think these targets helpful in making clearer to the public the abstract process of stabilizing the value of paper money. We can also collaborate with central banks which attach less importance than we do to monetary indicators, as well as with central banks which set less store by monetary stability. But those who are counting on our constructive involvement in "blueprints" of international economic and monetary policy cooperation should please bear in mind: participation in cooperative international strategies—both within the EEC and worldwide—should be expected of us only if preservation of the stability of the purchasing power of money continues to be regarded as the principal contribution which monetary policy can make to the maintenance of favorable global growth conditions. This is what German monetary policymakers are prepared to do—no more, but no less; in point of fact, they feel positively under an obligation to act along these lines.

Comment

Martin Feldstein

Jacques Polak has given us a fascinating and very useful review and analysis of the changes in macroeconomic policy during the past 25 years. It is especially helpful that he looks at the process of policy formation in each of Group of Five countries and does so within a common analytic framework. The result is a paper that traces the intellectual development of macroeconomic policy during the past quarter century as well as the changes in the policies themselves.

I agree completely with the key theme of Polak's analysis. He characterizes the development of the past quarter century as a retreat from macroeconomic policy activism. This retreat has not been the result of an ideological shift but of the recognition of the limits of activist government stabilization policy. Polak presents substantial evidence dealing with the experience in all of the major countries. His conclusion is undeniable.

A recurrent theme of the analysis is the growing emphasis on monetary policy as countries recognized that incomes policy and Keynesian fiscal policy are ineffective or actually destabilizing. The combination of reduced activism and a shift to monetary policy also paralleled a change in the focus of macroeconomic policy from the discretionary stabilization of employment and economic activity to a reduction of the rate of inflation.

At one point in his paper Polak discusses the shift in macroeconomic policy in the language of Jan Tinbergen as a shift away from some instruments and suggests that this was because of a change in preferences about the instruments per se. Although this idea that policy officials could have preferences about "instruments" as well as about "targets" is familiar to economists because of the work of Hans Theil, I think Polak's argument is not convincing. As he himself shows, the instruments of fiscal policy and of incomes policy were dropped not because of a "political aversion" to these instruments but because experience had shown them to be counterproductive.

Guidelines for Monetary Policy

Polak's discussion raises a central issue in the design of monetary policy. He correctly emphasizes the distinction between targeting monetary aggregates and using the management of monetary aggregates to target nominal GNP. I wish he had said more about this important issue.

I find nominal GNP targeting a very attractive approach. While it may not be the best of all ways to guide monetary policy, I think it is preferable to traditional targeting of monetary aggregates. Its key virtue is that it provides a practical and non-arbitrary way of adjusting monetary aggregates to exogenous shifts in velocity.

Nominal GNP targeting would avoid the inflationary excesses of the type observed in the United States and elsewhere in the 1970s. It would also provide an understandable guide to what the monetary authority is doing and therefore a better basis for confidence that observed changes in interest rates or money growth rates do not represent a weakened resolve to prevent increased inflation.

There are three commonly proposed alternatives to nominal GNP targeting: pure fixed money growth; ad hoc judgment without any nominal GNP anchor; and targeting exchange rates. I think that the nominal GNP approach is better than any of these alternatives.

A fixed money growth rate does prevent secular increases in inflation but would in practice (even if not inevitably in theory) lead to excessive short-term fluctuations of real activity and of employment when changes in financial institutions and banking rules lead to shifts in the demand for money.

A policy of "using good judgment"—that is, permitting any ad hoc action—is frightening to financial markets when the decision makers are seen to have very diverse views and when the financial markets do not have great confidence in the understanding and judgment of the monetary authorities. This is an even greater problem in countries where the central bank is subject to direct political influence.

Polak discusses the targeting of exchange rates as an alternative guide for monetary policy. It is not clear from the text whether he is advocating this or just describing it. My own view is unambiguous: targeting the exchange rate is a bad idea that confuses a real and a nominal magnitude.

Changes in real exchange rates play an important role in guiding the international allocation of resources. For example, an increase in real energy prices requires an offsetting realignment of real exchange rates. Since Japan is very dependent on imported oil, a rise in the price of oil requires a yen depreciation. A change in technology or tastes also requires offsetting real exchange rate adjustments. The increased capability of the newly industrialized nations to produce a range of intermediate technology products and high technology products requires a relative decline in the real value of the countries whose products they displace internationally.

Shifts in national saving rates also require offsetting shifts in real exchange rates. When the United States stimulated a sharp drop in the national saving rate by increasing budget deficits significantly, the real value of the dollar rose and the resulting increase in the current account deficit permitted a major capital inflow.

Of course, shifts in the observed nominal exchange rate may reflect nothing more than changes in the underlying price levels or the expected rates of inflation. A rise in the price level induces a currency devaluation while a rise in inflation that makes a currency more risky may also cause a fall in the value of the currency. The advocates of targeting exchange rates see it as a way to control such inflation-driven changes in exchange rates.

The danger in this process however lies in using changes in monetary policy to alter the nominal exchange rate when there are real exchange rate shifts. When the United States slowed the growth of money in 1987 in an attempt to stop the decline of the dollar it caused a rise in interest rates that slowed the economy's expansion and was a precipitating factor in the stock market decline. Earlier in the decade, there were many who advocated that the United States ease money as a way of stopping the dollar's sharp rise. That increase in the real value of the dollar was caused by the decline in the U.S. national saving rate and the dollar rise provided the mechanism for transferring capital to the United States from the rest of the world. The primary effect of an expansionary monetary policy that stopped the nominal rise in the dollar would have been a rise in the U.S. inflation rate while the real value of the exchange rate would have remained essentially unaffected.

Structural Tax Policy Changes

Polak's discussion of this topic completely ignores a major area of national economic policy: changes in tax structure. This is perhaps natural since such structural changes are not aimed at cyclical or price level conditions but at long-term resource allocation and economic growth. But structural tax policy has been a central instrument of government policy in dealing with these longer-term goals and has recently moved to center stage in the policy debate in a number of countries.

The key distinction that must be emphasized in this context is between the traditional Keynesian use of tax changes as fiscal policy instruments aimed at changing disposable income in order to stabilize economic activity with the structural use of tax policy to change relative prices and therefore long-run resource allocation.

During the 1980s the United States reduced the top individual income tax rates from 70 percent to 50 percent and then to 28 percent. Such tax rate reductions are now being copied worldwide. The purpose of these changes is to increase the incentives for individual effort, saving, and entrepreneurship. Lower tax rates also reduce the temptation to enter into investments that are driven by tax considerations rather than by pretax real rates of return. If these tax reforms are successful, they should increase the rate of economic growth and improve the allocation of resources.

Reducing personal tax rates is only one form of targeted tax policy. Other tax changes have been aimed at increasing personal saving rates and increasing investment in plant and equipment. The recent U.S. tax reforms were advocated as a way of making investment "more efficient" by reducing inter-asset distortions in effective tax rates (for instance, between equipment and structures) but may have been counterproductive by inadvertently increasing other inter-asset distortions even more (for example, between business investment and owner-occupied housing investment and between physical capital investments and investments in training and advertising).

Structural tax policies can play another role in the international economy. As the international mobility of capital increases, countries cannot control their own real interest rates. They can however influence the mix between consumption and investment by tax rules that influence the demand for investment at any given real interest rate.

I might add in this context that my emphasis on tax policies even in this international context is on the development of good national policies and not on the international coordination of structural tax rules. What is needed in this area of economic policy as elsewhere is better national policies and not more attention to the international coordination of policies.

As we look to the future of macroeconomic policy, it will be important for governments to consider more explicitly the structure of tax rules as well as other microeconomic policies that influence the allocation of resources. The paper by Polak provides a very useful historical analysis on which to base such a discussion of the redirection of economic policy in the future.

Comment

Toyoo Gyohten

As a practitioner who, almost by accident, happened to be one of the junior participants in the series of Group of Five and Group of Seven meetings over the last three or four years, I found Jacques Polak's paper extremely intriguing. His very rich assessment and well-balanced, objective analysis also made the paper very persuasive. I particularly liked his finding about the role of fiscal policy—that at the moment it needs to be treated with a considerable dose of tender loving care to keep it in sufficiently good health for the uncertain tasks of the future. As a treasury man, I would very much like to compliment this finding.

Being stimulated by Polak's paper, I would like to remark briefly on the progress of national economic policy coordination, particularly in the 1980s because that decade is still with us and has seen a very dramatic change. In retrospect, the decade of the 1970s was not very pleasant for all of us. It brought the collapse of the Bretton Woods regime, two oil price crises and ensuing stagflation, and, toward the end of the decade, the rather unfortunate experience of the so-called locomotive theory. I think these experiences made policymakers less confident, because it was quite clear that the industrialized world alone could not decide the destiny of the world economy. We also suffered a sense of loss because the world economic system seemed to have lost its anchor. So monetary authorities became more cautious and more conservative in establishing and formulating their policy objectives and the means to attain them. At the same time, this situation provided the rationale for the more self-oriented policy postures in many countries that became very apparent in the early part of the 1980s.

So when the 1980s set in, the macroeconomic policies of the major countries were, I am afraid, rather disorganized. But as I said earlier, there was during the 1980s a very dramatic shift from self-oriented policy formulation to a more world-oriented stance, and, in my view, the single most important determinant of the shift was the very serious international disequilibria which became most obvious in the early 1980s. The policy coordination efforts initiated by the industrialized countries like the Group of Five or the Group of Seven were certainly a product of such developments. These series of efforts to produce better coordination among the major industrialized countries can, in my view, be broadly categorized into three different stages. Interestingly enough, these three different stages were not planned beforehand; rather I think they evolved according to a learning process.

A predominant feature of the first stage of coordination was the strong emphasis on exchange rate realignment. By September 1985 everybody was of the view that the dollar was overvalued and something had to be done to rectify the situation. The famous Plaza Accord which was agreed in September 1985 had made that point very clear, as the communiqué shows. Although we talked about lists of macroeconomic policies to be pursued by the members, it was very obvious that the overwhelming thrust was on the exchange rate realignment, and how to weaken the dollar. Since the five countries agreed to make strong concerted actions in the exchange market to achieve that goal, the exercise as a whole involved the intervention and exhortation mentioned by Polak in his paper rather than coordinated action on macroeconomic policy. However, the strategy worked; the dollar depreciated very rapidly. Why? In my view, it was only because the dollar was definitely overvalued at that time. The yen's exchange rate vis-à-vis the dollar was 240 at the time of Plaza and is, as you know, 125 yen per dollar at present—a very successful outcome of the Plaza coordination effort.

As 1986 went by, a very gradual but subtle change took place in the minds of the policy authorities and the emphasis gradually shifted from exchange rate realignment to macroeconomic policy coordination. This was the second stage of the exercise. The first reason for the shift into this second stage was, I think, that exchange rate realignment had been successful. But while its beneficial impact was beginning to be evident from the trade performance of the major countries, for various reasons (including a J-curve effect), progress was not rapid. Meanwhile, the rapid change in exchange rate relationships had started to exert a rather unfavorable impact on the surplus countries' economic performance. These countries became discouraged because of this over-rapid change in exchange rates and the danger that their domestic economies might slacken. In the deficit countries too, the over-rapid change in exchange rates created a new concern about the credibility of their currency and also the credibility of the economy as a whole.

As a result, as was very clearly demonstrated at the now-famous Louvre Accord of February 1987, the major thrust was clearly shifted to macroeconomic policy coordination. As you recall, the Louvre Accord declared that the exchange rate realignment had been adequate and the priority was now more stability rather than a further change in exchange rate relationships. The ultimate purpose of this macroeconomic policy coordination, in my view, was how to shift the growth patterns of the major economies via fiscal and monetary policies.

In hindsight, these efforts proved reasonably successful if you look at the growth pattern of the major three countries. For instance, in 1987, GNP growth in the United States for the first time exceeded domestic demand growth: GNP grew at 2.9 percent while domestic demand grew at 2.5 percent. On the other hand, in the surplus countries, the Federal Republic of Germany and Japan, there was a reverse pattern of the growth. In Japan in 1987, domestic demand grew at 5.1 percent, but because of the negative contribution of net exports, GNP grew at only 3.7 percent. In Germany, domestic demand grew by 2.9 percent, but GNP grew by 1.7 percent. In other words, the shift in the growth pattern of major deficit and surplus countries was achieved. This point is probably one of the rare cases where Polak is not very accurate. He notes that it seems surprising that the coordination effort has paid domestic demand so little attention. But in fact, the importance of the relationship between domestic demand growth and the external balance has been one of the major interests of the finance ministers and the governors of the central banks in recent discussions of the Group of Five and Group of Seven. This point should be emphasized.

After making reasonable progress in macroeconomic policy coordination, we seem to be in the third stage now, when the emphasis is on structural measures. The ultimate purpose of these measures is how to secure lasting adjustment. As I noted, reasonable progress was made on exchange rate realignment and macroeconomic policy measures. Nevertheless, there has been a strong and persistent concern that these changes may not be sustainable unless more fundamental shifts take place. I believe this is the reason that we now pay considerable attention to this new stage of coordination.

In Japan, structural measures imply both public and private initiatives. I think this is the case in every country. Public initiatives in Japan have so far involved deregulation, privatization, subsidy cuts and market opening, reductions in working hours, and the abolition of tax incentives for savings. But it should be stressed that in our structural reform, private initiative is extremely important. Major industrial restructuring by market mechanisms is, I believe, taking place. Some industries, like coal mining, ship-building and some steel, aluminum and textiles, are really dying now. And other industries that are import competitive or export oriented are reallocating their production facilities offshore. This will certainly contribute to the lasting change in the trade pattern. In addition, in view of very strong domestic demand growth, many industries are shifting their major market from overseas to domestic markets.

But this third stage, as I said, has just started and I am not sure how much we can really achieve in it. But having said that, of the four policy objectives described in Polak's paper, I think the three goals of high growth, low inflation, and low unemployment still remain very valid. However, I believe that the balance of payments equivalent objective has changed somewhat. Under the Bretton Woods regime, the burden of adjustment fell mostly on the deficit countries, because if a deficit continued, the country had to sacrifice growth and employment. But now it seems to me that the burden of adjustment is falling more on the surplus countries. If a surplus persists, the country must suffer from rising protectionism in export markets and from international condemnation.

In conclusion, I think it is very important for all of us to realize that because of the very much greater international flows of capital, goods, and services, there has been a tremendous increase in interdependence among the major economies. As you know, various markets are also becoming more and more globalized. Therefore, policy objectives must now be pursued in an internationally harmonious way. This very important point is now recognized by the policy authorities in the major countries. I mentioned that we are now in the third stage of coordination. I do not know whether we will have a fourth stage. But I think that probably in the near future the major countries will make an effort to combine the three stages in a better way. I am sure that exchange rates will continue to have a significant role, as will macroeconomic policies and structural reforms.

Comment

Erik Hoffmeyer

I can go a long way along the lines indicated by Jacques Polak in his interesting paper on the broad policy changes over the last thirty to forty years.

First and foremost, it is clear that a change in priorities has occurred, with price stability becoming more important than full employment. I think, however, that the change has been a gradual process, developing through the latter part of the 1970s as a consequence of the combination of stagnation and high levels of inflation, and cannot easily be connected with the transition to conservative governments in the major countries.

The attitude toward economic policy has also undergone a substantial evolution. This is basically for three reasons. First the mechanistic view of policymaking has had to be abandoned. We were brought up with post-Keynesian thinking which taught that economic instruments were mutually independent and had a one-way impact. The latter characteristic meant that the economy was assumed not to react to the type of instrument used, nor to the intention of the politicians using it. This has proved to be an erroneous proposition, which the political system—and also professional economists—have found hard to learn.

The central issue is the role of credibility and expectations in the use of instruments. The use of exchange rate changes and the accommodation of inflation, for example, both create serious questions of attitude later on. Economic policy management is much more difficult than has been assumed.

Second, it was also expected that econometric models would become more and more reliable in forecasting economic developments. They have not, and this has been a great disappointment. I do not, of course, expect reliable forecasts of exogenous shocks, of which there have been many, but it was expected that endogenous developments in growth, inflation, key currency exchange rates, and so on could be forecast more reliably. Because they are not, it is not at all always clear whether economic policy should be changed and, if so, how much. Furthermore, explanations of economic performance have a tendency to degenerate into loose casuistic judgments instead of careful analysis. One consequence of this uncertainty is that the level of ambition in policymaking has been severely reduced.

Third—and connected with the second point—is the uncertainty in the interpretation of important events, particularly in the international sphere. I refer to the endeavors to move from the level of discussions and information in international relations to what could be called the coordination of policymaking.

The most illustrious cases are the Bonn Agreement of 1978, the Plaza Agreement of 1985, the Louvre Accord of 1987, and the Japanese expansion of 1987. In each case a really wide range of interpretations is possible—one extreme being that there was hardly any impact of the agreement, the other that it was of major importance. I am most inclined to the view that the impact has been very limited. This means that the level of ambition on coordination of international policymaking must be low.

I have been assigned to say something from a small country point of view but this presupposes that there are basic differences between big and small countries. It is certainly true that small countries do not have much influence in international negotiations, but if policy coordination is of limited importance—if it is, so to speak, one of the empty boxes—the problem does not deserve much comment. As regards the basic issues of policymaking, I do not think that conditions differ among big and small countries.

The balance of payments constraint was important for the United States in the late 1960s and is again now, as it has been for the United Kingdom and France very often and even for the Federal Republic of Germany in the late 1970s. Inflation has been a constraint for all countries—Japan, the United States, the United Kingdom, France, and Germany. Small countries have had the same problems and the same experiences with instruments that are not independent and with one instrument having an impact on several variables. In this respect I have never been over-fascinated by Tinbergen's propositions. I tend to believe that economic laws do not distinguish between big and small countries.

I am not entirely happy about the philosophy in Polak's paper in one respect. He argues that policy objectives were earlier directed at real magnitudes but are now rather concentrated on nominal goals. I do not find this convincing. When forecasts or objectives are put before parliaments there is always a distinction between real and nominal magnitudes, and as price stability has become more important—which is rightly pointed out in Polak's paper—this really means that the distinction is taken more seriously than before. I agree—for reasons I have mentioned earlier—that ambitions have had to be scaled back but the awareness of real versus nominal targets has definitely not.

Furthermore, I am inclined to argue that fiscal and monetary policies are used more actively than before, although I would agree they are not used for fine tuning. Experience over the last ten years suggests that it gives the wrong impression to argue that less importance has been given to these two instruments. In both big and small countries fiscal policy has been used to adjust the overall savings rate—a basic Keynesian proposition—and monetary policy has emancipated itself from being tied conventionally to nominal interest rates instead of real rates. I would not maintain that results have been entirely satisfactory but I think that the learning process has had some useful results which should not be overlooked.

In that respect, I am more optimistic than Polak but perhaps not on the issue of reconciling price stability with full employment, on which I wrote a book almost thirty years ago and on which I do not think that we have come much closer to a solution.

To sum up, I agree that there has been a shift of priorities in economic policy. I do not attach much importance to international policy coordination. I do not agree that the distinction between real and nominal targets has much weight and I do not think that fiscal and monetary policies can be said to be used less than in previous periods.

CHAPTER 2

International Adjustment and the Dollar: Policy Illusions and Economic Constraints

William H. Branson[1]

A reader of the daily press in 1987 and 1988 could easily gain the impression that the finance ministers of the Group of Seven countries think that today's constellation of exchange rates is an equilibrium constellation, regardless of the date or the actual values of the rates. A reader of the Fund's *World Economic Outlook* could easily gain the impression that the same group of people think that a shift in the fiscal mix between the United States and the rest of the Group of Seven would substitute for further depreciation of the dollar, despite the lessons they were taught many years ago by the fathers Mundell and Fleming. These views seem to be held firmly although they are contrary to most generally accepted analyses of exchange rates and fiscal policy. The fact that they are professed publicly may even hinder progress toward actual international adjustment.

This paper attempts to provide a comprehensive but concise analysis of the relationship between fiscal policies and exchange rates and outlines alternative feasible macroeconomic policy options, including their implications for exchange rates. Fiscal policies are treated at the aggregate level, as if the control variable were undifferentiated government purchases. This provides one limit to the discussion, avoiding the territory already covered by Frenkel and Razin (1987). The theoretical discussion is limited to two-country examples, but the empirical simulations cover three areas, the United States, Japan, and Europe, sometimes represented by the Federal Republic of Germany.

---

[1]This paper was written while the author was resident at the Banca d'Italia. He thanks the Research Department for providing technical support and an excellent research environment. Special thanks to Grazia Marchese for preparing the empirical analysis in the paper.

The analysis also avoids the complications of cyclical fluctuations by assuming constant levels of output. One justification for this procedure is that adjustment policies should succeed at full employment; permanent recession or inflation would not seem to be an appropriate part of the plan.

The methodology of the paper is to proceed from the relatively simple to the relatively complex, using only as much theoretical apparatus as is needed for the issue at hand. This means moving from the long run to the short, from comparative statics to dynamics, from analysis of the real equilibrium to nominal variables, from theory to empirical results.

The next section of the paper discusses the long-run outlook for the dollar, and concludes that perhaps 15 percent more real depreciation is needed. The following section focuses on fiscal policy and the exchange rate, concluding that depreciation is the very mechanism through which a fiscal shift would restore international balance. Fiscal policy in a real "fundamentals" model (that is, a two-country version of the model in Branson (1985)) is then analyzed. The model in Genberg and Swoboda (1987) is quite similar to the model of this section, and has essentially the same results. Nominal variables and dynamics are brought into the story in the following section, in a two-country version of the model in Dornbusch (1976). Based on these models, the argument is then made for a combination of fiscal tightening in the United States and monetary ease in the Federal Republic of Germany and Japan. This would provide more short-run exchange rate stability and reduce world real interest rates, to the benefit of developing country debtors.

The final sections discuss the Haas-Masson (1986) Minimod as an empirical representation of the theoretical models of the earlier sections and analyze recent policy adjustment scenarios by the International Monetary Fund and the Organization for Economic Cooperation and Development (OECD), using the theoretical spotlight from previous sections. These reinforce the point that a shift in the fiscal mix will be accompanied by further dollar depreciation, and the view that monetary expansion would be better than fiscal expansion in the rest of the OECD.

Long-Run Equilibrium for the Dollar

Two major long-run issues of adjustment among the industrial countries, represented here by the United States, the Federal Republic of Germany, and Japan, are the effect of the change in the international position of the United States from creditor to debtor during the 1980s, and the effects of differential trends in productivity and output growth. If the output bundles of goods in the three areas are imperfect substitutes in demand, these will require adjustments in real exchange rates to maintain current account balance at a standardized level of employment in the three areas, even if they begin in balance. In this section, we begin the analysis with a simple real model of the current account that highlights these adjustments.

For any of the three areas, the current account balance can be represented as the sum of the trade surplus, X, and the surplus on investment income, rF. Here F is the net foreign investment position and r is the rate of return on F. If the country is a net debtor, F is negative. The surplus on current account is then given by

(1) $CAB = X(c, Y/Y^*) + rF.$

Here the trade surplus X is assumed to depend on competitiveness, c (measured by weighted relative unit labor costs), and relative real GNP. Throughout the paper, a "*" represents the "foreign" variable. These should generally be interpreted as weighted averages of the relevant foreign economies. An increase in c represents an increase in competitiveness, and results in an increase in X. An increase in Y/Y^* is assumed to reduce X. The long-run equilibrium is represented by the condition that CAB is constant, and for simplicity, we will assume this constant is zero. So in the long run we have

(2) $CAB = X(.) + rF = 0.$

The competitiveness measure is relative unit labor costs. It can be written as

(3) $c = EW^*q/Wq^* = eq/q^*,$

where W is the nominal wage rate, E the nominal exchange rate, q is labor productivity, and e is the real exchange rate in terms of relative wages. This way of expressing c will facilitate the analysis of differential productivity trends later. The model of equation (1) and the definition of long-run equilibrium can be used to show the consequences of the shift in the U.S. international asset position and the likely long-run trend for the equilibrium value for the dollar, in real effective terms.

U.S. Asset Position and Real Exchange Rate

During the 1980s, the United States shifted from an international net creditor to debtor position. To see the implications of this shift for the long-run equilibrium of the dollar, we can ask what this shift implies for the equilibrium trade balance. Let 1980 represent initial equilibrium, with a U.S. current balance of about zero and a trade deficit of about 1 percent of GNP, financed by investment income, rF. During the 1980s, the current account and trade balance were substantially in deficit, and the international investment position turned negative in 1985. If we assume that the United States will return to current account balance sometime in the first half of the 1990s, it will have a debt service requirement, represented by a negative rF. This, in turn, will require a trade surplus to finance the debt service for current account balance.

The eventual size of the debt service depends on when and how the adjustment to the long-run equilibrium is made. Estimates by Blanchard (1987) put it in the range of 0.5 to 2.5 percent of GNP. His best estimate would be at the lower end of the range. The U.S. Committee for Economic Development (1987) estimates the debt service to be about $55 billion in the early 1990s. This is about 1 percent of projected GNP in 1992. So an estimate of eventual debt service of 1 percent of 1990s' GNP seems acceptable as a working hypothesis. This, in turn, implies a swing of 2 percent of GNP in the trade balance from the original equilibrium of 1980 to the eventual equilibrium of the early 1990s.

To see the implication for the equilibrium real exchange rate of the dollar, as measured by the competitiveness variable c, consider how large a real depreciation relative to 1980 would be needed to achieve a swing of 2 percent of GNP, holding relative real output Y/Y^* constant. Dornbusch and Frankel (1987) present econometrics that estimate that a 13.5 percent real depreciation is needed to achieve an increase of 1 percent of GNP on the trade balance. This is consistent with the "conventional wisdom" estimate of the semi-elasticity of the trade balance reported by Marris (1985), that a 1 percent real depreciation would yield a $3 billion improvement in the trade balance. With 1985 GNP at $4.0 trillion, $3 billion is 0.075 percent, so Marris' estimate implies that a 13.5 percent depreciation would yield 0.975 percent of GNP, which is close enough to 1.0. On these estimates, a swing of 2 percent of GNP in the trade balance would require a real depreciation of the dollar of 26 percent in effective terms relative to 1980.

Most estimates put U.S. competitiveness at the end of 1987 slightly higher than in 1980. (Remember that on our measure, up is an improvement.) For example, the OECD (1987) shows it improved by about 10 percent. This suggests that, in the absence of other important shifts in the world economy since 1980, a further real depreciation of about 15 percent, in effective terms, would be needed to move the U.S. current balance to equilibrium. If the currencies of some of the major trading partners of the United States, such as Canada, do not appreciate much against the dollar, others, such as the yen, would have to appreciate more.

Most of the changes in the world environment since 1980 that would be relevant for modifying this conclusion seem to work in the direction of increasing the estimate of the necessary further real depreciation to bring the U.S. current account back into balance at standardized levels of real output. Table 1 shows estimates of growth of real domestic demand and labor productivity in manufacturing for the United States, Japan, and the Federal Republic of Germany, for 1980–86. U.S. demand growth was stronger than that in Japan or Germany. Most estimates of income elasticities of trade show a substantially higher elasticity for U.S. imports than for U.S. exports. The combination of stronger demand growth and asymmetric income elasticities in the United States implies the need for a greater real gain in competitiveness.

Table 1. Growth in Domestic Demand and Labor Productivity in Manufacturing, 1980–86
(Average annual growth rates, in percent)

	Labor Productivity	Real Domestic Demand
United States	3.7	3.6
Japan	4.7	3.1
Germany, Fed. Rep. of	3.7	0.8

Source: Bank of Japan (1987).

Table 1 shows that growth in labor productivity in manufacturing in the United States was about the same as in Germany and a percentage point less than in Japan over the period 1980–86. Since the competitiveness variable is relative unit labor cost, slower productivity growth in the United States means that a greater real depreciation in terms of wages is needed to achieve a given gain in competitiveness. In addition, the depression in Latin America attendant on the debt crisis reduces the demand for U.S. exports relative to those of Japan or Europe. All of these factors suggest that the estimate of a required further real depreciation for the dollar in effective terms of 15 percent is on the low side.

Long-Run Equilibrium Trend

The calculations in the previous section should be interpreted as giving the needed real depreciation of the dollar that would return the current balance to equilibrium in the early 1990s. However, this does not suggest that holding the dollar at that level in real effective terms would maintain equilibrium. The estimates in Table 1, and the asymmetry of the U.S. trade income elasticities, imply that the dollar would have to depreciate in real terms continuously along a long-run trend to maintain equilibrium. In this section we briefly present the calculation of that long-run trend. Estimating its long-run value would require detailed study beyond the scope of this paper, and the parameter values will change before the dollar is back on the equilibrium path. So here we present only the qualitative results.

The definition of equilibrium as current account balance implies a constant net foreign debt position, and a constant flow of debt service, for given interest rates. This, in turn, implies a constant level of net exports, x, to finance the debt service. The net export function from equation (1), with the definition of competitiveness filled in from equation (3), is

(4) $X = X(eq/q^*, Y/Y^*)$.

The rate of change of net exports is given by

(5) $\hat{X} = n_{xc}(\hat{e} + \hat{q} - \hat{q}^*) + n_{xy}(\hat{Y} - \hat{Y}^*)$,

where n_{xc} is the positive elasticity of net exports with respect to competitiveness, n_{xy} is the negative elasticity with respect to relative growth, and a "^" over a variable denotes its growth rate.

The focus here is on the rate of real depreciation of the dollar in terms of relative wages, e, needed to set $\hat{X}$ at zero, given relative growth in productivity and demand. From equation (5), with $\hat{X} = 0$, this is

(6) $\hat{e} = (\hat{q}^* - \hat{q}) - n_{xy}/n_{xc}(\hat{Y} - \hat{Y}^*)$

The rate of real depreciation along the equilibrium path is equal to the weighted differential in productivity growth less the weighted differential in demand growth times the ratio of the negative income elasticity with respect to relative demand to the positive price elasticity with respect to competitiveness. Both factors are likely to contribute to a needed real depreciation of the dollar along the equilibrium trend. U.S. productivity growth is slower than that of its major trade competitors, its demand growth is faster, and the asymmetry of income elasticities will raise the value of n_{xy}.

Thus it appears that the long-run trend for the dollar that would maintain equilibrium on the current account is depreciation in real effective terms. It also appears that a further real depreciation is needed to get the dollar back on that equilibrium trend.

Fiscal Policy and the Real Exchange Rate

Before moving on to models of the determinants of exchange rates and international adjustment, it will be useful to deal at the clearest and simplest level with one specific issue regarding the relationship between fiscal policy and real exchange rates. This is because the view in policy discussions in the context of the Groups of Five and Seven seems to be that a contractionary shift in fiscal stance in the United States and an expansionary shift in Europe and Japan would substitute for real depreciation of the dollar in restoring current account balance among those three areas. The argument in the previous section says that a further real depreciation is necessary, and is therefore contradictory to this new view of the Group of Seven. So it seems best to confront this issue directly before moving to a more complex level of analysis.

The view of the Group of Seven that an international shift in the fiscal mix can substitute for a change in the real exchange rate is expressed in the October 1987 issue of the *World Economic Outlook* of the International Monetary Fund (p. 17).

> "It is important, therefore, to consider what role policies might play in avoiding the sharp exchange rate movements . . . of the finance constrained scenario . . . A harmonized realignment of fiscal positions would tend to restrain the growth of domestic demand in the United States, while fostering it in the surplus countries. If accompanied by a moderate movement in exchange rates, this could be consistent with a gradual reduction in external imbalances . . . ."

The problem with this view is that, in general, a balanced fiscal package with no change in world aggregate expenditure will change the composition of world expenditure toward the expanding area's goods, away from the contracting area's. This will require a rise in the relative price of the expanding area's goods, that is a real appreciation, to rebalance supply and demand in both markets. This is shown by the following illustration, taken from Krugman (1987).

Consider a two-area example, with both areas producing a given amount of output, perhaps full-employment output. The home area has a marginal propensity to spend on imports out of total absorption of m, with 1–m spent on home goods. Likewise, the foreign area's marginal propensitites are m* and 1–m*. Then total spending on the two areas' goods is given by

(7a) $\quad d = (1-m)a + m^*a^*;$

(7b) $\quad d^* = ma + (1-m^*)a^*,$

where a and a* are real absorptions and d and d* are real demands.

Suppose now that a balanced fiscal package reduces a and increases a* by equal amounts, with no change in output of either area's goods. This means that $\Delta a^* = -\Delta a$. Then the changes in demands for the two areas' goods are given by

(8a) $\Delta d = (1 - m - m^*)\Delta a$, and

(8b) $\Delta d^* = (m + m^* - 1)\Delta a$.

If the sum of the two marginal propensities to import is less than one, the demand for home goods falls, and for foreign goods rises, by the same amount in this two-area case. This requires a reduction in the relative price of home goods, that is, a real depreciation of the home currency, to eliminate the excess supply of the home good and the excess demand for the foreign good. This need for a real depreciation of the home currency is caused by the fiscal shift. It is how the fiscal shift generates the adjustment. In this sense, real depreciation is a complement to the fiscal shift, rather than a substitute.

Krugman's illustration assumes two areas, both specialized in production, so there are two goods. McKinnon (1988) produces an example with three goods. Each area produces an exportable (X), an importable (M), and a nontraded good (N). Here the terms of trade is P_x/P_m. The real exchange rate is the ratio of the average price of traded goods to P_n. McKinnon points out that the effect of a fiscal shift on the terms of trade is uncertain in this setting. Tighter fiscal policy at home reduces the demand for both the exportable and the importable, for example. McKinnon takes this result as refuting Krugman's point. But in the three-good example, the relevant variable is the real exchange rate, and the result still holds. Tighter fiscal policy at home and easier fiscal policy abroad will reduce the demand for the home nontraded good, and increase it for the foreign nontraded good. So the relative price of the home nontraded good must fall to restore equilibrium. This means the real exchange rate must rise, that is, the home currency must depreciate in real terms.

Given this analysis, it is reasonable to ask how the Group of Seven view came into existence. One possibility is that the implicit model underlying it assumes a traded versus nontraded structure. Here each country or area produces a common, perfectly substitutable, traded good, and a unique nontraded good. For each country, the real exchange rate is the ratio of the prices of the traded and nontraded goods.

In this case, or in the three-good McKinnon example, if the fiscal shifts resulted purely in a shift in the composition of demand for the traded goods, with no spillover onto the nontraded goods, there would be no need for a change in either real exchange rate. However, if the contraction in the home area and expansion abroad in the examples fell partially on the nontraded goods, the home nontraded would have to fall in price relative to the foreign nontraded to reestablish equilibrium in the two markets for nontraded goods. This requires a real appreciation in the expanding area and a depreciation in the contracting area.

Thus, the Group of Seven view could hold up if the fiscal shift affected relative demands only for a perfectly substitutable traded good. But most of government exhaustive spending is on nontraded goods, such as construction and wage and salary payments. So the Group of Seven view is unlikely to hold in this implicit framework, either. The basic conclusion is that a change in the real exchange rate is a complement to a fiscal shift, except under most unusual circumstances.

Fiscal Policy in a Fundamentals Model

Shifts in fiscal policy will have important implications for the international pattern of real interest rates, as well as real exchange rates. This section explores these, using a minimal two-country framework that focuses on the effects of shifts in real exogenous variables on real interest rates and the real exchange rate. The model is a two-country version of the "fundamentals" model presented in Branson (1985) and modified in Branson (1988). It is called a fundamentals model because it focuses on the real variables that rational markets should consider in forming their expectations. A precursor of the two-country version was presented in Krugman (1985). The model expands the previous discussion by explicitly incorporating budget positions and financial market equilibrium into an explanation of movements in real interest rates and the real exchange rate. First we set up the model briefly, and then discuss the effects of fiscal shifts.

Fundamentals Model

This subsection will present only enough detail to support the discussion of fiscal policy in the subsection on the long-run equilibrium trend. A full discussion of the model and results is in Appendix I. The model consists of the two countries' national income equilibrium conditions and the arbitrage equation linking their financial markets. These three equations determine movements of real interest rates and the real exchange rate as dependent on relative bond stocks, and the long-run equilibrium real exchange rate from the earlier section.

The two national income equilibrium conditions are given by

(9a) $D = S(r) - X(e - \bar{e})$,   (Home country)

(9b) $D^* = S^*(r^*) + X(e - \bar{e})$.   (Foreign country)

These two equations say that the (real) budget deficits D and D* must equal the sum of (real) net private saving S and S* and the current balance X. With two countries, one's X is the other's $-X$. Net private saving is assumed to be an increasing function of the real interest rate. Net exports of the home country X are assumed to be an increasing function of the real exchange rate relative to its long-run equilibrium value $\bar{e}$. Movements in $\bar{e}$ reflect the considerations discussed in the section on the long-run equilibrium. When $e = \bar{e}$, the current account is in balance.

Financial market equilibrium can be summarized by the arbitrage condition across real interest rates and the expected rate of change in the real exchange rate e:

$$r = r^* + \hat{e} + \rho(B/B^*).$$

Here ρ is the risk premium on home currency, an increasing function of the home bond stock relative to the foreign. The exchange rate is expected to move toward its long-run equilibrium following the proportional adjustment process given by

$$\hat{e} = \theta (\bar{e} - e).$$

Combining these two relationships gives us the arbitrage condition that is the third equation of the fundamentals model:

(10) $e - \bar{e} = (1/\theta) (r^* - r + \rho(B/B^*))$.

This arbitrage condition says that if r is higher than r* plus the risk premium, then e must be sufficiently below its long-run equilibrium value that its expected rate of increase maintains the arbitrage equality.

Equations (9) and (10) can be used to obtain solutions for r, r*, and e as functions of D, D*, B/B*, and $\bar{e}$. The algebra is relegated to Appendix I. Here we move to the graphical analysis.

Equations (9a) and (9b) can be combined into one condition in the two interest rates. Summing the two equations gives us the world saving-investment balance:

(9c) $D + D^* = S(r) + S^*(r^*)$.

This condition is represented by the negatively sloped RR line in Chart 1. For a given total fiscal deficit $D + D^*$, an increase in one interest rate requires a reduction in the other to maintain world

Chart 1. Equilibrium in the Fundamentals Model

Chart 2. Two Fiscal Scenarios

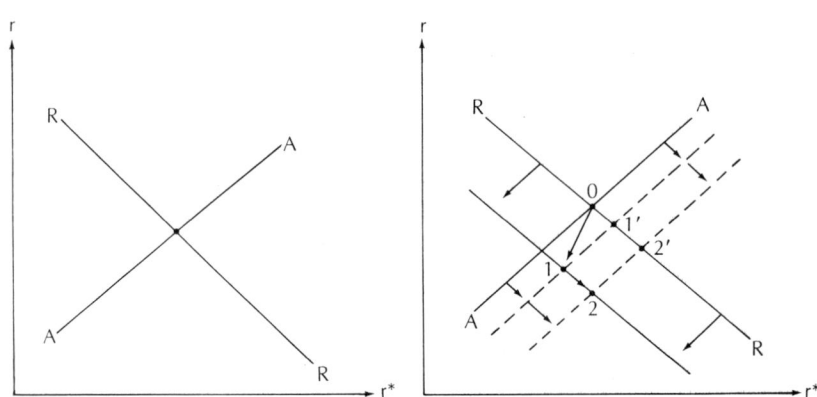

saving-investment balance. An increase in either deficit shifts the RR line up, requiring a rise in real interest rates. A reduction in one deficit, matched by an increase in the other, would not move the RR line.

Equation (9c) introduces the point that world real interest rates will be reduced by an industrial country fiscal package that reduces the aggregate deficit, but not by one that simply rearranges its composition, as is suggested in the passage from the April 1987 *World Economic Outlook* cited earlier. Thus to reduce the burden of debt service on developing countries, the policy mix should reduce the aggregate deficit.

The positively sloped AA line in Chart 1 represents financial market equilibrium, as specified in equation (10). The AA line has a slope of unity. It is shifted up by an increase in the risk premium or by a decrease in $e - \bar{e}$. In any long-run equilibrium, $e - \bar{e} = 0$, and the position of the AA line is determined by the risk premium that controls the equilibrium real interest differential. The equilibrium values of r and r^* at any time are determined by the intersection of RR and AA. In the background behind the position of the AA line is the equilibrium value of $e - \bar{e}$. How this is determined is best discussed in the context of a shift in one of the basic exogenous variables, D or D^*.

Fiscal Policy

Two common medium-term scenarios in analyses by the Fund, the OECD, and the European Community of the economic outlook involve a fiscal contraction in the United States alone, or a fiscal contraction in the United States matched by a fiscal expansion in Europe and Japan. These two cases are shown in Chart 2. Consider first the case of a U.S. contraction.

The analysis proceeds in two steps. First, consider the impact of the shift in the budget position. This shifts both RR and AA. Second, consider the effect of the new path of debt accumulation; this alters the risk premium and shifts the AA curve only, leading to the final equilibrium.

A reduction in the home deficit D shifts the RR line, as shown in Chart 2. What happens to the position of the AA line? To answer this question, refer back to equations (9a) and (9b). In (9b), there is no change in D^*, by supposition. If the position of the AA line were unchanged, r^* and S^* would fall. This would require an increase in $e - \bar{e}$, a depreciation of the home currency, to maintain saving-investment balance in the foreign country. Less excess private saving to finance the given D^* requires an increase in the current account deficit (or reduction in the surplus). In equation (9a), the increase in $e - \bar{e}$ reduces the current account deficit, splitting the decrease in D between a fall in S and an increase in X. So the initial depreciation of the home currency maintains saving-investment balance abroad, and cushions the effect on the real interest rate at home.

The increase in $e - \bar{e}$ accounts for the initial downward shift of the AA line in Chart 2, taking the equilibrium from point 0 to point 1. Both interest rates must fall. If AA shifted enough that r^* increased, moving from 0 to 1, the previous reasoning on the movement of $e - \bar{e}$, based on equation (9b), would be reversed, producing an upward shift in AA, which would contradict the premise that r^* increased in the first place. So the initial effect of the reduction in D is for both real interest rates to fall, r by more, and the home currency to depreciate, moving from point 0 to point 1 in Chart 2.

At this point the two economies have not yet reached the final equilibrium, because the reduction in D implies an eventual reduction in the relative debt stock B/B^* and in the risk premium. This will shift the AA curve down further, bringing the two economies to a final equilibrium at point 2 in Chart 2, where r^* is back at its original level, r has fallen by the decrease in the risk premium, and $e = \bar{e}$. In equation (9b), with D unchanged and X back to zero, r^* must be the same as the original value.

The long-run equilibrium $\bar{e}$ will have decreased in the movement from point 0 to point 2 due to the reduction in debt service of the home country with a reduced ratio B/B^*. So the actual value of the exchange rate rises (home currency depreciates) from point 0 to point

1, and then falls from 1 to 2. It ends up below its initial value due to the long-run effect of reduced debt service. The reduction of average interest rates in this unbalanced fiscal scenario also implies a reduction of debt service of the developing countries.

The case of an equal reduction in D and increase in D* is shown in Chart 2 by the movement from points 0 to 1' to 2'. The balanced fiscal package leaves the RR line undisturbed. But a depreciation of the home currency is required to maintain the arbitrage condition (10) as r falls and r* rises. The depreciation shifts the AA line down, producing the movement from point 0 to point 1'. The depreciation also reduces the home country's current account deficit, cushioning the movement in relative interest rates in the movement from 0 to 1'.

Again, at point 1', further adjustment comes with the reduction in the risk premium implied by the fall in B/B*. This moves the economies to the final equilibrium at point 2', with a lower r and higher r*. At 2', $\bar{e}$ is below its original value, and $e = \bar{e}$, so the path of actual e is reversed in the movement from points 0 to 1' to 2'. The net results from the balanced fiscal package are a change in relative interest rates and the risk premium, offsetting changes in the government deficit and excess private saving in the two industrial countries, and no reduction in debt service for the developing countries.

Nominal Dynamics and Monetary Policy

The fundamentals model, due to its focus on real variables and equilibrium positions, says nothing about the dynamics of price and nominal exchange rate adjustment, expectations, and monetary policy. To introduce these elements into the discussion of policy alternatives, we turn to a modified two-country version of the Dornbusch (1976) model of exchange rate and price dynamics. This expands the fundamentals model to include the two price levels, the nominal exchange rate, and monetary policy. Price adjustment is assumed to be gradual, while the exchange rate and interest rates can jump in anticipation of future developments. Movements of real variables between equilibria then depend on combinations of sluggish adjustment of price levels and instantaneous adjustment of asset prices. The fundamentals model gives the real equilibria; the model developed in this section gives the paths between them. In the following subsections, we first outline the model in the minimum necessary detail, and then apply it to the analysis of fiscal and monetary policies.

Two-Country Dynamics Model

This subsection presents only enough exposition to support the subsequent discussion of fiscal and monetary policy. The details of the algebra are in Appendix II. Here we add money-market relationships and dynamics to the fundamentals model. Since for analysis we will use the assumption that the two countries are symmetric to reduce the dimensionality of the model, the assumption that parameters are the same in both countries is applied from the outset.

The two money-market relationships are given by:

(11a) $\quad m - \alpha p - (1-\alpha)p^* - (1-\alpha)E = \phi y - \lambda i$ (Home)

(11b) $\quad m^* - \alpha p^* - (1-\alpha)p + (1-\alpha)E = \phi y^* - \lambda i^*$. (Foreign)

Here all variables except the nominal interest rates i are expressed in logs, making λ the semi-elasticity of the demand for real balances with respect to the interest rate. The deflator for money balances is the consumer price index, with weights α for home goods and $(1-\alpha)$ for imports. Real outputs are assumed to be exogenous. The semi-log form is used only to impose homogeneity in nominal variables. It ensures that if the ratios of money supplies and price levels, and the exchange rate, all change by the same proportion, the real equilibrium will remain undisturbed.

The arbitrage condition from the fundamentals model also applies across nominal interest rates and the expected rate of change of the nominal exchange rate. This gives the arbitrage condition linking the two money markets,

(12) $\quad i = i^* + \dot{E} + \rho,$

where ρ is the risk premium, still dependent on B/B^*. Since E is the log of the exchange rate, $\dot{E}$ is the rate of change. In the dynamics of this section, exchange rate expectations will be assumed to be formed in an unbiased manner, that is, with zero average forecast error over time. This defines expectations as rational. So $\dot{E}$ in equation (12) is both the expected and actual rate of change of the exchange rate.

The two domestic goods prices are assumed to adjust gradually over time to eliminate excess demand, which is $X-S+D$ from the national income equilibrium equations (9) of the fundamentals model. The dynamic versions of equations (9) are given by

(13a) $\quad \dot{p} = \pi[X(E+p^*-p-\bar{e}) - S(i) + D].$ (Home)

(13b) $\quad \dot{p}^* = \pi[-X(E+p^*-p-\bar{e}) - S(i^*) + D^*].$ (Foreign)

Here the price levels adjust to excess demand with a speed given by π. The real exchange rate in the net export function is expressed in terms of its components. To avoid excessive complexity, excess private saving is written as a function of the nominal interest rate, which will be the same as the real rate in equilibrium.

Long-run equilibrium of this model can be analyzed by setting $\dot{p}$, $\dot{p}^*$, and $\dot{E}$ equal to zero in equations (11)–(13). Then the five equations determine values for the two price levels and interest rates, and the exchange rate. This analysis is discussed in Appendix II. Here the focus is on dynamic adjustment to equilibrium. To do the dynamic analysis, we can reduce the model to two equations in the relative price level $p-p^*$ and the exchange rate E and proceed graphically.

Subtraction of equation (11b) from (11a), and substitution of $\dot{E}+\rho$ for $i-i^*$ from equation (12) yields the relative money-market equilibrium condition

(11c) $\quad m - m^* + (1 - 2\alpha)(p - p^*) - 2(1 - \alpha)E$
$\quad\quad = \phi(y - y^*) - \lambda(\dot{E} + \rho).$

If α, the share of home goods in consumption, is between 0.5 and 1.0, the coefficient of $(p-p^*)$ is negative and the coefficient of E is positive. To obtain the equation for the inflation differential $\dot{p}-\dot{p}^*$, we assume that the saving functions are linear (so one can be easily subtracted from the other) and subtract (13a) from (13b) with the same substitution for $i-i^*$. This yields

(13c) $\quad \dot{p} - \dot{p}^* = \pi[2X(E + p^* - p - \bar{e}) - S(\dot{E}+\rho) + D - D^*].$

The two equations (11c) and (13c) are a dynamic system in the relative price level $p-p$ and the exchange rate E. The dynamics can be analyzed readily using a variant of the diagram introduced by Dornbusch (1976).

Setting $\dot{E} = 0$ in equation (11c) yields the negatively sloped line in Chart 3. This is the locus of points along which the money markets are in equilibrium with zero expected change in the exchange rate. An increase in the exchange rate requires a reduction in the domestic price relative to the foreign if neither consumer price index is to change, and therefore neither money market equilibrium disturbed. The dynamics of the exchange rate relative to the $\dot{E} = 0$ line can be understood by considering a point above it, such as point A in Chart 3. At point A, the home price relative to the foreign, $p-p^*$, is higher than would be consistent with expected $\dot{E} = 0$. A higher home price level means lower real balances and a higher interest rate than the foreign, that is $i-i^*>0$. If i is greater than i^*, then from the arbitrage condition (12), expected $\dot{E}$ must be positive for point A to be consistent with money-market equilibrium. With rational expectations, this means that at point A, E must be rising. In a sense, only an expectation of a further increase can justify an already high exchange rate. This line of analysis yields the direction of the horizontal arrows in

Chart 3. Above the $\dot{E} = 0$ line, E rises; below it, E falls. The $\dot{E} = 0$ line provides the unstable element of the dynamics.

Setting $\dot{p} - \dot{p}^* = 0$ in equation (13c) yields the positively sloped line that is so labeled in Chart 3. This is the locus of points along which the goods market is in equilibrium. (To derive the expression for the slope of $\dot{p} - \dot{p}^* = 0$, one must substitute from equation (11c) for $(\dot{E} + \rho)$ in (13c); see Appendix II.) Below this line, for example at point A, the relative price of home goods is too low to be consistent with equilibrium. There is excess demand for home goods and excess supply of foreign, so $p - p^*$ rises. This reasoning yields the direction of the vertical arrows in Chart 3. The $\dot{p} - \dot{p}^* = 0$ line provides the stable element of the dynamics.

The intersection of the $\dot{E} = 0$ and $\dot{p} - \dot{p}^* = 0$ lines in Chart 3 is the long-run equilibrium of the system, given the two money stocks, the two deficits, and the risk premium. It will be useful to notice that the equilibrium real exchange rate is given by the slope of the ray from the origin to the equilibrium. This is P/EP*, the inverse of the real exchange rate. So any disturbance that moves the equilibrium to a flatter ray raises the real exchange rate, that is, depreciates the home currency.

With one stable and one unstable element in the dynamics, there is one unique stable path to the equilibrium in Chart 3. This is the path labeled ss; in the technical literature it is called the "saddle path." It has two essential properties: (a) it leads to the equilibrium, and (b) along it, expectations of changes in the exchange rate are realized. As suggested by the arrows moving away from the ss path in Chart 3, all other paths are unstable; they are "speculative bubbles." Along them, expectations are realized from one period to the next, but they do not

Chart 3. Equilibrium and Dynamics

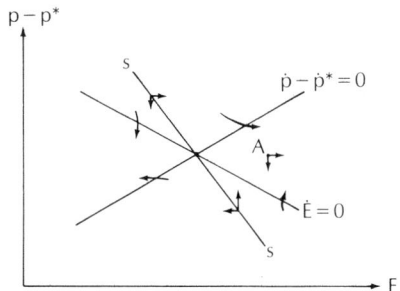

Chart 4. Relative Monetary Expansion Abroad

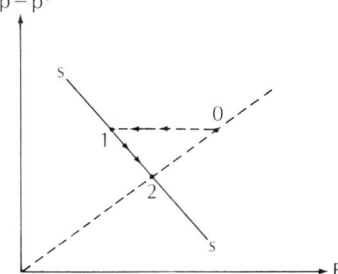

lead to the equilibrium. The market abhors these bubble paths, and searches for the ss path that does lead to the equilibrium.

After a disturbance, the relative price $p - p^*$ cannot adjust instantaneously, by assumption, but the exchange rate can jump onto the new ss path that leads to the new equilibrium. So following a disturbance that will lead to future relative price adjustment, the market attempts to find the value for the exchange rate that lies on the ss path, so expectations could be expected to be realized if the economy were to proceed to the equilibrium with no further disturbances.

Monetary Policy

A brief discussion of the case of an unanticipated shift in monetary policy will provide a clear example of dynamic adjustment and set the stage for the subsequent analysis of policy options. The effects of a relative easing of monetary policy abroad are illustrated in Chart 4. The original equilibrium is at point zero. A reduction of $m - m^*$ shifts both the $\dot{E} = 0$ and $\dot{p} - \dot{p}^* = 0$ lines proportionately toward the origin. The long-run equilibrium moves down the ray from the origin to point 2 in Chart 4. Eventually the relative price level and the exchange rate will change by the same proportion as the relative money supply.

A new stable ss path leads to the new long-run equilibrium at point 2. For the initially given value of $p - p^*$, the exchange rate jumps to the ss path at point 1. In anticipation of the future fall in the relative price level, the home currency appreciates immediately. The relative price level, $p - p^*$, and the exchange rate then move gradually along the ss path to point 2. This illustrates the well-known "overshooting" result in response to monetary disturbances.

The initial jump downward of the exchange rate to point 1 has to be consistent with the expectation that it will rise gradually to point 2. With no initial change in relative prices, initially the interest rate at home rises relative to that abroad, consistent with the expectation that the exchange rate will rise. As the adjustment then proceeds from point 1 to point 2, the interest differential closes as the home price level rises relative to the foreign.

Fiscal Policy

The results of a relative fiscal contraction in the home country are shown in Chart 5. The fiscal variables do not appear in equation (11c) for $\dot{E} = 0$, so a fiscal contraction in the home country shifts the $\dot{p} - \dot{p}^* = 0$ line down along the original $\dot{E} = 0$ line. The new long-run equilibrium point 2 is on a flatter ray from the origin, reflecting a real depreciation of the home currency. The new ss path runs into the long-run equilib-

Chart 5. Relative Fiscal Contraction at Home

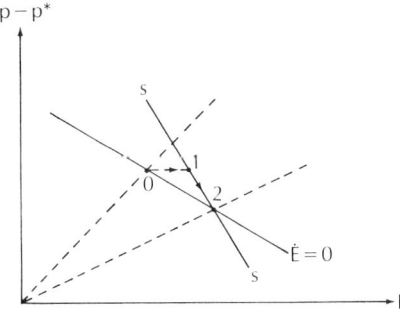

Chart 6. Policy Scenario: Fiscal Contraction in the U.S.; Monetary Expansion Abroad

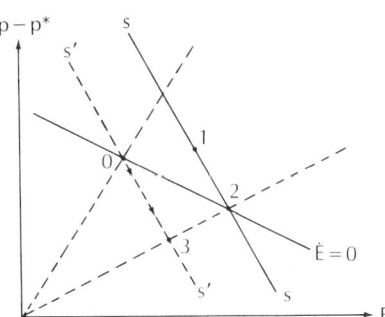

rium. The exchange rate jumps onto the ss path at point 1 in Chart 5, and then the relative price level and the exchange rate move gradually toward point 2. This is an example of undershooting in response to a real disturbance.

The path of the exchange rate in Chart 5 breaks the movement from point 0 to point 2 into two pieces. The real depreciation from 0 to 2 is determined by the fundamentals model. The additional result here is the prediction of an initial jump as the market anticipates the subsequent further real depreciation of the home currency.

Policy Scenario: U.S. Fiscal Contraction with Exchange Rate Stability

In anticipation of the later discussion of empirical policy scenarios, it may be useful at this point to use the dynamics model to illustrate a scenario that could provide short-run exchange rate stability with an international shift in fiscal policy. This scenario would combine a tightening of fiscal policy in the home country, the United States, and easing of monetary policy abroad, the Federal Republic of Germany and Japan. The scenario is partially suggested by the evident desire of the Group of Seven to avoid any further sudden movements in exchange rates. It has the additional benefit that by increasing world saving it would reduce real interest rates and developing country debt service. The scenario essentially combines Charts 4 and 5.

Let us begin by interpreting Chart 5 as illustrating the result of a U.S. fiscal contraction. In the absence of any additional policy action, the dollar would show a jump depreciation in nominal and real terms, and then a further gradual depreciation. This is the theoretical result in Chart 5, and it is the empirical result in the Fund's Multimod model and scenarios to be reviewed below. It is shown as the movement from points 0 to 1 to 2 in Chart 6, which reproduces Chart 5 to this point.

Let us now assume that the initial jump in the exchange rate from 0 to 1 is undesirable. How can policy prevent it? By altering monetary policy so that the original equilibrium point 0 lies on the new s's' path. The shift in the U.S. fiscal position establishes a new equilibrium real exchange rate given by the fundamentals model, and shown in Chart 6 by the ray through point 2. But an expansionary monetary policy in Germany and Japan can shift the new equilibrium in along this ray until the new s's' path goes through point 0. This combination of fiscal tightening in the United States and monetary expansion in Germany and Japan would result in a gradual depreciation of the dollar from point 0 to point 3 with no initial jump.

The gain in exchange rate stability here comes at the cost of additional adjustment of relative price levels and nominal dollar depreciation between points 2 and 3 in Chart 6. This tradeoff could be evaluated in quantitative terms using the Fund's Multimod. This scenario has the additional benefits of lower world real interest rate and a stimulus to demand in Germany and Japan to offset any potential contraction in the United States.

Empirical Representation: Minimod

The theoretical models discussed in the previous sections have a close empirical representation in Minimod, a two-country model developed at the Fund. The model is presented in detail in Haas and Masson (1986). It includes empirical specifications of equations (11)–(13), and options for adaptive or rational expectations solutions. Haas and Masson present simulation results that correspond closely to the policy experiments described analytically in Charts 2, 4, and 5, plus the result of an increase in the risk premium, which is described in Appendix Charts 10 (Panel 4) and 11 (Panel 6).

In the simulations, the authors first solve the model forward from the first quarter of 1985, using the baseline assumptions on policy provided by the Brookings Institution model project (see Haas and Masson, footnote 13). They then change the path of a policy or other exogenous variable by a specified amount, and re-solve the model under the two alternative expectations assumptions. For each endogenous variable, the difference from the baseline path, in percentage terms, is the effect of the policy change. The simulations of policy effects over time should correspond to the analytical experiments of the earlier sections of this paper. They do, fairly closely.

The effects of an unanticipated, permanent reduction of real government purchases by 1 percent of GNP in the United States, beginning in the first quarter of 1985, on the dollar exchange rate and the U.S. and foreign absorption deflators are shown in Chart 7. This corresponds to the experiment analyzed in Charts 2 and 5 earlier. Chart 7 shows percentage deviations from baseline, beginning in 1985. The heavy line in each figure shows the rational expectations result, and the light line shows the adaptive expectations result. Note that in the Haas-Masson model, as in the analytical models of the earlier sections, an increase of the exchange rate is a depreciation.

The top panel of Chart 7 shows a jump depreciation of the dollar by 4 percent following the fiscal action. This is followed by a slight further depreciation, and then a slow path of appreciation. The depreciation comes as the initial response to the fiscal contraction for a given debt ratio B/B^*. Then gradually the debt ratio falls relative to baseline. This reduces the risk premium and leads to a gradual appreciation. Eventually, the argument of the above section says the dollar would appreciate, due to lower debt service relative to the baseline. This reversal is also noted by Haas and Masson (p. 735), although it occurs past the horizon of their illustrations.

The bottom panels of Chart 7 show the fall in the U.S. price level relative to the foreign as is also shown in Chart 5. The initial jump in the price levels in the Minimod is due to the direct effect of the exchange rate on the absorption deflator. The price levels in Chart 5 are prices of home and foreign output, while Minimod works with absorption.

The effects of a foreign monetary expansion in the Minimod are shown in Chart 8, which corresponds to the earlier Chart 4. The foreign money supply is increased permanently by 4 percent, with the increase spread evenly over the first four quarters of the simulation. The top panel of Chart 8 shows an initial appreciation of the dollar by 7 percent, followed by a gradual depreciation, as is also shown in Chart 4. The bottom panels of Chart 8 show the fall of the U.S. relative price, mainly from an increase in the foreign price level. Again, the initial jump down in the U.S. price and up in the foreign price comes from the direct effect of the exchange rate on the absorption deflators.

We can see how the policy scenario of the previous section could be implemented, at least as estimated by the 1986 Minimod, by comparing the top panels of Charts 7 and 8. Chart 7 shows a 1 percent of GNP fiscal contraction in the United States producing a 4 percent depreciation, while Chart 8 shows a 4 percent increase in the foreign money

Chart 7. Minimod Simulation: Reduction in U.S. Government Purchases

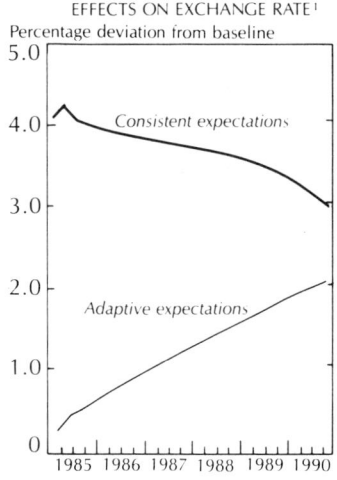

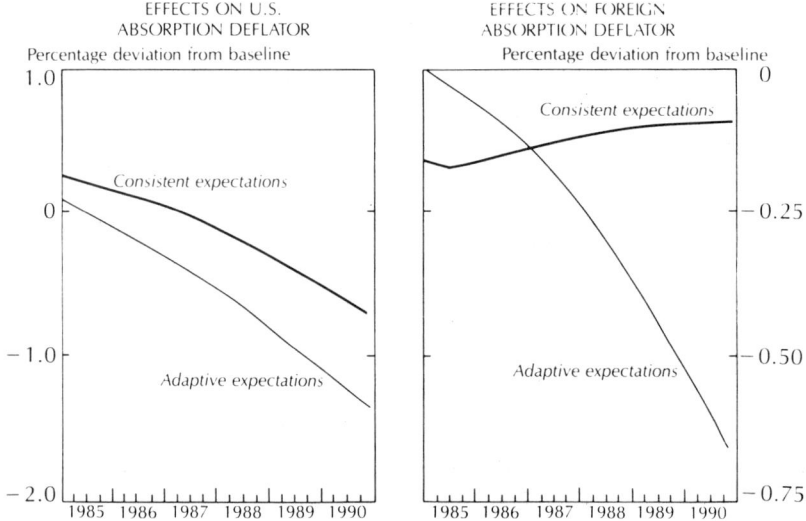

Source: Haas and Masson (1986), Chart 1.
[1]Increase indicates dollar depreciation.

Chart 8. Minimod Simulation: Non-U.S. Monetary Expansion

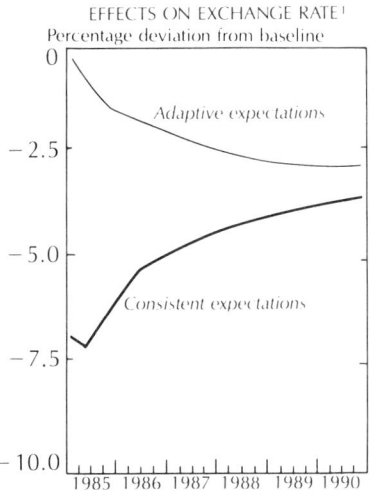
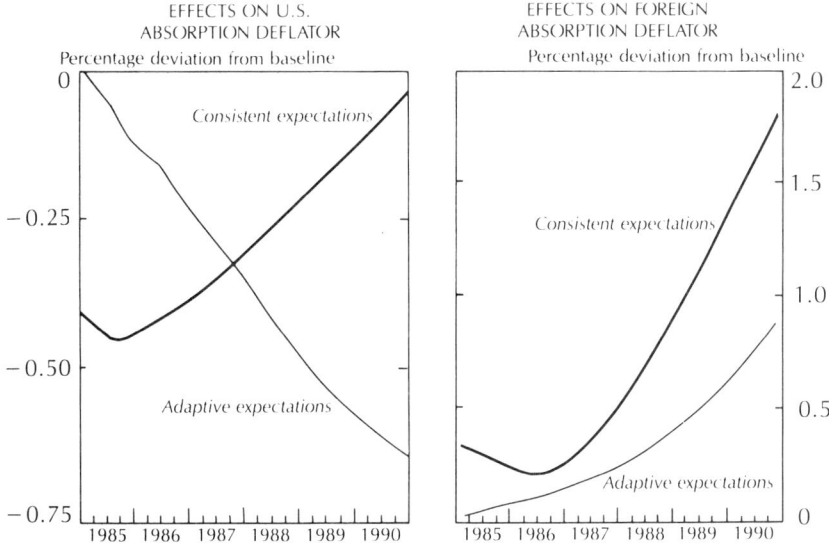

Source: Haas and Masson (1986), Chart 4.
[1]Increase indicates dollar depreciation.

supply producing a 7 percent appreciation. So scaling the fiscal contraction up to 1.75 percent of GNP, and combining it with a 4 percent increase in the foreign money supply (in the Federal Republic of Germany and Japan) would leave the exchange rate approximately unchanged, as illustrated in Chart 6. Subsequently, the dollar would gradually depreciate, as also shown in Chart 6. This can be seen in the flatter path of the exchange rate in Chart 7 compared with Chart 8. Thus the policy scenario of the previous section seems quite feasible in the context of the Minimod simulations.

The effects of the addition of a constant 1 percentage point to the risk premium on dollar assets in the Minimod, beginning in 1985, are shown in Chart 9. This corresponds to Appendix Chart 10, Panel 4 and Chart 11, Panel 6. The top panel of Chart 9 shows an initial depreciation of about 7 percent in the rational expectations case, and a gradual depreciation with adaptive expectations. In the case of an increase in the risk premium, the latter might be the more appropriate assumption. Rather than following on a policy announcement, as in the two previous cases, the increase in the risk premium may come about more gradually as the market comes to understand the long-run consequences of current policies, if they were to continue indefinitely. This upward movement is shown most clearly in Chart 11, Panel 6. Whether it takes the form of a jump depends on expectations.

The bottom panels of Chart 9 show the initial effects on the two absorption deflators from the jump in the exchange rate in the rational expectations case. With adaptive expectations, the U.S. relative price rises slowly. This fits the ambiguity of the relative price movement with an increase in the risk premium in Chart 12, Panel 6 and Table 4.

Alternative Policy Scenarios and the Dollar

The theoretical structure of the earlier sections is reflected to differing degrees in the simulation models used by the international organizations. The Fund's Multimod, or multi-region econometric model, is an expanded version of Minimod. It includes endogenous determination of exchange rates and arbitrage equations with terms for risk premia. So policy simulations with Multimod produce endogenous variations in exchange rates. In addition, simulations can be performed with exogenous variations in risk premia and endogenous variation in exchange rates. The OECD Interlink model takes nominal exchange rates as exogenous. This results in small variations in real exchange rates in the policy simulations. To simulate the effects of market-determined variations in exchange rates, Interlink must be given exogenous input.

Chart 9. Minimod Simulation: Increase in Risk Premium on U.S. Dollar Assets

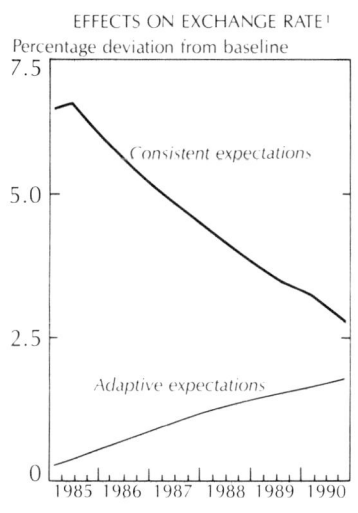

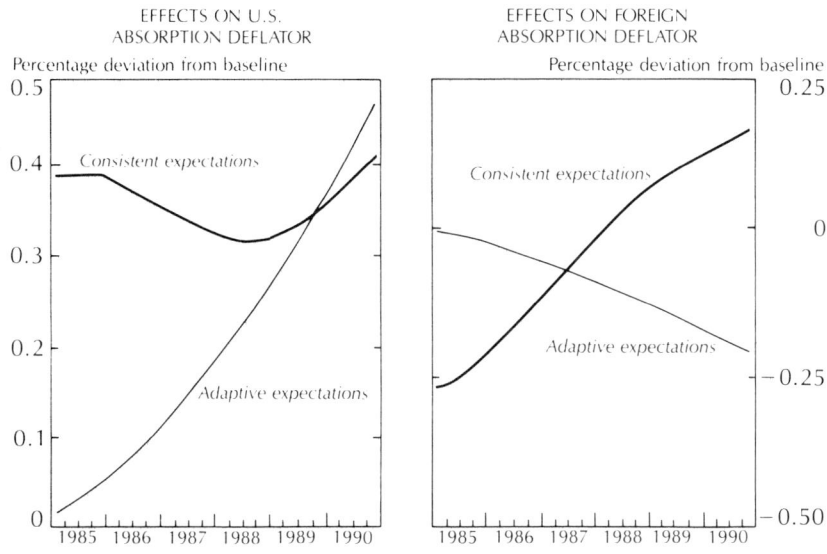

Source: Haas and Masson (1986), Chart 5.
[1]Increase indicates dollar depreciation.

Table 2. Alternative Policy Scenarios

Multimod: Alternative Scenarios

	1 Pure Dollar Depreciation				2 Fiscal Restriction in U.S.				3 Fiscal Restriction in U.S., Expansion in Japan, Germany and Endogenous Dollar Depreciation			
	1989		1992		1989		1992		1989		1992	
	(A)	(B)	(A)	(B)	(A)	(B)	(A)	(B)	(A)	(B)	(A)	(B)
United States												
Real GNP	3.2	−1.5	2.9	−0.8	3.1	−0.4	2.8	−0.4	3.0	−0.4	2.8	−0.4
GNP deflator	3.9	0.4	3.2	0.2	3.5	0.0	3.3	−0.2	3.6	0.1	3.4	0.1
Current balance												
In billions of dollars	−91.8	36.6	−41.9	86.1	−118.2	10.2	−91.3	36.7	−118.2	10.2	−85.2	42.8
In percent of GNP	−1.8	0.7	−0.7	1.4	−2.3	0.2	−1.5	0.6	−2.3	0.2	−1.4	0.7
Japan												
Real GNP	3.3	−1.6	4.1	0.7	3.5	−0.6	3.7	0.0	3.6	−0.1	3.7	−0.2
GNP deflator	−0.3	−2.9	0.8	−6.6	1.1	−1.0	1.2	−2.3	1.2	−1.0	1.3	−2.1
Current balance												
In billions of dollars	70.2	−4.4	64.0	−11.0	68.7	−5.9	75.9	0.9	67.5	−7.1	78.7	3.7
In percent of GNP	2.2	−0.2	1.6	−0.4	2.2	−0.2	1.9	−0.1	2.1	−0.3	1.8	−0.2
Real exchange rate (Yen/$)	148.9	−7.1	155.9	−2.7	155.7	−2.8	149.6	−6.6	151.8	−5.3	139.1	−13.2
Germany, Fed. Rep. of												
Real GNP	0.8	−2.9	2.8	0.5	1.4	−0.9	2.5	0.1	1.8	−0.2	2.5	0.6
GNP deflator	0.3	−2.8	1.7	−5.3	1.4	−0.9	2.1	−1.8	1.3	−1.2	2.2	−2.0
Current balance												
In billions of dollars	37.5	−4.0	50.7	3.1	38.8	−2.7	50.0	2.4	37.5	−4.1	44.8	−2.8
In percent of GNP	2.7	−0.4	3.0	0.0	2.8	−0.3	2.8	−0.2	2.7	−0.4	2.5	−0.5
Real exchange rate (DM/$)	1.71	−8.0	1.78	−4.2	1.78	−4.3	1.7	−11.1	1.79	−3.9	1.66	−10.7

Interlink: Alternative Scenarios

	1 Pure Dollar Depreciation				2 Fiscal Restriction in U.S.				3 Fiscal Restriction in U.S., Expansion in Japan, Germany and Endogenous Dollar Depreciation			
	1989		1992		1989		1992		1989		1992	
	(A)	(B)	(A)	(B)	(A)	(B)	(A)	(B)	(A)	(B)	(A)	(B)
United States												
Real GNP	2.3	1.4	1.6	−1.0	1.1	−1.2	1.4	−3.5	1.2	−0.5	2.5	−0.6
Consumption deflator	6.9	3.7	5.7	9.6	3.7	−0.2	3.4	−1.8	4.2	1.0	4.8	2.5
Current balance												
In billions of dollars	−101.0	4.0	−79.0	37.0	−89.0	16.0	−66.0	50.0	−85.0	20.0	−47.0	69.0
In percent of GNP	−1.9	0.2	−1.2	0.7	−1.8	0.3	−1.1	0.8	−1.7	0.4	−0.8	1.1
Japan												
Real GNP	1.7	−1.6	3.3	−3.8	2.7	−0.4	3.0	−1.4	3.5	1.1	3.3	1.7
Consumption deflator	0.8	−1.4	0.8	−3.8	1.8	−0.1	1.6	−0.8	1.8	−0.4	2.1	0.0
Current balance												
In billions of dollars	76.0	−3.0	71.0	−22.0	75.0	−4.0	79.0	−14.0	71.0	−8.0	55.0	−38.0
In percent of GNP	2.2	−0.6	1.6	−1.0	2.7	−0.1	2.3	−0.3	2.4	−0.4	1.5	−1.1
Real exchange rate (Yen/$)	145.7	−15.9	145.7	−15.9	173.1	−0.1	171.5	−1.0	172.2	−0.6	174.2	0.5

Table 2. Alternative Policy Scenarios (concluded)

Interlink: Alternative Scenarios

	1 Pure Dollar Depreciation				2 Fiscal Restriction in U.S.				3 Fiscal Restriction in U.S., Expansion in Japan, Germany and Endogenous Dollar Depreciation			
	1989		1992		1989		1992		1989		1992	
	(A)	(B)	(A)	(B)	(A)	(B)	(A)	(B)	(A)	(B)	(A)	(B)
Germany, Fed. Rep. of												
Real GNP	1.1	0.0	2.4	−1.1	0.9	−0.4	1.9	−1.1	0.9	−0.5	2.0	−1.0
Consumption deflator	1.3	−0.5	0.8	−1.8	1.5	−0.1	1.1	−0.6	1.4	−0.3	0.8	−1.8
Current balance												
In billions of dollars	37.0	5.0	30.0	−4.0	30.0	−2.0	26.0	−8.0	30.0	−2.0	26.0	−8.0
In percent of GNP	2.5	0.0	1.6	−0.4	2.4	−0.1	1.7	−0.5	2.3	−0.2	1.7	−0.5
Real exchange rate (DM/$)	1.75	−11.4	1.75	−11.4	1.98	−0.1	1.95	−1.2	1.96	−0.7	2.02	2.3

Notes: (A) Percentage growth rates, except as otherwise marked. (B) For GNP, deflator and exchange rate, percentage deviations from reference scenario; for current account balance, absolute deviations. Figures under (A) have been obtained applying deviations from baseline derived from simulations carried out by the Fund in August 1987 with the reference scenario. For scenario 2, figures under (A) have been obtained applying deviations from baseline derived from simulations carried out by the OECD in August 1987 with the reference scenario.

Source: Bank of Italy estimates.

Table 2 summarizes recent alternative policy scenarios produced using the Multimod and Interlink. The baseline scenarios (not shown) assume generally unchanged policy and roughly constant real exchange rates. The alternative scenarios add to the most recent baseline the effects of assumed changes in policy or in the economic environment. Three of these are summarized in Table 2. These are the cases of market-determined dollar depreciation with no change in policy, a shift toward fiscal restraint in the United States, and a combination of a shift in the international fiscal mix and market-determined dollar depreciation. Details of the simulation assumptions are given in the notes to the table.

Let us focus on the behavior of exchange rates and the U.S. current account in Table 2. Consider first the Fund's Multimod scenarios in the top bank of figures. The case of pure dollar depreciation reflects an exogenous increase in the risk premium. This is shown in the movement of the real exchange rates of the yen and DM against the dollar. The yen appreciates by 7.1 percent against the dollar in 1989 and 2.7 percent in 1992, relative to the baseline. The corresponding numbers for the DM are 8.0 and 4.2. These follow the path of sudden depreciation of the dollar with rational expectations shown in Chart 9. The consequence is a reduction in the U.S. current account deficit of $86.1 billion by 1992, the largest reduction of all the alternatives in Table 2.

Table 3. Key Assumptions for Scenarios
Pure Dollar Depreciation[1]

MULTIMOD	INTERLINK
Fiscal policy: unchanged policy setting with respect to the reference scenario and endogenous revenues.	*Fiscal policy:* unchanged policy setting with respect to the reference scenario and endogenous revenues.
Monetary policy United States: monetary conditions are tightened in order to avoid inflationary consequences of dollar depreciation; interest rates rise above the level in the reference scenario. Japan and Federal Republic of Germany: interest rates decline somewhat with the appreciation of the currencies, as monetary growth rates remain unchanged.	*Monetary policy:* broadly non-accommodating. In particular: United States: short-term interest rates are driven up to 9 percent as a counter to inflation and then fall to 7 percent as output weakens and inflation pressures ease; long-term interest rates rise from 9 to 11 percent over the projection period. Japan and Germany: interest rates decline as inflation falls, with a floor on short-term rates at 2 percent.
Exchange rates: a constraint is imposed over the ratio of U.S. net foreign indebtedness to GNP, that must not exceed 15 percent in 1995, as against 22 percent in the reference scenario. Therefore, the exchange value of the dollar is assumed to decline in a way consistent with the reduction of U.S. current account deficit that keeps the foreign debt ratio at the desired level in 1995; the adjustment takes place in 1988, with the U.S. dollar depreciating by 15 percent in nominal terms against the other major currencies.	*Exchange rates:* during 1988, the U.S. dollar depreciates by 20 percent against the yen and 15 percent against the DM in nominal terms. Then exchange rates are constant in nominal terms in 1989, and broadly stable in real terms in the following years.

Fiscal Restriction in the United States[2]

MULTIMOD	INTERLINK
Fiscal policy United States: federal government non-interest expenditure is reduced by amounts rising from $42 billion in 1988 to $91 billion in 1992 from the levels assumed in the reference scenario. Japan and Germany: unchanged policy setting with respect to the reference scenario and endogenous revenues.	*Fiscal policy* United States: federal government expenditures is gradually reduced by about $70 billion and proceeds from income taxes increase by about $50 billion by the end of 1992 from the levels assumed in the reference scenario. Japan and Germany: unchanged policy setting with respect to the reference scenario and endogenous revenues.
Monetary policy: interest rates decline in the United States in order to keep money growth on target; a reduction of interest rates is also projected, to a lesser extent, for Japan and Germany.	*Monetary policy:* U.S. money supply growth decelerates broadly in line with nominal income leaving short-term rates unchanged from the levels in the reference scenario; in Japan and Germany, interest rates also remain at the reference level.
Exchange rates: endogenous variations.	*Exchange rates:* nominal exchange rates unchanged from the levels in the reference scenario.

Table 3. (concluded) Key Assumptions for Scenarios
Coordinated Fiscal Action and Dollar Depreciation[3]

MULTIMOD	INTERLINK
Fiscal policy	*Fiscal policy*
United States: the same policy setting as in scenario 2.	United States: starting from 1988, the general government financial deficit is cut back over four years by a further 2 percent of GNP, compared with the reference scenario, action being concentrated on government expenditure.
Japan: higher fiscal expenditures in 1988–1990 by an amount equal to 0.5 percent of GNP.	
Germany: lower tax revenues by an amount growing from DM 7.6 billions in 1988 to DM 20 billions in 1991. As a ratio to GNP, the fiscal stimulus is roughly the same as in Japan.	Japan: starting from 1988, the general government financial deficit is increased over four years by a total of 1 percent of GNP compared with the reference scenario, action being concentrated on government expenditure; housing investment is increased by 3 percent per annum compared with the reference scenario.
Monetary policy: interest rates decline in the United States and rise in Japan and Germany, in order to keep money growth on target.	
Exchange rates: endogenous variations.	Germany: the same policy setting as in the reference scenario and endogenous revenues.
	Monetary policy: is assumed to be broadly non-accommodating. In particular:
	United States: unchanged money growth and lower interest rates compared with the reference scenario.
	Japan: interest rates are assumed to be initially slightly higher than in the reference scenario before falling toward the end of the projection period.
	Germany: interest rates are rather lower than in the reference scenario reflecting weaker output growth and lower inflation.
	Exchange rates: steady decline of the U.S. and Canadian dollar against other OECD countries of 2 percent per annum in nominal terms relative to the reference scenario.

[1] Simulation carried out in August 1987 for Multimod and in February 1988 for Interlink.
[2] Simulation carried out in August 1987 for Multimod and in April 1987 for Interlink.
[3] Simulation carried out in August 1987 for Multimod and in February 1988 for Interlink.

The Multimod scenario of fiscal restriction in the United States illustrates one of the main points of this paper. In this scenario the dollar depreciates in real terms against the yen by 2.8 percent in 1989 and 6.6. percent in 1992, and against the DM by 4.3 percent in 1989 and 11.1 percent in 1992. In the scenario with fiscal expansion in Germany and Japan as well as fiscal contraction in the United States, the depreciation against the yen is much greater; against the DM it is a bit smaller. The point here is that the fiscal scenarios all include further depreciation of the dollar. This raises the question: why do the Group of Seven finance ministers and some of their central banks profess the illusion that fiscal action can eliminate the need for further dollar depreciation? This undermines their own credibility.

The OECD Interlink model takes nominal exchange rates as exogenous, so the simulations in the bottom bank of figures in Table 2 are quite different from Multimod's in the behavior of exchange rates. In the first simulation, the dollar is devalued against the yen by 15.9 percent and against the DM by 11.4 percent in real terms and held at that level. Oddly, the effect on the U.S. current account is less than half of that in the corresponding Multimod simulation, which has less than half the dollar depreciation. In the Interlink simulation of fiscal restriction in the United States, the real exchange rate hardly moves. This does not support the Group of Seven view, of course; it is due to an inconsistent assumption.

The simulations, as well as theory, show that a degree of restoration of fiscal balance in the United States, with its concomitant dollar depreciation, would contribute to the restoration of international balance. The curious point remains the idea of the need for fiscal expansion outside the United States. If the secondary objective is to stabilize the dollar in the short run, fiscal expansion is counterproductive. Monetary expansion in Japan and Europe could do the job. It would also support demand and ward off fears of a world recession as the United States rights its fiscal balance. And, by increasing world saving, this package would reduce real interest rates and the debt service of the developing countries.

Appendix I

Two-Country Fundamentals Model

This Appendix sets out the algebra of the two-country version of the "fundamentals" model presented in Branson (1985 and 1988). The model analyzes the effects of changes in real variables such as the deficit or risk premium on other real variables, namely real interest rates and the real exchange rate. It abstracts from cyclical effects by holding output constant.

The model delivers the comparative statics of real disturbances for real endogenous variables. It does not analyze their dynamic paths, which are composed of changes in nominal variables, some of which are sticky (goods prices), and some free to jump (asset prices). The dynamics of nominal adjustment are discussed in Appendix II, which has the same real comparative static properties as the fundamentals model here. So it may be useful to view this model as giving a concise description of the movement of equilibrium position in real terms, and the dynamic model as describing the nominal paths between equilibria.

Model

The model is three equations, describing national income equilibrium in each country, and the real arbitrage condition linking the two countries' financial markets. The national income equilibrium conditions are

(14) $\quad D = S(r) - X(e - \bar{e}, \alpha)$, (Home country)

(15) $\quad D^* = S^*(r^*) + X(e - \bar{e}, \alpha)$ (Foreign country).

These say that the budget deficits (D, D^*) must equal the sum of net private saving (S, S^*), and the current account surplus $(X>0)$ or deficit $(X<0)$. Net saving is assumed to depend on the domestic interest rate with S', $S^{*'}>0$. Net exports of the home country depend on the real exchange rate and a shift parameter to reflect changes in demand patterns, with $X_e>0$ and $X_\alpha>0$. When $e = \bar{e}$, the current account is in balance.

Financial equilibrium is characterized by the arbitrage condition on real interest rates developed in Branson (1988):

$r = r^* + \hat{e} + \rho\,(B/B^*)$,

where $\hat{e}$ is the expected rate of change of the real exchange rate and ρ is a risk premium that depends on the relative supplies of government debt, assumed to be denominated in home currency. We add the perhaps reasonable assumption that the exchange rate is expected to move toward the long-run equilibrium:

$\hat{e} = \theta\,(\bar{e} - e)$.

Combining these two relationships yields the arbitrage condition that is the third equation of the fundamentals model:

(16) $\quad e = \bar{e} + \dfrac{1}{\theta}[r^* - r + \rho\,(B/B^*)]$.

Equations (14) – (16) serve to determine the real interest rates r and r^* and the real exchange rate e, as functions of the real budget deficits D and D^*, the shift parameter α, the relative real debt stock B/B^*, and the underlying long-run equilibrium real rate $\bar{e}$.

Comparative Statics

The total differential of the model can be written in matrix form as equation (17):

$$
\begin{array}{c}
(14) \\
(15) \\
(16)
\end{array}
\overset{A}{\begin{bmatrix} S' & 0 & -X_e \\ 0 & S^{*\prime} & X_e \\ 1 & -1 & \theta \end{bmatrix}} \begin{bmatrix} dr \\ dr^* \\ de \end{bmatrix} = \overset{B}{\begin{bmatrix} 1 & 0 & X_\alpha & 0 & -X_e \\ 0 & 1 & -X_\alpha & 0 & X_e \\ 0 & 0 & 0 & \rho' & -\theta \end{bmatrix}} \begin{bmatrix} dD \\ dD^* \\ d\alpha \\ d\dfrac{B}{B^*} \\ d\bar{e} \end{bmatrix}
$$

The determinant $|A| = S'[\theta S^{*\prime} + X_e] + S^{*\prime}X_e > 0$.

The comparative statics results can be obtained by substituting columns of the B matrix into the A matrix following Cramer's Rule. These results are given in Table 4. Since total differentiation linearizes the model, effects of combinations of changes in D and D* can be obtained by summing or differencing the entries in the dD and dD* rows. For example, a reduction in D and an increase in D* by the same amount would reduce r and increase r* by

$$dr = -\frac{S'\theta}{|A|} dD^*; \qquad dr^* = \frac{S^{*\prime}\theta}{|A|} dD^*.$$

The effect on e would be an increase (depreciation) by

$$de = \frac{S^{*\prime} + S'}{A} dD^*.$$

Table 4. Comparative Statics Results of Fundamentals Model

Exogenous Variables	Endogenous Variables		
	dr	dr^*	de
dD	$\dfrac{S^{*\prime}\theta + X_e}{|A|} > 0$	$\dfrac{X_e}{|A|} > 0$	$\dfrac{-S^{*\prime}}{|A|} < 0$
dD^*	$\dfrac{X_e}{|A|} > 0$	$\dfrac{S'\theta + X_e}{|A|} > 0$	$\dfrac{S'}{|A|} > 0$
$d\alpha$	$\dfrac{S^{*\prime}\theta X_\alpha}{|A|} > 0$	$\dfrac{-S'\theta X_\alpha}{|A|} < 0$	$\dfrac{-X_\alpha(S' + S^{*\prime})}{|A|} < 0$
$d(B/B^*)$	$\dfrac{\rho' X_e S^{*\prime}}{|A|} > 0$	$\dfrac{-\rho' X_e S'}{|A|} < 0$	$\dfrac{S'S^{*\prime}\rho'}{|A|} > 0$
$d\bar{e}$	0	0	1

The effects of policies on the interest differential $r - r^*$ can be obtained by the difference of the entries in the relevant row. For example, an increase in D will raise the interest differential $r - r^*$ by

$$d(r - r^*) = \frac{S^{*\prime}\theta}{A} dD,$$

holding the existing relative debt stocks B/B^* constant.

Graphical Analysis

The two-country model has three endogenous variables, r, r^*, e. For a graphical analysis in r, r^* space, we can collapse the model into two equations as follows. The total differentials of the two national income equations (14) and (15) can be summed to yield

(18) $dD + dD^* = S' dr + S^{*\prime} dr^*$.

In the r, r^* space of Chart 10, Panel 1, this is the RR line with a negative slope $dr/dr^* = -S^{*\prime}/S'$. An increase in either D or D^* shifts RR out, tending to increase both interest rates. The arbitrage condition (16) is the AA line in this panel, which has a slope of unity. Its position is conditional on $(e - \bar{e})$ (which is endogenous) and B/B^*. An increase in $(e - \bar{e})$ shifts the AA line down; an increase in $\rho(B/B^*)$ shifts it up.

We can now describe the results of Table 4 graphically. An increase in either D or D^* shifts RR out, as in Chart 10, Panel 2. If the increase is in D, the real exchange rate e falls (home currency appreciates), and the AA line shifts up, moving the equilibrium to point 1 from point 0. The home interest rate rises more than the foreign rate. If the increase is in D^*, the AA curve shifts down or e rises, and the equilibrium moves to point 2 from point 0. In both cases, both interest rates rise because world saving is reduced; this is clear from Panel 1.

A shift in demand from foreign to home goods, reflected in an increase in α, causes the real exchange rate to fall (home currency appreciates), shifting the AA line up along RR, raising r and reducing r^*. This is shown in Panel 3. Similarly, an increase in the risk premium $\rho(B/B^*)$ shifts the AA curve up.

The text analysis of the effects of an increase in D, such as occurred in the 1980s in the United States, is illustrated in Chart 10, Panel 4. The initial increase in the deficit carries the system from point 0 to point 1, with an increase in r, r^*, and $r - r^*$, and a fall in e (appreciation). This generates a current account deficit $(X < 0)$. As dollar debt accumulates, B/B^* rises, shifting the AA curve up further. During this phase the exchange rate is rising (depreciation). This can be seen from $de/d(B/B^*) > 0$ in Table 4. This process continues until the current account deficit is closed at a point like 2. There r has risen enough, and r^* fallen enough, to raise S and reduce S^* enough to make room for debt service in the current account X. This would be represented in Table 4 by an increase in $\bar{e}$.

Chart 10. Comparative Statics Results of Fundamentals Model

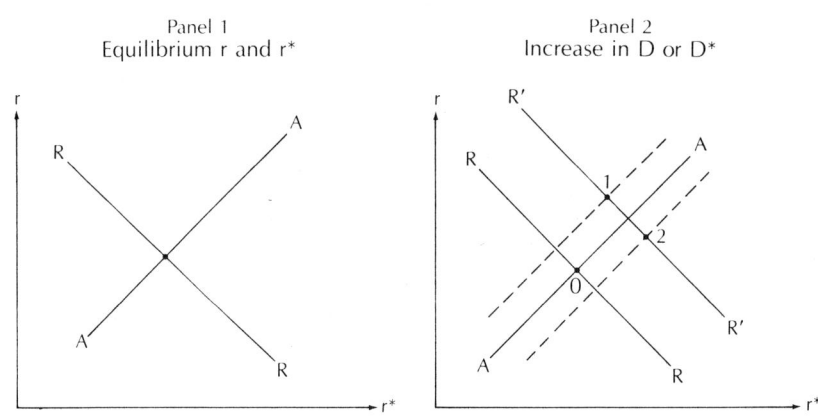

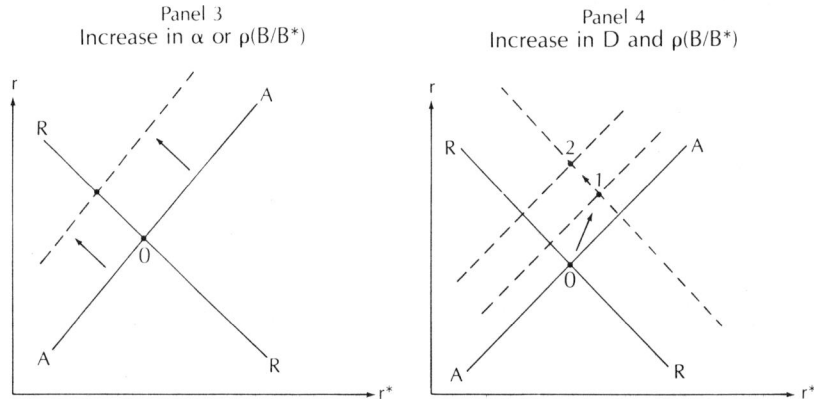

Appendix II

Nominal Dynamics in Two-Country Dornbusch Model

This Appendix sets out the algebra of the two-country version of the dynamic exchange rate model presented first in Dornbusch (1976). The model can be used to analyze the effects of changes in monetary and fiscal policies on the price level and the nominal exchange rate. In the version presented here, real output is held constant to avoid the complications of cyclical effects.

This model delivers the comparative statics of nominal disturbances for nominal variables, and the dynamic paths of adjustment of these variables. After setting out the model, we will first present the long-run comparative statics, and then the dynamics. This model contains the fundamentals model of Appendix I as the determinant of real variables, but adds the dynamics of nominal adjustment. Here we focus on the latter.

Model

Here we add money-market relationships and nominal variables to the fundamentals model, and then reduce the model by assuming symmetry to focus on relative price levels and the nominal exchange rate. So as the model is introduced, we assume the parameters are the same in both countries.

The two money-market equilibrium conditions are

(19) $\quad m - \alpha p - (1-\alpha)p^* - (1-\alpha)E = \phi y - \lambda i \quad$ (Home)

(20) $\quad m^* - \alpha p^* - (1-\alpha)p + (1-\alpha)E = \phi y^* - \lambda i^* \quad$ (Foreign).

All variables except the nominal interest rates i and i^* are in logs, so λ is the semi-elasticity of money demand. The deflator for nominal money balances in each case is the consumer price index, with a home goods share α and an import share $(1-\alpha)$. We assume $\alpha > 0.5$. The exchange rate enters both equations through the import content of consumer prices. E is the log of the nominal exchange rate.

The nominal arbitrage condition is given by

(21) $\quad i = i^* + \dot{E} + \rho$,

where ρ is the risk premium. In the dynamic analysis we will assume exchange rate expectations are formed rationally.

Gradual adjustment of prices to excess demand in the goods markets is assumed. The two price-adjustment equations are

(22) $\quad \dot{p} = \pi [X(E + p^* - p - \bar{e}) - S(i) + D] \quad$ (Home)

(23) $\quad \dot{p}^* = \pi [-X(E + p^* - p - \bar{e}) - S(i^*) + D^*] \quad$ (Foreign).

Here prices adjust gradually to the excess of demand, given by $X - S + D$. The components of demand are the same as in the fundamentals model. Since in the long-run equilibrium inflation is zero, in the long run $i = r$ and $i^* = r^*$.

Long-run equilibrium of the model can be analyzed by setting $\dot{p}$, $\dot{p}^*$, and $\dot{E}$ equal to zero in equations (19)–(23). In that case, the five equations serve to determine long-run equilibrium movements in the two price levels, the two interest rates, and the nominal exchange rate, in response to changes in the money supplies m and m*, the fiscal deficits D and D*, and the risk premium ρ. Total differentiation of (19)–(23) with $\dot{p} = \dot{p}^* = \dot{E} = 0$ yields the 5×5 matrix equation (24):

$$
\begin{array}{c}
(19) \\ (20) \\ (21) \\ (22) \\ (23)
\end{array}
\overbrace{\begin{bmatrix}
-\alpha & -(1-\alpha) & -(1-\alpha) & \lambda & 0 \\
-(1-\alpha) & -\alpha & (1-\alpha) & 0 & \lambda \\
0 & 0 & 0 & 1 & -1 \\
-X_e & X_e & X_e & -S' & 0 \\
X_e & -X_e & -X_e & 0 & -S'
\end{bmatrix}}^{A}
\begin{bmatrix} dp \\ dp^* \\ dE \\ di \\ di^* \end{bmatrix}
= I
\begin{bmatrix} -dm \\ -dm^* \\ d\rho \\ dD \\ dD^* \end{bmatrix}
$$

where I is the unit diagonal matrix.

Rather than analyzing the entire 5×5 system, we simplify it into two parts. The fundamentals model of Appendix I combines p, p*, and E into one variable e and focuses on the real part of the system. The A matrix in equation (17) is the bottom right-hand 3×3 matrix in A in (24), with θ in place of 0 in the diagonal. Here we focus on nominal adjustment and dynamics by eliminating i and i* and reducing the system to two equations in $p - p^*$ and E. Here the assumption of symmetry is important.

If we subtract equation (20) from (19) and substitute from (21) $\dot{E} + \rho$ for $i - i^*$, we obtain

(25) $\quad m - m^* + (1 - 2\alpha)(p - p^*) - 2(1-\alpha)E = \theta(y - y^*) - \lambda(\dot{E} + \rho)$.

The assmption that $\alpha > 0.5$ makes the coefficient of $(p - p^*)$ negative. To obtain the equation for the inflation differential $\dot{p} - \dot{p}^*$, we assume the savings functions are linear and subtract (23) from (22) with the same substitution for $i - i^*$. This yields

(26) $\quad \dot{p} - \dot{p}^* = \pi[2X(E + p^* - p - \bar{e}) - S(\dot{E} + \rho) + D - D^*]$.

The two equations (25) and (26) can be used to analyze the comparative statics and dynamics of the relative price level $p - p^*$ and the exchange rate E.

Long-Run Comparative Statics

Long-run equilibrium can be analyzed by setting $\dot{p} = \dot{p}^* = \dot{E} = 0$ in equations (25) and (26). The total differentials of the resulting equilibrium system are given by the 2×2 matrix equation (27):

$$
\begin{array}{c} (25) \\ (26) \end{array}
\overbrace{\begin{bmatrix} -(1-2\alpha) & 2(1-\alpha) \\ -2X_e & 2X_e \end{bmatrix}}^{A}
\begin{bmatrix} d(p-p^*) \\ dE \end{bmatrix}
=
\overbrace{\begin{bmatrix} 1 & \lambda & 0 & 0 \\ 0 & S' & -1 & 1 \end{bmatrix}}^{B}
\begin{bmatrix} d(m-m^*) \\ d\rho \\ dD \\ dD^* \end{bmatrix}
$$

The determinant of the $|A|$ matrix is $2X_e > 0$.

The comparative static results are given in Table 5. The symmetry of the model is obvious. An increase in the relative money supply $(m - m^*)$ raises $(p - p^*)$ and E proportionately. An increase in the home deficit D reduces E (appreciation) and an increase in the foreign deficit increases it. An increase in the risk premium raises E but has an ambiguous effect on $(p - p^*)$.

The effect here of a change in either deficit or in the risk premium on the real exchange rate e ($= E + p^* - p$) can be obtained by subtracting the entry for $(p - p^*)$ from the entry for E in Table 5. The results are given by

$$\frac{dE - d(p-p^*)}{dD} = -\frac{dE - d(p-p^*)}{dD^*} = -\frac{1}{2X_e} < 0$$

$$\frac{dE - d(p-p^*)}{d\rho} = \frac{S'}{2X_e} > 0.$$

As in the fundamentals model, an increase in the home budget deficit or reduction in the foreign budget deficit generates an appreciation of the real exchange rate, and an increase in the risk premium, a depreciation.

Table 5. Comparative Statics in Two-Country Dornbusch Model

Exogenous Variables	Endogenous Variables	
	$d(p-p^*)$	dE
$d(m-m^*)$	1	1
$d\rho$	$\lambda - \frac{S'}{X_e}(1-\alpha) \gtrless 0$	$\lambda - \frac{S'}{2X_e}(1-2\alpha) > 0$
dD	$\frac{(1-\alpha)}{X_e} > 0$	$\frac{(1-2\alpha)}{2X_e} < 0$
dD^*	$-\frac{(1-\alpha)}{X_e} < 0$	$-\frac{(1-2\alpha)}{2X_e} > 0$

Dynamics

We can study dynamics in the $(p - p^*)$, E space by sketching the locuses for $\dot{E} = 0$ from equation (25) and $(\dot{p} - \dot{p}^*) = 0$ from equation (26). Setting $\dot{E} = 0$ in (25) gives the downward-sloping locus in Chart 11, Panel 1, with a slope given by

Chart 11. Comparative Statics in Two-Country Dornbusch Model

Panel 1
Money-market equilibrium

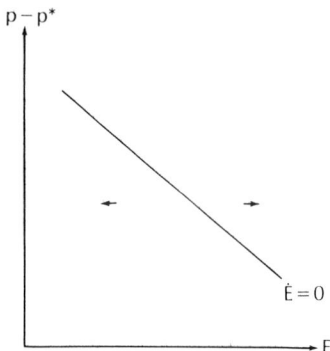

Panel 2
Goods market equilibrium

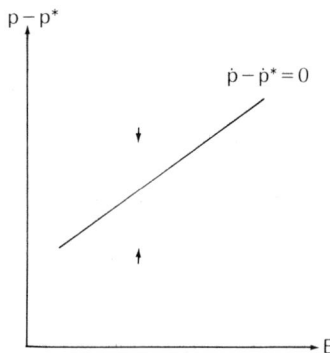

Panel 3
Saddle-path equilibrium

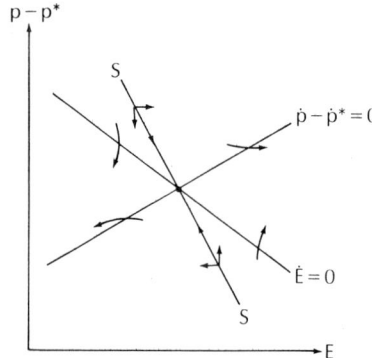

Panel 4
Monetary disturbance

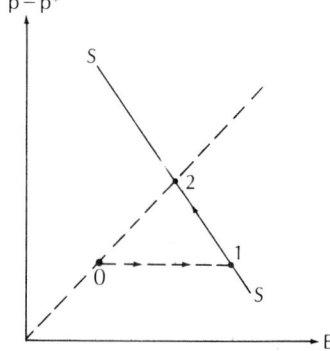

Chart 11. (concluded) Comparative Statics in Two-Country Dornbusch Model

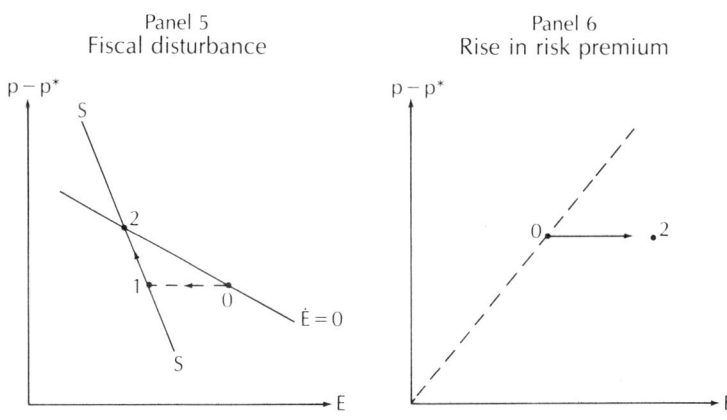

Panel 5
Fiscal disturbance

Panel 6
Rise in risk premium

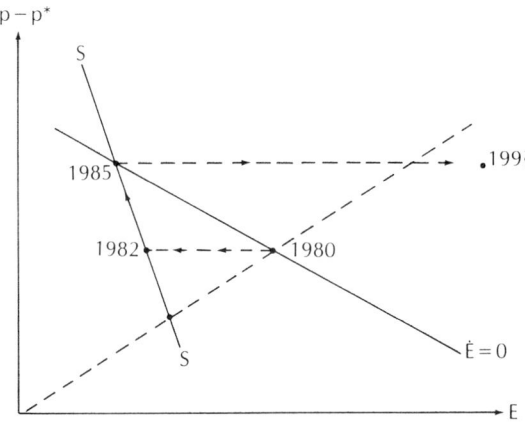

Panel 7
Fiscal shift followed by rise in
risk premium: the dollar in the 1980s

$$\left.\frac{d(p-p^*)}{dE}\right|_{\dot{E}=0} = \frac{2(1-\alpha)}{1-2\alpha} < 0 \quad \text{if} \quad \alpha > 0.5.$$

The dynamics of E relative to the $\dot{E}=0$ locus under rational expectations are given by the horizontal arrows in Panel 1. For a value of the exchange rate above the $\dot{E}=0$ locus to be consistent with money-market equilibrium, the exchange rate must be expected to rise. An increase in the exchange rate reduces relative real balances and increases $i-i^*$, requiring from the arbitrage condition a positive $\dot{E}$. Below the $\dot{E}=0$ locus, the exchange rate must be expected to fall. With rational expectations, the actual movement is the same as the expected.

The slope of the locus where $\dot{p}-\dot{p}^*=0$ can be obtained as follows. Totally differentiate equation (25) allowing $(p-p^*)$, E, and $\dot{E}$ to change, and solve for $d\dot{E}$. Then totally differentiate equation (26) with $\dot{p}-\dot{p}^*=0$, and substitute the expression from (25) for the term in $d\dot{E}$. This yields for the $\dot{p}-\dot{p}^*=0$ locus in Chart 11, Panel 2, a slope of

$$0 < \left.\frac{d(p-p^*)}{dE}\right|_{\dot{p}-\dot{p}^*=0} = \frac{2X_e - \frac{s'}{\lambda} 2(1-\alpha)}{2X_e - \frac{s'}{\lambda}(1-2\alpha)} < 1.$$

The slope of the $\dot{p}-\dot{p}^*=0$ locus is flatter than unity due to the $\dot{E}$ term in equation (26). As $(p-p^*)$ rises, $\dot{E}$ increases because $i-i^*$ rises, so saving increases and the depreciation needed to maintain goods market equilibrium is less than the original increase in $(p-p^*)$. The vertical arrows in Panel 2 show the direction of price adjustment toward the $\dot{p}-\dot{p}^*=0$ locus.

Dynamic adjustment to the long-run equilibrium where both $\dot{p}-\dot{p}^*$ and $\dot{E}=0$ is shown in Panel 3. As usual in a model with expectations dynamics, there is a unique stable saddle path into the equilibrium, labeled SS. (This is the QQ path in Dornbusch (1976)). Other paths diverge to an asymptote normal to the SS path. Following a disturbance, the market searches for a level of the exchange rate in the SS path, which has two essential properties: (a) it leads to equilibrium, and (b) along it, expectations of $\dot{E}$ are realized.

Dynamic adjustment can now be analyzed as follows. First, the movement of the equilibrium point is given by the multipliers of Table 5. This locates the new SS path. Then the exchange rate jumps to the new SS path at the pre-existing value of $p-p^*$. Finally both E and $p-p^*$ were along SS to the new equilibrium.

The effect of an unanticipated increase in $(m-m^*)$ is shown in Panel 4. The long-run equilibrium moves out proportionately from point 0 to point 2, with both locuses shifting up. The exchange rate jumps from point 0 to point 1 on the new SS path, and then E and $p-p^*$ move gradually to point 2. This is the famous overshooting result in the two-country model.

The effect of an increase in $D-D^*$, the relative fiscal stance, is shown in Panel 5. Here only the $\dot{p}-\dot{p}^*=0$ locus shifts, since $D-D^*$ is not in the $\dot{E}=0$ equation. The long-run equilibrium moves from point 0 to point 2 as the

$\dot{p} - \dot{p}^* = 0$ locus (not shown) shifts up. The exchange rate jumps (appreciation) to point 1 on the new SS path, and then both E and $p - p^*$ adjust gradually to point 2. The model exhibits "undershooting" with respect to the (real) fiscal disturbance. A decrease in $D - D^*$ would move the equilibrium down the $\dot{E} = 0$ locus in Panel 5, with the exchange rate depreciating. This would be the consequence of a tightening in the U.S. fiscal position and an easing of fiscal policy in Germany and Japan.

The effect of an increase in the risk premium is shown in Panel 6. From Table 5, we see E rises but the sign of the effect on $p - p^*$ is unclear. If the latter were zero, then the equilibrium would move from point 0 to point 2, with both locuses shifting right. The exchange rate would follow the shift with no effect on $p - p^*$. If the new equilibrium is above point 2, that is, $p - p^*$ rises, then the exchange rate would overshoot. If it is below point 2, the exchange rate would undershoot. Thus we can expect an erratic path of depreciation in response to an increase in the risk premium.

The movement of the U.S. dollar since 1980 can be roughly replicated in this model if we assume first an increase in $D - D^*$ as the U.S. fiscal position shifted, and later in 1985 an increase in the risk premium as the market came to understand the implications of the increase in the stock of dollar debt. This is shown in Panel 7. The initial budget shift yielded a jump appreciation of the dollar across 1981 as the market came to understand the implications for the deficit. The dollar continued to appreciate along an erratic path to early 1985, as the market continued to digest new information on the size and duration of the deficit. The turnaround in 1985 can be interpreted as resulting from a gradual rise in the risk premium as the market contemplates the eventual size of the stock of dollar debt. The final equilibrium position in 199? will have to be below the ray from the origin to the initial 1980 point, since the equilibrium real exchange rate ē will have risen. This is necessary to provide the trade surplus to finance debt service at eventual current account balance.

REFERENCES

Bank of Japan, "U.S. Competitiveness in Manufacturing," Special Paper No. 153, September 1987.

Blanchard, O.J., "Reaganomics," *Economic Policy Review* (Cambridge), No. 5, (October 1987), pp. 15–56.

Branson, William H., "Causes of Appreciation and Volatility of the Dollar," in Federal Reserve Bank of Kansas City, *The U.S. Dollar—Recent Developments, Outlook, and Policy* (Kansas, 1985).

———, "Sources of Misalignment in the 1980s," in R.C. Marston, ed., *Exchange Rate Misalignment* (Chicago: University of Chicago Press, forthcoming, 1988).

Committee for Economic Development, "Report on U.S. Debt," cited in *International Herald Tribune*, February 20–21, 1988.

Dornbusch, Rudiger D., "Exchange Rate Dynamics," *Journal of Political Economy* (Chicago), Vol. 84 (December 1976), pp. 1161–76.

———, and Jeffrey A. Frankel, "Macroeconomics and the Dollar," in R.M. Stern, ed., *U.S. Trade Policies in a Changing World Economy* (New York: MIT Press, 1987), pp. 77–130.

Frenkel, Jacob A. and Assaf Razin, *Fiscal Policies and the World Economy* (Cambridge, Mass.: MIT PRess, 1987).

Genberg, Hans and Alexander Swoboda, "Current Account and Policy Mix Under Flexible Exchange Rates," International Monetary Fund Working Paper WP/87/70, October 1987.

Haas, Richard, and Paul R. Masson, "Minimod: Specification and Simulation Results," *Staff Papers*, International Monetary Fund (Washington), Vol. 33 (December 1986), pp. 722–67.

International Monetary Fund, *World Economic Outlook* (Washington: IMF, 1987).

Krugman, Paul R., "Exchange Rates and International Adjustment," New York University, The Center for Japan-U.S. Business and Economic Studies Working Paper No. 39 (September 1987).

———,"Fiscal Policy, Interest Rates, and Exchange Rates: Some Simple Analytics," Mimeograph, M.I.T., August 1985.

Marris, Stephen N., "The Decline and Fall of the Dollar: Some Policy Issues," *Brookings Papers on Economic Activity: 1* (1985), The Brookings Institution (Washington), pp. 237–44.

McKinnon, R.I., "An International Gold Standard Without Gold," Mimeograph, Cato Institute Sixth Annual Monetary Conference, February 25–26, 1988.

Organization for Economic Cooperation and Development, *Economic Outlook* (December 1987).

Comment

Niels Thygesen

William Branson identifies three policy illusions in the analysis by the International Monetary Fund and the Group of Seven Finance Ministers of the issue of international policy coordination. Taking the Fund's recent *World Economic Outlook* and Group of Seven communiqués announcing the so-called Louvre Accord of February 1987 and the follow-up in December 1987 as representative expressions of the official view, Branson is highly critical of three conclusions:

(1) that "today's constellation of exchange rates is an equilibrium constellation";

(2) that "a shift in the fiscal mix between the United States and the rest of the Group of Seven would substitute for further depreciation of the dollar"; and

(3) that there should be fiscal expansion in the surplus countries in the OECD area to match fiscal contraction in the United States.

Branson disagrees on all three points and provides a cogent empirical and theoretical analysis in support of his alternative views: a further depreciation of the dollar of at least 15 percent in effective real terms is required to eliminate the U.S. current account deficit; fiscal policy adjustments cannot substitute for depreciation, as both expenditure reduction and expenditure-switching measures have to be set in motion in the U.S. economy; while, finally, monetary expansion outside the United States would be preferable to fiscal expansion to smooth exchange rate changes. My comments take issue with all three of Branson's points. While there are good reasons for believing that the officially expressed views contain elements of wishful thinking and of inconsistent assumptions, Branson's conclusions seem to me too severe. Without endorsing the official view, which Branson identifies on the basis of a mixture of explicit statements and implicit assumptions, my own interpretation of it is more sympathetic. Let me take the three in turn.

Equilibrium Exchange Rate for the Dollar

Branson's reasoning is loyal to the bulk of the empirical analysis on the determinants of the U.S. current account deficit which has become available in recent years. The official institutions (the Fund and the OECD) and the large econometric models surveyed in the long-term research program on macroeconomic interactions and policy design in interdependent economies, jointly sponsored by the Brookings Institution and the Centre for Economic Policy Research (see notably Bryant, and Holtham and Hooper (1988)), invariably reach pessimistic conclusions about the course of the U.S. current account deficit over the next three to four years. After a small correction in 1986–88, the deficits widen again from 1989 on the basis of the assumptions of unchanged policies and exchange rates. Branson's estimate of the real exchange rate depreciation it would take to bring the U.S. current account into approximate balance by the early 1990s is not only in line with the results of the authors he quotes—Dornbusch and Frankel and Marris—but also with most of the large models. Had the paper been written in mid-1988 rather than early 1988, Branson would have been justified in increasing from 15–20 percent the required real depreciation, since the dollar has been allowed to rise by approximately 5 percent in nominal effective rate terms in recent months—

which is surprising in view of the general recognition that the dollar was not undervalued when it reached its temporary low in early 1988. Branson adds that even 15 (or 20) percent real depreciation—which would correspond to at least 25–30 percent nominal depreciation of the effective rate and more vis-à-vis the major industrial competitors, implying a dollar rate of less than 100 yen and less than DM 1.25 by 1991—would not be the end of exchange rate adjustment. Because of the weaker trend performance in output per manhour in the United States than in some of its competitors, and because of the asymmetry between the income elasticities in U.S. import demand and in the demand in the rest of the world for U.S. exports, the dollar will require further gradual downward adjustment, though at a much slower rate, after the major depreciation of the near future which Branson sees as necessary to restore external balance for the United States.

I have two critical comments to these calculations and their implications, while accepting Branson's analysis as a good reflection of mainstream macroeconomic analysis. The first relates to his choice of external objective for the United States, while the second raises a more basic doubt about the elasticity pessimism which is reflected in the calculated effects of past changes in the U.S. dollar.

As regards the former point, setting the objective for the U.S. current account at zero by the early 1990s appears unnecessarily ambitious. There is nothing compelling in such a scenario. The financial constraint on the United States in the sense of keeping the risk premium on dollar-denominated assets constant, is likely to be looser. For example, as long as U.S. net indebtedness is growing no faster than international financial portfolios, there should be no relative upward pressure on U.S. interest rates. Furthermore, foreign investors in dollar assets are likely to put more emphasis on the direction of change in the U.S. current account than on the level. Tentatively, but clearly as arbitrarily as for full elimination, one might argue that aiming for a gradual reduction of the current account deficit toward a level of 1 percent of GNP by the early 1990s would be sufficient to assume smooth financing through private net inflows. If such a course were to be firmly set, foreign central banks would also find the task of sustaining the dollar more manageable during brief periods of doubt in private markets, if such action were to be required. If the objective is "only" to swing the current account toward a deficit of 1 percent of GNP, the required real depreciation is cut by 8–10 percentage points according to Branson's own calculations (after taking into account the additional interest service, because U.S. net indebtedness will be higher in such a scenario).

As regards the second point, it seems reasonable to question whether the collective wisdom accumulated in the econometric models has moved toward excessive pessimism with respect to the price sensitivities of trade flows. The estimates based on these models are dominated by the experience of the 1970s and 1980s with their short-run volatility and medium-term cycles. This experience is reflected partly in a slower pass-through of exchange rate changes into prices—a phenomenon which is taken into account in well-specified models—and partly in greater reluctance to engage in international trade and investment. A detailed justification for inertia and a wait-and-see attitude has been provided (in recent work by Krugman (1987)).

At the present time, a lengthening of the lags with which firms producing internationally traded goods respond to relative price changes may offer an important part of the explanation of the apparent conflict between the massive improvement in U.S. competitiveness over the period since 1985 (confirmed in surveys of U.S. manufacturing industry by the Conference Board and others as largely sufficient to make U.S. products fully competitive with those of its main industrial competitors in the OECD area), and the slowness with which these changes show up in the trade flows (even in constant dollars). U.S. exporters are hesitating to engage in major efforts in foreign markets, and those U.S. producers who have been squeezed hard by foreign competition have delayed their decision to hit back aggressively while awaiting a clearer message as to how far and how fast the dollar was to be brought back to a sustainable level.

Last, but not not least, international investment in the United States and the repatriation of some U.S.-owned production facilities abroad have been delayed by the uncertainty surrounding the prospects of the dollar and by the many verdicts by economists that it was bound to fall significantly further. It is my contention that we are some distance from having observed the full effects of the downward adjustment of the dollar that had taken place up to early 1988—provided that adjustment had been regarded as permanent and definitive.

Turning to the shorter-term outlook, it adds to the uncertainty about the nature of the medium-term cycle of the dollar against the other main currencies that the dollar has been allowed to rise in recent months. One may disagree, as I do, with respect to the degree of overvaluation relative to a longer-term sustainable equilibrium estimated by Branson, but there could hardly be any disagreement about the medium-term required change, which—for the two reasons mentioned above—I would put at less than half the figure estimated by Branson.

Can Fiscal Policy Substitute for Depreciation?

It is correct and important to point out that fiscal adjustment in the United States, possibly combined with similar measures in the opposite direction abroad, cannot by themselves achieve both internal and external balance. A package of fiscal changes designed to bring the current accounts of the major countries into sustainable equilibrium—not necessarily zero—while pegging exchange rates in real (or, even more so, in nominal) terms could well lead to an overall deficiency in demand. Some exchange rate adjustment will be required, unless rather stringent assumptions are met, as mentioned by Branson, if departures from internal balance are to be contained. This is orthodox transfer theory and has been well absorbed into the textbook version of international adjustment following the contributions of Meade, Johnson, Fleming, and Mundell. It is only the juxtaposition with the recent official view that makes it look controversial. It is a virtue of Branson's paper that this conflict is put in the open. I believe it to be more apparent than real for essentially three reasons.

The first, briefly recognized by Branson, is that he adopts a too aggregative and Keynesian view of fiscal policy which is taken to be synonymous with short-term changes in public expenditure. Fiscal policy is not easily reducible to this one dimension, as, for example, the work of Frenkel and Razin (1987) on temporary versus permanent fiscal changes and on different fiscal instruments has shown. A more differentiated approach is required, even for assessing the broad macroeconomic issues raised by Branson. The international institutions are already taking this into account in their policy recommendations, though the implications are to make advice less qualitative and more difficult.

The second point is, as was the first, more a counsel of perfection than an objection which can easily be quantified. By focusing in his discussion of fiscal policy on public expenditure changes, Branson gives maximum weight to the departure from the assumptions under which fiscal policy could be sufficient for bringing about external adjustment between two countries while preserving internal balance in both. These assumptions are, as Branson fairly notes, either that one abstracts from bringing nontraded goods into the analysis, or that the sum of the marginal propensities to import in the two areas is one. Neither of these justifications is likely to hold if we think of opposite changes in public expenditures in the two countries. They would be less unrealistic if one thought of tax changes impinging largely on consumer spending or on corporate investment.

My third point in partial justification of the view attributed by Branson to the officials of Group of Seven starts from the observation

Chart 1. Internal and External Balance and Dollar Devaluation

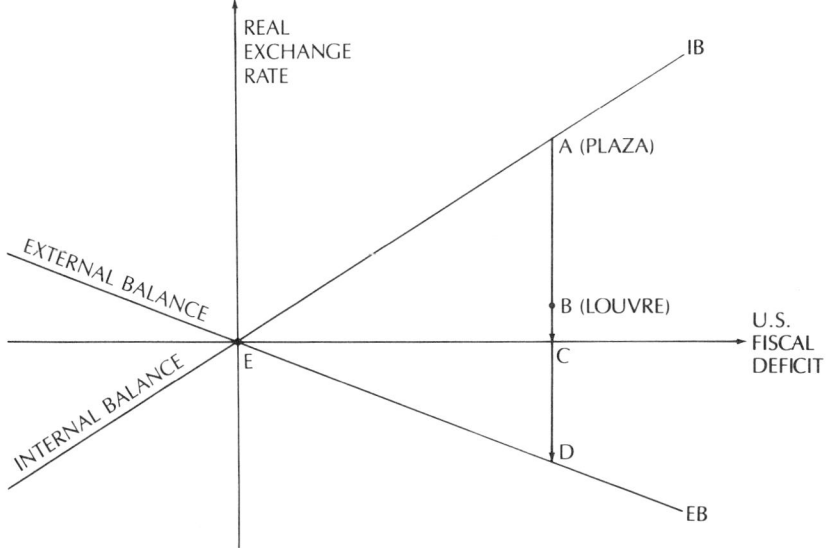

Source: *After the Louvre: Promoting Exchange Rate Stability* (Report of the Croham Committee, Public Policy Centre, London, 1988).

that, in the perspective of most non-U.S. officials and of an increasing number of U.S. officials, the U.S. economy is in an overheated state, in which both internal and external considerations suggest a need for fiscal tightening. Without it the risk of accelerating inflation and a collapse of the dollar is seen as considerable. This line of thinking is illuminated in Chart 1.

The chart, which takes policy outside the United States as given, shows in the traditional way combinations of the real exchange rate and the stance of fiscal policy (possibly measured by the structural budget deficit) at which the U.S. economy is in external and internal balance. As the fiscal deficit grows, the dollar has to appreciate in real terms to provide internal balance; this is approximately what happened during the later stages of the U.S. expansion and appreciation of 1983–85. A growing fiscal deficit requires real depreciation to pursue current account equilibrium; hence the external balance line has a negative slope.

The story starts at point A, marked Plaza. (One could have started it from the peak of the dollar in February 1985 above the internal balance line with a combination of even greater overvaluation of the dollar in an external sense and some unutilized resources.) On that occasion the Group of Five Finance Ministers argued that further depreciaton of the dollar should be encouraged. At their Louvre meeting 17 months later, with the dollar nearing what would be a sustainable level of the U.S. currency, *provided* a U.S. fiscal contraction, possibly combined with fiscal expansion abroad, was launched, the Group of Five chose to put the main emphasis on the fiscal prerequisites, while encouraging their central bankers to sustain the dollar where it was. One may see interventions and the supporting monetary policies essentially as a means of affecting the speed with which the dollar moves along the vertical trajectory in the absence of other policy changes. The dollar had to fall further after the stock market crash in October had prompted the U.S. monetary authorities into a relative easing of policy which was incompatible with the Louvre Accord. But in December 1987 the Group of Five reiterated in a statement their view that the dollar had fallen enough. To be fair, the U.S. fiscal stance has been tightened slightly in late 1987 but it is near enough to being unchanged to justify the crude illustration in the diagram.

The strategy of the Group of Five would appear to be to say to the financial markets: we believe that relying on further dollar depreciation without an important fiscal contraction would be counter-productive. The further distance from C to D in the chart may not be very long in real terms—say, at most 10 percent from mid-1988 levels, or about half of Branson's figure—but in nominal terms it could be dramatic, because the depreciation would feed quickly into domestic costs and prices. It could also force a drastic adjustment of U.S. monetary policy. In these circumstances it is in the joint interest of the United States and other countries to try to constrain the adjustment path as closely as possible to CE, rather than to follow CDE (or a more unfavorable path with the dollar falling temporarily further than required by external balance, possibly interpreted as it was above in the sense of a small, but sustainable deficit). Recognizing that fiscal contraction on any major scale is unlikely in 1988, the Group of Five have effectively chosen to try to stay near or just above C for the time being.

This reasoning may be tactically motivated and risky, but it is not as inconsistent as Branson's criticism implies. The strategy is designed to avoid an inferior outcome of rapid dollar depreciation and the need for brutal correction rather than a full blueprint for how adjustment to both internal and external balance could be achieved. The illustration fails to take explicitly into account that the external balance line, representing the sustainable flow equilibrium of the current account will itself shift gradually downward to the extent that the net external indebtedness of the United States grows and the risk premium required to encourage investors into dollar assets increases. But these effects are, within the range of policy options considered, sufficiently small to leave the basic message of the official view coherent enough to warrant serious attention, despite their apparent conflict with received theory.

Symmetric Adjustment Outside the United States?

In accordance with the traditional view that the responsibility for correcting balance of payments imbalances should not fall solely on the deficit countries, most official statements over the past few years have stressed that the surplus countries have to facilitate adjustment by fiscal or other means to keep the growth of their domestic demand well above the growth of output. This prescription seems particularly appropriate in countries where the growth of output has in recent years been insufficient to prevent substantial underutilization of resources, resulting in high unemployment. The problem raised by Branson is whether this responsibility of the surplus countries should be exercised through fiscal or monetary expansion.

Branson is surely right in saying that fully compensating fiscal expansion outside the United States to offset contraction there would be inappropriate. His main reasons for saying so are that such a package would keep interest rates too high and accentuate downward pressures on the dollar which official opinion proclaims to wish to avoid. Instead, he argues, as always with good and discriminating use of economic theory, that the contribution of the surplus countries should take the form of additional monetary ease to contain an otherwise likely jump downwards of the dollar.

The former part of the argument seems to me more convincing than the latter. It would be desirable to have some net tightening of fiscal policy in the OECD area both because fiscal contraction in the United States seems an urgent problem and because the fiscal position in the aggregate outside the United States is not initially such as to suggest any major room for expansion. Japan has already acted significantly, but may have to do more; the Federal Republic of Germany could do more, though the growth of domestic demand there too is running well ahead of output growth. Germany's expansion may, however, have to be offset to some extent by fiscal tightening in other parts of Europe, where high deficits and/or high debt/GNP ratios severely constrain investment. The need to minimize the risk of pushing interest rates higher, hence reducing investment and making the debt-servicing problems of the international debtor countries more difficult, must encourage the industrial countries to collectively reduce their public deficits, making the U.S. contraction larger than the fiscal expansion abroad.

Branson's argument that a symmetrical adjustment would be a recipe for exchange market instability and undershooting of the dollar seems more questionable to me. The scenario underlying Branson's Charts 5 and 6 implies that a fiscal contraction in the United States would prompt a decline in U.S. interest rates and a downward jump of the dollar. This jump would become larger if fiscal expansion outside the United States was to be announced simultaneously because relative interest rates would then move further in favor of nondollar-denominated assets. While logically correct within the framework of the Dornbusch overshooting model, this reasoning is in conflict with the dynamics of exchange rates as seen by market participants and intended by officials.

An announced fiscal tightening of some significance in the United States would be likely to reduce U.S. interest rates, but the impact on the dollar is uncertain, because the fall in internal rates would largely reflect lower inflationary expectations. And it is certainly arguable that the initial effect on the dollar of the anouncement of a program for reducing the U.S. deficit gradually over three to four years would initially push the dollar up; only gradually, as the new policy showed up in lower borrowing, would there be a lower dollar to accompany the lower interest rates. Similarly, outside the United States, it is not obvious that an increase in interest rates prompted by larger government borrowing in Germany or other European currencies would strengthen the respective currencies. Early empirical work by Oudiz and Sachs (1984) on policy coordination did not find such effects outside the United States, and on the whole the transmission through interest rates to exchange rates of fiscal changes are not well explained in the models.

My conclusion is that Branson has taken the overshooting model of exchange rates too literally. The arguments he finds in that model against a partly symmetrical fiscal response in the United States and elsewhere constitute no serious impediment to the adoption of such a program.

Branson recommends expansionary monetary policy in Europe and Japan to smooth the course of the dollar. His policy prescription may already be said to have been followed in Japan and Germany over the past couple of years, during which money growth has run well ahead of what the authorities expected or intended, partly as a result of dollar interventions. A similar remark could be made about the United Kingdom. In this situation, where domestic liquidity is already considered ample and as posing some inflationary risks, for the monetary authorities of the United Kingdom, Japan, Germany and possibly others to announce a step up in the rate of money creation would be hazardous. But the authorities of these countries may continue to follow, quietly and without announcing that as their contribution to international policy coordination, a course of intervening occasionally to sustain the dollar while minimizing in their domestic markets the liquidity effects of these interventions.

Jacques Polak said in his perceptive paper in this volume on national policies that a good deal of loving tender care had to be applied to fiscal policy to keep it in good shape for future and more difficult tasks. A similar observation may be made about monetary policy outside the United States; by permitting the rate of money creation to be stepped up significantly from already high rates, these countries would find themselves with serious difficulties of monetary management—as they have done in past periods where a weak dollar has left them with excessive liquidity. Branson's prescription would push the policy mix outside the United States still further in a direction in which it is already lopsided.

REFERENCES

Bryant, R.C., G. Holtham, and P. Hooper, eds, *External Deficits and the Dollar: The Pit and the Pendulum* (Washington: The Brookings Institution, 1988).

Croham, Lord et al., *After the Louvre: Promoting Exchange Rate Stability*, Report of an International Committee chaired by Lord Croham, Public Policy Centre (London, 1988).

Frenkel, Jacob A., and Assaf Razin, *Fiscal Policies in the World Economy* (Cambridge, Massachusetts: MIT Press, 1987).

Krugman, P.R., "Exchange Rates and International Adjustment," The Centre for Japan-US Business and Economic Studies Working Paper No. 39 (New York: New York University, 1987).

Oudiz, Gilles, and Jeffrey D. Sachs, "Macroeconomic Policy Coordination Among the Industrial Economies," *Brookings Papers on Economic Activity*, 1 (1984), The Brookings Institution (Washington), pp. 1–75.

Comment

Alexander K. Swoboda

William Branson's paper, together with most popular discussions of contemporary international adjustment problems, focuses on the need to achieve a reduction in the large current account deficit of the United States. Branson pays particular attention to the role of the dollar in the adjustment process as well as to the impact of fiscal and monetary policies. His argument proceeds in piecewise fashion. He begins with a simple model of the long-run equilibrium *real* value of the dollar consistent with a given target value of the current account and goes on to derive the implications of fiscal policy for the real exchange rate from a version of the classical transfer criterion. Branson then presents a "fundamentals" two-country model which determines both real interest rates and real exchange rates from the requirements of saving-investment balance and the fulfillment of an arbitrage condition that includes a risk premium related to relative bond stocks. He then investigates monetary policy and "nominal dynamics" with the help of a two-country variant of the Dornbusch single-country model. These analytical exercises are supplemented by preliminary empirical investigations with the help of the Fund's Minimod and lead, in conclusion, to a fairly specific policy recommendation: fiscal tightening in the United States and monetary ease in the Federal Republic of Germany and Japan.

This is clearly a rich paper that covers a vast territory and does so well and efficiently. Individual analytical points are made simply, clearly, and forcefully. I have few qualms with the various models that are presented as long as their explicit (and implicit) assumptions are clearly kept in mind.[1] Yet I do have serious reservations about some of the conclusions.

Branson's main conclusions are conveniently summarized in the introduction to his paper. The first is that, as far as the long-run outlook for the dollar is concerned, "perhaps 15 percent more real depreciation is needed." The second is that "depreciation is the very mechanism through which a fiscal shift would restore international balance." Third, the proposed combination of fiscal tightening in the United States and monetary ease in Germany and Japan would "provide more short-run exchange rate stability and reduce world real interest rates, to the benefit of developing country debtors."

---

[1] Branson's reader should be aware (and beware) that the assumptions underlying the various models used in the paper differ. For instance, the real exchange rate is sometimes endogenous, and sometimes exogenous; in some parts the effects of foreign bond accumulation are at the heart of the analysis, while in others they are assumed away (as, for example, in the monetary dynamics model); sometimes the relevant exchange rate variable is the nominal rate, and at other times it is the real rate. The ratio of domestic to foreign output is kept fixed through much but not all of the analysis; furthermore fixity of that ratio sometimes but not always implies fixity of the ratio of domestic to foreign absorption—and savings is assumed to be simply proportional to output.

In the next part of my comment I question the contention that the dollar will or should depreciate by some 15 percent in real terms by the early 1990s. In the following part I argue, and here I do not think Branson would sharply disagree, that depreciation or appreciation is only one of the mechanisms through which international balance is restored in response to fiscal shifts. I then introduce some general considerations on the role of monetary and fiscal policy under fixed and flexible exchange rates which shed some light on the appropriate policy package to deal with current international imbalances.

Long-Run Outlook for the Dollar

There are three main steps in Branson's argument that perhaps 15 percent more real depreciation of the dollar is needed. The first step is to identify 1980 as an initial current account equilibrium where income on net foreign assets represented about 1 percent of GNP and was matched by an equivalent trade deficit. Since by the mid-1990s income on the foreign asset position of the United States is forecast to have turned negative to the tune of roughly minus 1 percent of GNP, re-equilibrating the current account will require a change of the trade balance from a 1 percent deficit to a 1 percent surplus (of GNP), or a total turnaround of some 2 percent of GNP. The second step is to refer to "standard estimates" of the elasticity of the trade balance with respect to the real exchange rate which indicate that the dollar must depreciate by 26 percent in real terms from its 1980 level to achieve such a 2 percent turnaround. Since roughly 10 percent real depreciation has already occurred, some 15 percent remains. The third step is to note that these calculations are valid only "in the absence of important shifts in the world economy since 1980." Branson argues that such shifts, mainly changes in productivity, would, if anything, call for even more dollar depreciation.

There are at least two questions that one can address to Branson's argument. First, how credible, or reliable, is his conclusion *as a forecast* of what will actually happen to the dollar? Second, what are the *policy implications* of the statement that the dollar must (will?) decline by another 15 percent or so in real terms?

With respect to the first question, there are three requirements for the forecast to be credible. First, the initial equilibrium (here 1980) must pertain not only to the current account but also to other endogenous variables, notably the real exchange rate. Second, one must identify the sources of the disturbance to the initial equilibrium, that is, one must know or forecast the paths of important exogenous (monetary, fiscal, or foreign) variables and trace their implications for the endogenous variables of interest (here the current account and the real exchange rate) with the help of a model, however simple, which includes the path of other important endogenous variables, such as interest rates, saving, and investment. Finally, one must have credible statistical estimates of the relationship among the main variables of interest.

The 15 percent depreciation forecast seems to me not to meet the above three criteria. Take them in reverse order. The "standard estimates" of the Marris type are based on a simple regression of the trade balance on the real exchange rate over a specific sample period. They are not a properly derived reduced-form estimate from an appropriately specified economic model. They completely ignore that the real exchange rate and the trade account are jointly determined endogenous variables. Second, and related, it is clear from all reasonable general equilibrium models, however simple, that the path of the real exchange rate associated with any given improvement of the current account will depend both on the source of the initial disequilibrium and on the adjustment policies being pursued. Therefore naive "trade balance elasticity" estimates only capture the relationship between the trade balance and a relative price variable yielded by a particular constellation of shocks.

As an example, compare an improvement in the U.S. trade balance brought about by an "exogenous" increase in the risk premium on dollar assets (such as a tax on capital movements) on the one hand, and by a decrease in government spending on the other. Theoretical and empirical considerations suggest that both the path and the eventual change in the real exchange value of the dollar (as well as in other variables) will differ substantially in these two cases. For instance, a Minimod-based simulation of these two cases undertaken by my colleague Hans Genberg in Geneva suggests that the real depreciation of the dollar eventually brought about by an increase in the risk premium is substantially larger than that associated with a decrease in government spending; moreover, while the first of these "policies" results in an increase in real interest rates in the United States, the second produces a fall in real U.S. interest rates; potential output as well as other macroeconomic variables are affected differently in the two regions.

Finally, there is the important question of the nature of the initial equilibrium. If 1980 was a year of current account equilibrium, what of the real exchange rate, real interest rates, output, absorption, and so forth? And how much of the adjustment in these other variables has already taken place today? The answer to these questions bears crucially on whether one would expect the dollar to have to depreciate, or for that matter appreciate, further. To illustrate, consider Chart 1,

Chart 1. Response of Real U.S. Dollar Exchange Rate to One-Period Fiscal Deficit of 3 Percent of GNP

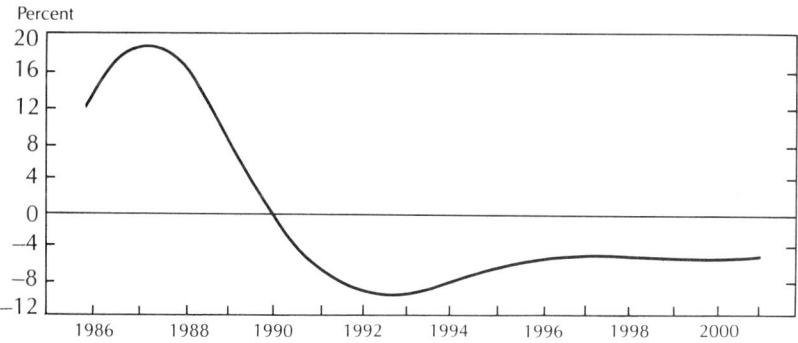

Source: Reproduced from Morris (1988), p. 3.

which represents the path of the dollar real exchange rate in response to a one-period fiscal deficit of 3 percent of GNP simulated from the estimated version of a fairly complete but simple model (due to Dirk Morris) which corresponds rather closely to Branson's "fundamentals" model.[2] In the model, the current account goes into deficit and remains in deficit for some seven years; it eventually returns to equilibrium. Note that the real depreciation from peak to trough is over 25 percent, while from initial to final equilibrium it is roughly 5 percent. Now backdate the fiscal shock to 1981 and reckon that, as Morris suggests, the fiscal shock in Chart 1 should be multiplied by (slightly less than) three "to get close to the actual size of US debt financing over the mid-1980's."[3] Then the eventual real depreciation of the dollar would be of the order of 15 percent and not 26 percent, and perhaps we have already reached the trough and should expect the dollar to appreciate rather than depreciate in real terms in the future.

The upshot of this discussion is simply that, as a forecast, the statement that "15 percent more real depreciation of the dollar is

---

[2]See Morris (1988).
[3]*Ibid.*, p. 3.

needed" is, to say the least, unreliable. I would argue, furthermore, that such a statement is devoid of policy implications beyond suggesting that policy should not seek to resist trend changes in real exchange rates, a proposition that can be justified on general analytical grounds independently of any specific forecast of the future value of the real exchange rate. As the real exchange rate is an endogenous variable under both fixed and flexible exchange rates, one should not want to make it a fixed target of policy although one may want to smooth its path. The statement that the dollar must depreciate in real terms does imply that prices in the United States must decline relative to those in the rest of the world, but that can occur either through nominal depreciation, or through movements in price levels, or through a combination of both. It thus tells us little per se about the inherent merits or demerits of stabilizing nominal exchange rates.

Arguing that the dollar must depreciate by x percent in order to improve the balance trade is fraught with danger if one does not have much confidence in the accuracy of that forecast, or in the realization of the circumstances upon which it is conditional. It distracts attention from the actual policies needed to restore balance and risks recourse to protectionism as a "last resort" if depreciation is not associated with an improvement in the trade balance (cf. 1985–87).

Fiscal Shifts, Exchange Rate, and International Balance

In the third section of his paper, Branson appeals to the classical transfer problem criterion for a change in the terms of trade to argue that "depreciation is the very mechanism through which a fiscal shift would restore international balance." If the words "one of the possible mechanisms" were substituted for "the very mechanism" in this statement, one could have no qualms about it.

Although it is true that a change in the real exchange rate (or the terms of trade) will have to occur if the sum of the marginal propensities to import is different from unity, that change is only one of several mechanisms that concur to restore trade or current account balance. These include the direct expenditure effects of the fiscal shift, possible changes in saving behavior, expectations, and output changes if economies do not continuously stay at full employment. They also include those mechanisms so correctly emphasized in Branson's "fundamentals" model, that is, the asset accumulation process and its relationship to risk premia and real interest rates.

If, among these, one wants to emphasize "the principal mechanism" of trade balance adjustment one might as well take, as Branson does in other parts of the paper, a saving-investment (or absorption) approach to the current account. Take, for instance, the first equation (9a) of Branson's "fundamentals" model. Assuming the exchange rate to be equal to its long-run equilibrium value we have: $X = S(r) - D$. The most direct determinants of the trade account are the budget deficit and net private saving; the crucial adjusting variable is the real interest rate; though this is not in the equation, there could also possibly be a direct terms-of-trade, Laursen-Metzler, effect on net saving. Such an absorption approach may prove useful if one were to ask what policies should be undertaken to adjust the current account or to speed up its adjustment to some target long-run value. It is to this issue that I turn next.

Role of Monetary and Fiscal Policy

In what follows I assume that current accounts are targets of policy without questioning the wisdom of such targeting. I also assume that there is agreement on what value of the current account represents "equilibrium."[4] Rather than asking by how much the real exchange rate will or should change to bring the current account back into equilibrium after some initial fiscal or other disturbance, I want to ask what policies are best assigned to the trade or current account, what policies to other objectives. To do so, I will draw on some recent work carried out with Hans Genberg (see Genberg and Swoboda (1987a)).

To keep things simple, take the long-run case analyzed by Branson where output is given at full employment and consider a two-country model with perfect capital mobility. This last assumption allows one to concentrate on the world rate of interest and ignore risk premia and interest-rate differentials; incorporating the latter would not make a major difference for present purposes.[5] Table 1 shows the assignments of instruments to targets that suggest themselves under fixed and flexible rates (the latter being the case analyzed by Genberg and Swoboda).

---

[4]The legitimacy of current-account targeting is briefly discussed in Genberg and Swoboda (1987a). Note two problems with current-account targeting. First, the case for adopting a current account target frequently rests, in practice, on the existence of (policy-induced) distortions in other sectors of the economy and the first-best intervention would be to remove these distortions directly. Second, it is difficult to estimate what is a sustainable, or appropriate, path for the current account in view of the complicated path that variable would follow in accordance to a "stages of the balance of payments" cycle or in response to various real shocks.

[5]Such risk premia could be incorporated in Chart 2 and further in the text to provide a better match with Branson's model, but at the cost of some complication. See also Genberg and Swoboda (1987b) for an analysis of the effects of foreign asset accumulation.

Table 1. Long-Run Assignments

Target	Instrument	
	Fixed E	Floating E
P		M
P*		M*
P_w	$M_w = M + M^*$	
E	$M - M^*$	
CA	$G - G^*$	$G - G^*$
r_w	$G + G^*$	$G + G^*$

Note: G = government spending; M = money stock; P = price level; E = nominal exchange rate; CA = current account; and r_w = world interest rate.

An asterisk identifies foreign variables, the subscript w identifies world variables; and the real exchange rate, e = EP*/P is endogenous under both exchange rate regimes.

Four policy instruments are considered: monetary and fiscal policy at home (unstarred) and abroad (starred). Four targets can be reached with these four instruments. The targets differ under fixed and flexible exchange rates. A fixed exchange rate ties national price levels together and endogenizes the distribution of the world money stock among the two countries (national monetary policy loses its autonomy and must be devoted to keeping the nominal exchange rate, E, fixed). The nominal targets under fixed rates are therefore the world price level and the nominal exchange rate to which the sum of the national money stocks (the world money stock, M_w) and their difference (the distribution of M_w) must respectively be assigned. The real targets are the current account and the world rate of interest to which the difference and the sum of government spending in the two countries (given taxes) must respectively be assigned.

The same assignment of instruments to real targets obtains under flexible exchange rates. Here, however, the nominal exchange rate is no longer a target of policy but an endogenous variable; national monetary policy regains its autonomy and should be assigned to the national price level (or rate of inflation). Note that under both exchange rate regimes, the real exchange rate is an endogenous variable, the exchange rate regime impinging on whether the real exchange rate adjusts through inflation differentials, through nominal exchange rate changes, or both.

Three broad conclusions emerge from this simple long-run framework.[6] First, as far as policy toward the current account is concerned,

---

[6]For additional, especially short-run, implications under floating rates, see Genberg and Swoboda (1987a).

the focus should be on fiscal policy, more specifically on the difference in fiscal stances—and the real exchange rate should be left free to adapt under both exchange rate regimes. As, in addition, the world fiscal stance plays an important role in determining the world level of real interest rates, coordination of fiscal policies is required if the real variables are targets of policy. Second, under fixed exchange rates some agreement on the desirable evolution of the world money stock and some means for achieving it are required to achieve the target world price level or rate of inflation.

Finally, the fact that, under both exchange rate regimes, the real exchange rate is an endogenous variable which presumably adjusts to changes in tastes, technology, and endowments (and relative asset positions), suggests that targeting that variable as in some "target zone" proposals is likely to be destabilizing. There are two main reasons why this should be so. First, unless the target value of the real exchange rate happens to correspond to that which would represent an equilibrium given all policy and behavior parameters, disequilibrium will build up in other variables of the system. Second, target zone proposals typically propose that the target real exchange rate be reached by means of monetary policy. The assignment of monetary policy to the current account via that policy's effect on the real exchange rate is clearly inappropriate if Table 1 is to be believed. It is interesting to note, in this context, that the paper by Frenkel, Goldstein, and Masson (1988) presented at this conference (see Chapter 4 in this volume) provides some empirical evidence which confirms the potentially destabilizing character of the typical assignment proposed by advocates of the target zone system.

Dealing with Current International Imbalances

The general principles outlined in the preceding section do have some implications for the proper policy packages to deal with current international imbalances. The design of such packages requires first that current imbalances be identified, second that there be some agreement on the goals to be reached, and third that there be some agreement on the way the world economy functions, that is, on a minimal model of the world economy.

I will illustrate with a very simple model of the world economy under floating exchange rates that corresponds to the general principles of the previous section and does not differ sharply from Branson's "fundamentals" model. The model, drawn from Genberg and Swoboda (1987a), will allow us to appraise Branson's policy proposals

Chart 2. Three Paths Toward Current Account Equilibrium

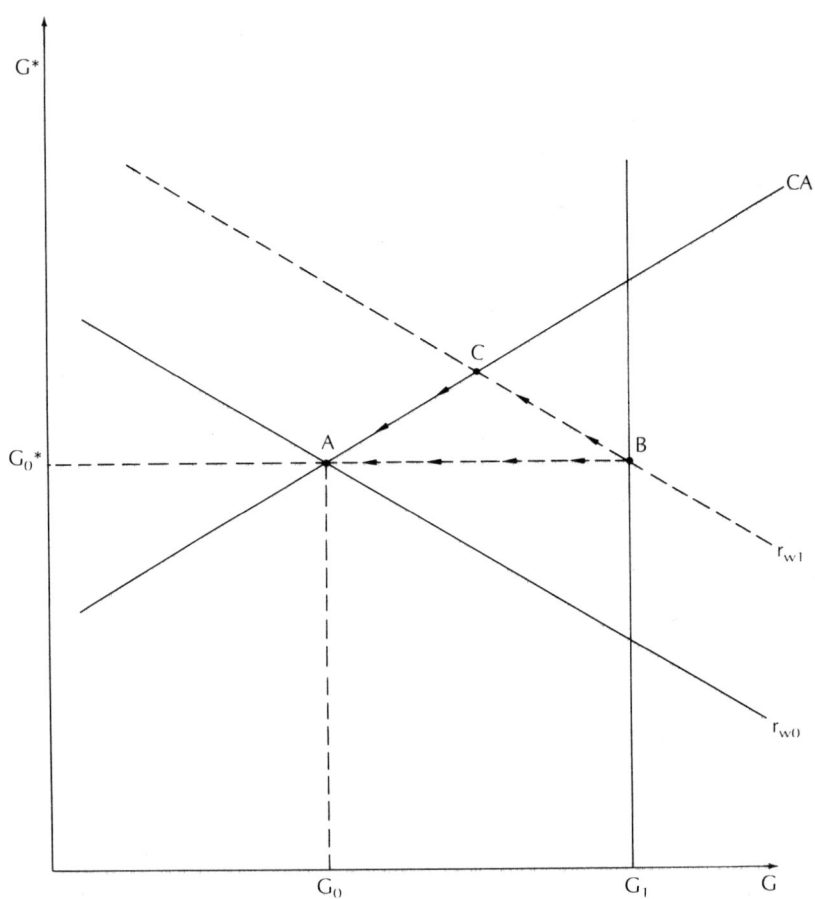

Three paths away from B and toward current account equilibrium:
(1) B to C (Group of Seven view?)
(2) B to A (Branson view?)
(3) B to C to A (cautious view?)

and to compare them with some alternatives.

The model is pictured in Chart 2. G stands for government expenditure in the United States or, if you prefer, the stance of U.S. fiscal policy, while G* stands for fiscal policy in the rest of the world, Europe and Japan if you wish. The line CA represents the combinations of fiscal policies in the two regions which given current values of all other exogenous and pre-determined variables would yield current account equilibrium (or an agreed target value of the current account). Similarly, the r_{w0} line represents those combinations of the two fiscal policies that would yield an appropriate, or target level of real interest rates in the world.[7] Assume that there is general agreement that r_{w0} and current account equilibrium are legitimate and desirable goals of policy in the long run.

The remaining questions are: where are we today and how do we get from wherever we are to the target real interest rate and to current account equilibrium? Answers to the first question differ. Nevertheless, there is probably fairly general agreement that the U.S. current account deficit is too large, that is, that we are below and to the right of the CA line in Chart 2, and that current levels of real interest rates are too high—that is, that we are above and to the right of the r_{w0} line. This, in turn, implies that U.S. government expenditure is too high; it is above G_0, say at G_1. There is less agreement as to where European fiscal spending is. Suppose for simplicity that it is G_0^* so that we are currently at B in Chart 2. The combinations of the two countries' government expenditures which would maintain real interest rates at their current (high) level is given by the dotted line labelled r_{w1}.

Suppose first that there is no change in fiscal stances, that is that G remains at G_1 and G* remains at G_0^*. What would happen? Presumably current account equilibrium would eventually be re-established by the mechanisms described in Branson's "fundamentals" model. Increasing indebtedness of the United States would lead to a risk premium on the dollar, real interest rates would rise in the United States and fall in the rest of the world. Net private saving would rise in the United States, fall abroad, and the CA curve would gradually shift to the right until it intersected the r_{w1} curve (now to be interpreted as a given *average* real interest-rate line) at B. The dollar would probably, though not necessarily, depreciate in real terms in the process. But the target real interest rate would not be reached.

Alternatively, fiscal policy could be used to speed convergence to

---

[7] With symmetry of behavior parameters and perfect capital mobility, the r_w lines would be 45° lines; that is, the world rate of interest would depend only on the sum of government spending in the two regions.

policy targets. Branson's suggestion would seem to amount to moving directly from B to A, leaving it to expansionary monetary policy in Germany and Japan both to cushion the possible recessionary impact of a reduction in U.S. government spending in the short run and to avoid too sharp a short-run nominal depreciation of the dollar. The view of the Group of Seven, as characterized by Branson, would seem to call for a movement from B to C, where the matching of the decrease in U.S. government spending with an increase in government spending abroad would result in a return to current account equilibrium at the currently high level of real interest rates. The increase in fiscal spending abroad that the latter strategy implies could again be justified by fear of the recessionary impact of the reduction in G coupled with a fear of the inflationary consequences of monetary expansion in the surplus countries (as well as with disbelief in the effectiveness of monetary expansion). A third possibility would be to combine the U.S. budget cut with a temporary fiscal stimulus (if possible of the supply-side variety) abroad; this would amount to moving from B to C and then to A as the temporary stimulus is withdrawn.

Note that the basic element in all these policy packages is fiscal policy, particularly a reduction in the U.S. budget deficit. Little has been said about what would happen to the real exchange rate. Presumably the dollar would depreciate in real terms on impact, then appreciate in real terms. But this implies very little about what policy toward the nominal value of the dollar should be.

REFERENCES

Frenkel, Jacob A., Morris Goldstein, and Paul R. Masson, "International Coordination of Economic Policies: Scope, Methods, and Effects," this volume (1988).

Genberg, Hans, and Alexander K. Swoboda (1987a), "The Current Account and the Policy Mix under Flexible Exchange Rates," International Monetary Fund Working Paper WP/87/70 (Washington).

——— (1987b), "Policy and Current Account Determination under Floating Exchange Rates," International Monetary Fund Working Paper WP/87/69 (Washington).

Morris, Dirk, "International Policy Coordination: Popular Misconceptions," Swiss Bank Corporation, *Economic and Financial Prospects*, No. 1 (February/March 1988).

Comment

Hans-Eckart Scharrer

In his stimulating paper, William Branson addresses two important issues. The first issue concerns the long-run equilibrium level and path of the dollar, the second the potential contribution of fiscal restriction in the United States, and fiscal or monetary expansion in Europe and Japan, to the restoration of international balance. In this connection, Branson raises the question whether fiscal action can eliminate the need for further dollar depreciation. I have been assigned the task of focusing on aspects of trade policies, a topic not addressed in Branson's paper, and I should like to raise the question: Can *trade* policy action eliminate—or reduce—the need for further real dollar depreciation?

Before turning to that question, let me make a few remarks on the notion of long-run equilibrium. Branson defines long-run equilibrium by the condition that the U.S. current account balance is constant, "and for simplicity, we will assume this constant is zero." I have no problems in accepting a zero balance "for simplicity." Since Branson draws important analytical (and normative) conclusions from this assumption, it is necessary however, to emphasize that a scenario where a U.S. deficit on investment income is matched by a U.S. surplus on trade account, so that the sum equals zero, is by no means the only conceivable, sustainable current account position. Quite the contrary: current account equilibrium in that sense has been the exception rather than the rule during the entire postwar period, and many economies (including the United States, Japan, and the Federal Republic of Germany) have even been in "fundamental" surplus or deficit—although it is true that earlier balances were generally smaller, as a percentage of GNP, than those experienced since the mid-1980s. The fact that in 1987 private agents have not been willing to finance a U.S. current account deficit of $161 billion, or 3.6 percent of GNP, at the given exchange rate and interest rate differentials, is therefore not at variance with the possibility that they might well be prepared to finance a current account deficit of, say, 1 percent of GNP—equal to the projected debt service payments—on a lasting basis in the 1990s. As long as the United States continues to grow faster than other major high-income regions, an assumption underlying Branson's deduction of the long-run equilibrium trend of the dollar, the expected real rate of return on U.S. investment is likely to be higher—or at least not lower—than in alternative locations. It is then not unreasonable to assume that investors will reinvest their earnings in the United States, and that the country will even be able to attract fresh money from abroad, so that the "investment income" portion of the current account (rF) will easily be financed. If that happened, which also implies that the U.S. internal investment/savings gap will not be closed fully, the swing in the trade account from the 1980 level would need to be only 1 percent rather than 2 percent of GNP, and the warranted one-time shift in the real exchange rate will be, accordingly, smaller.

This should not imply that such an outcome is absolutely more plausible than Branson's. It needs to be stressed, however, that economies can well live with current account deficits and rising net external indebtedness for quite some time, and that the preferences of analysts or policymakers for a balanced current account are not necessarily also the preferences of the market players.

With that in mind, let me turn to the relationship between the stance of trade policy, especially in Europe, and the percentage change in exchange rates required to reduce the U.S. deficit to a sustainable level (however defined). Branson has cited a number of estimates on the elasticity of the trade balance to changes in the real exchange rate. These estimates are based upon the trade regime prevailing in the 1970s and early 1980s. As a first observation it can be stated that the effect on trade flows of any given exchange rate change will be the greater, the more exposed to exchange rate movements the international sectors of the surplus countries are. In other words: if a major portion of the tradable goods sector of an economy is shielded from the impact of exchange rate changes by import restrictions, production subsidies or export subsidies, the trade effect of any given fall of the dollar will be smaller than without such protective devices, and the dollar will have to fall more to bring about the desired trade adjustment. Since the burden of that adjustment has to be fully borne by the exposed (and basically competitive) industries which will be subjected to an *excessive* profit squeeze, the allocative distortions—a byproduct of any policy of trade protection—are compounded.

These considerations are far from being irrelevant in practice. Twenty-five to 30 percent of world trade is estimated to be subject to nontariff barriers of one kind or another. In Europe, including the Federal Republic of Germany, major portions of the tradable goods sector are shielded from international competition. Protection is offered to agriculture, coal mining, steel, telecommunications equipment, consumer electronics, textiles and cloth, shipbuilding, the Airbus, railroad equipment, in certain countries also the car industry —to mention just the most conspicuous examples. In some of these products the United States is competitive, in others newly industrializing countries or traditional agricultural producers have a comparative advantage which they are, however, often unable to exploit: not only is the European market shielded but European producers are able, with the support of their national governments or the European Community, to engage in subsidized competition on third markets. As a result, redressment of bilateral and multilateral trade flows is obstructed, and an overshooting of real exchange rates is provoked.

The message is therefore clear: in a more competitive international trade regime, a redressment of the U.S. current account could be achieved at a lesser cost in terms of dollar depreciation and resource misallocation, whereas another sequel of protectionist moves would increase the "warranted" dollar variability. It is equally clear, however, that dismantling trade barriers in Europe is politically difficult to accomplish during a period of dollar weakness, high and protracted unemployment, and slow growth. It can succeed only in a climate of international trade liberalization backed by the United States, Japan, and the more advanced newly industrializing countries and with a major policy contribution of my own country which, as a principal exporter and importer of manufactures, has a foremost interest in an open world economy and steadiness in the dollar-deutsche-mark rate.

Under present conditions, a fair U.S. contribution would be to resist domestic pressures for new protectionist legislation or administrative action, and to promote actively the Uruguay Round of the GATT. As far as Japan and the newly industrializing countries are concerned, further opening of their markets for foreign commodities and a shift of their growth strategies toward more domestically led expansion would not only serve their own medium-term and long-term interests and the interest of the United States in a reduction of bilateral trade imbalances. It is also a necessary quid pro quo for increased access of their products to the European market. An important element of an enhanced growth and trade strategy of the major newly industrializing countries would be a reassessment of their exchange rate policies with a view to allowing stronger appreciation of their currencies against the dollar, in line with market forces. It is then up to U.S. firms to make use for the improved export opportunities and to recover domestic market shares.

Since the overall surplus of the European Community on current account of (roughly) $40 billion is mainly due to the German surplus of $44 billion, and most other Community countries are in deficit, the future stance of Community trade policy will crucially depend upon the German ability and readiness to offer "compensation" for a renunciation of existing as well as new trade barriers vis-à-vis the outside world. This is all the more true since the creation of a single European market by 1992 does not only offer macroeconomic efficiency gains estimated by the Cecchini Commission at $260 billion (or 5 percent of Community GNP) but will also bring about regional and microeconomic adjustment costs (plant closures or lay-offs). Various member countries appear little prepared to compound these costs by opening their markets for more competition from abroad—even though the macroeconomic benefits should be no different from the ones expected from the move for deepened integration.

What form could German compensation take? It is useful to start from the observation that of the toal German trade surplus of DM 118 billion in 1987, about one half—namely DM 62 billion—was generated with other Community countries, adn that this surplus has actually increased by 20 percent over 1986. For the current account surplus has actually increased by 20 percent over 1986. For the current account surplus of DM 80 billion, the same is true with respect to both proportion and trend. Support to other Community countries could be given either through a revaluation of the deutsche mark in the European Monetary System (EMS) or by a German growth initiative, or by both.

Present exchange rate management in the EMS is narrowly linked to cost and price inflation differentials with a further tendency of repressing realignments in order to discourage inflationary expectations. In view of the large disparities of current account positions among member countries, deficit countries have to accept real interest rates of 1–1½ percentage points above German rates in order to defend their currencies' bilateral parities against the deutsche mark. A shift to a wider concept of exchange rate policy, giving due weight to the variance in trade and current accounts and using real exchange rate changes in the EMS deliberately as a tool of internal *and* external adjustment, would allow member countries to grow faster, to absorb more imports from outside the Community—including the United States—rather than from Germany, and to lessen the adjustment costs.

Yet, in view of the low price elasticities of imports cited in Branson's paper, more could be gained by deliberate growth efforts in Germany. In addition to fostering coherence in Europe and enabling Germany as well as its European partners to adjust better to international competition, this would have a direct impact on German imports from the United States and the dollar area at large. But how can more growth be generated?

Branson has ruled out fiscal expansion, and I share his conclusion, though partly for reasons different from those put forward in his paper. Monetary policy in German policy has already been rather relaxed, as is witnessed by a rate of growth of the central bank money stock of 8 percent against a growth rate of nominal GNP of 3.8 percent, and by the low level of short-term interest rates (the only rates which the Bundesbank can directly influence). The steep yield curve suggests that monetary policy is caught in a liquidity trap, so that little could be gained from additional monetary stimulation.

However, there is wide scope for action on structural policies in the broadest sense, that is:
- policies to overcome the rigidities in the labor markets which discourage regional and sectoral mobility;
- policies to reduce barriers to access and activity in the services sector which stand in the way of a speedy restructuring of the German economy in favor of the production of more home—rather than export—goods;
- policies to stimulate competition in the transport and telecommunications industries and in government procurement;
- policies to effectively cut back production subsidies, which, besides giving wrong signals to market participants are a burden to the economically sound sectors of the economy; and
- policies to encourage investment and thus to absorb a greater portion of savings domestically.

With these policy prescriptions we pass, of course, the frontiers of the Mundell-Fleming world, but that is inevitable given the limitations of the model. Quite in the spirit of Branson's paper, though, trade and economic policy adjustment in Europe should not be regarded as a substitute for but as a complement to restoration of fiscal balance in the United States which, because of its impact on the investment-savings gap, is a necessary condition for a return to a sustainable international current account and exchange rate pattern.

CHAPTER 3

Empirical Evidence of Effects of Policy Coordination Among Major Industrial Countries Since Rambouillet Summit of 1975

Günter GroBer

The past few years have seen renewed efforts at macroeconomic policy coordination among the major industrial countries, and the global turbulences on the equities and exchange markets in late 1987 have increased demands for improving coordination. The expected benefits are based on theoretical analyses of the advantages of cooperative policies compared with the results of noncooperative policies, though the outcome is ambiguous. In these circumstances, academic research has increasingly been aimed at furnishing empirical evidence for the conditions, the possible welfare gains and losses, and the limits of macroeconomic policy coordination.

Economic cooperation among industrial countries is exercised in many forms, extending from the mere exchange of information up to joint action.[1] In this hierarchy, policy coordination is tantamount to a rather intensive engagement by participating countries. In the academic literature it has been precisely defined as "the agreement by two or more countries to a cooperative set of policy changes, where neither would wish to undertake the policy change on its own, but where each expects the package to leave it better off relative to the Nash non-cooperative equilibrium, in which each sets its policies taking the other's as given."[2] A typical agreement of this kind is the focus of this paper—the ad hoc coordination of macroeconomic policies among interested parties.[3]

---

[1] See Cooper (1986), p. 5.
[2] See Frankel (1987), p. 1.
[3] For a review of types of coordination see Horne and Masson (1988).

The rise of international policy coordination as a new instrument was promoted by the transition to a regime of flexible exchange rates in the first half of the 1970s. Enlarged room for discretionary national action had increased external uncertainty, and concern about inconsistent policies was an important background for the first economic summit conference in 1975, when inflation and balance of payments disequilibria had upset the world economy. The subsequent annual meetings of the heads of governments of the seven major industrial countries became the most conspicuous setting for economic cooperation, though the execution of policy coordination was recently delegated to the Group of Five or Seven level. These activities are highly interrelated with the work of other institutions, such as the Group of Ten, the Interim Committee, and also the International Monetary Fund itself. Another important forum for economic cooperation among industrial countries is the Organization for Economic Cooperation and Development (OECD). Here again, the summit countries play a leading role in the discussion of appropriate economic policies. However, larger countries prefer to consult about possible changes in targets and policies in smaller groups.[4]

Apart from worldwide coordination efforts by major industrial countries, the European Community reflects a regional approach. However, even the elaborate proposal of "a cooperative growth strategy for more employment" submitted by the European Commission in November 1985 did not bring forward effective macroeconomic policy coordination among member countries. Against this, the European Monetary System (EMS) is an important example of institutionalized coordination, although not all Community members participate in the exchange rate mechanism.[5]

On the whole there is a very broad spectrum of economic cooperation among major industrial countries. The following analysis will differentiate between the few cases of policy coordination among major industrial countries and the overwhelming number of less intensive forms of cooperation; policy activities in participating countries will be compared with agreed policies. The empirical evidence for the effects of policy coordination will then be discussed.

Policy Coordination Since Mid–1970s

The loss of the reins for discretionary national decision making inherent in the Bretton Woods exchange rate system turned out to be an important stimulus to international economic cooperation. A sec-

---
[4]See Solomon (1984), p. 12–13.
[5]Nonparticipants are Greece, Portugal, Spain, and the United Kingdom.

ond stimulus was the poor economic performance of industrial countries after the 1974–75 recession. In the wake of the first oil price hike, persistent inflationary pressure combined with stubbornly high unemployment was a new experience for economic policy. When the United States succeeded in pushing growth up to pre-crisis levels, but not Japan and Western Europe, current account disequilibria and weakness of the dollar gave evidence of external disorder. This situation alone was fertile soil for the idea of cooperative policy efforts by major countries. Important features of this constellation of circumstances reappeared in the mid-1980s when the consequences of divergent policies and divergent growth performance of the United States on the one hand and Japan and Western Europe on the other confronted economic policymakers with the challenge of reconciling the urgent reduction of external imbalances with, at least, the continuation of the moderate growth achieved.

Forums for Policy Coordination

The main forums for ad hoc coordination of macroeconomic policies have been the economic summits of the heads of government and the Group of Five or Seven meetings of the ministers of finance and central bank governors. Originally, the objective of economic summits was an intense discussion of urgent problems rather than the elaboration of economic action programs. However, the critical situation of the world economy in the mid–1970s induced participants from the beginning to use common declarations to support confidence worldwide. Before long, the discussion on important policy issues led to aspirations to influence policy actions.

Ad hoc coordination of macroeconomic policies was exercised first at the 1978 Bonn Summit. After a pause of several years in the wake of the second oil price hike, similar endeavors started again in the 1980s. Activities were concentrated in the Group of Five and, since 1986, in the Group of Seven, which were entrusted with the task "to work together more closely and more frequently in the periods between the annual Summit meetings" (1986 Tokyo Economic Declaration). In general, at these meetings the finance ministers and central bank governors are joined by the Managing Director of the Fund, taking account of the goal of strengthening multilateral surveillance called for at the 1982 Versailles Summit. In this context, evidence of elements of policy coordination appeared in the Plaza Statement in September 1985, the Louvre Accord in February 1987, and the Statement of the Group of Seven in December 1987.

The EMS constitutes a different approach to policy coordination. It is aimed at increasing the internal and external stability of participating countries. Factually there is an unwritten agreement by its members to adopt a stable exchange rate against the deutsche mark, providing a "low inflation standard."[6] In this system, ad hoc coordination is limited to the requirement to agree on new parities between the currencies of the member countries in the case of realignments, eleven of which have been implemented since 1979, the last one in January 1987. Apart from this, the EMS is an example of institutional coordination based on the constraints of a fixed exchange rate system. To some extent, international monetary rules can work as a substitute for coordination of economic policies. However, theoretical analysis has concluded that EMS member countries have little incentive to cooperate in fiscal policies,[7] and empirical analysis considered apparent lack of progress in this field even as an element of uncertainty in the EMS.[8] Against this, empirical evidence of convergence in inflation rates at a low level was impressive, although this trend was not confined to EMS members.[9]

Character of Policy Coordination

While the EMS has represented policy coordination in the monetary field, economic summit meetings have been characterized by a very broad approach to problems and needs. Special emphasis was always laid on the objective of steady noninflationary growth and higher employment, and on macroeconomic policies to achieve these ends. The declarations covering these issues were heavily influenced by intended home use, either to endorse existing policies, or to increase acceptance of planned policies.

In general, summit declarations fell short of policy coordination in favor of a limited cooperative approach intended primarily to reduce risks and uncertainties for national policies. Discussion was directed at the harmonization of priorities of policy objectives, of judgment on the functioning of economies, and of national strategies. This was a continuous process, as economic problems changed, as did prevailing schools of thought, and the political orientation of governments. Sometimes the underlying changes were bigger than only marginally adjusted wording suggested.

Summarizing national policy intentions has recently become part of Group of Five and Group of Seven statements. Most actions mentioned originated in autonomous decisions, although account was

---

[6]See Pöhl (1987), Section VI.
[7]See De Grauwe (1986), p. 26.
[8]See Ungerer and others (1986), p. 27.
[9]See Horne and Masson (1988), pp. 275–79, and Scheide and Sinn (1987), pp. 21–23.

taken of available information on developments and policies in other countries. True policy coordination, however, would require participating countries to agree on national measures that are different from those implemented without coordination. In reality, this distinction is difficult to identify in view of the international flow of information. This holds in particular for situations when conformity of problems and priorities suggests parallel action.

Actually, ad hoc policy coordination of explicit and quantified measures has been confined to situations with pronounced imbalances calling for different policies in important countries. Efforts by participating countries were directed, to a large extent, at exploiting the presumed advantages of coordinated macroeconomic fine tuning compared with noncoordinated national actions.

Contents of Coordination Pledges

After the first oil price hike, the deterioration of structural conditions decisive for growth was generally underestimated, and the need to foster growth via stimulative macroeconomic policies was a common objective. In these circumstances a first, still qualitative, approach to policy coordination was undertaken at the 1977 London Summit Conference, when some countries promised unspecified expansionary measures in order to achieve their respective growth targets. However, it was not until one year later, at the 1978 Bonn Summit Conference, that agreement was reached on a detailed program of different actions. Apart from the inclusion of prior announcements by some countries, the main contributions to a coordinated macroeconomic strategy were the explicit commitments by the Federal Republic of Germany to initiate reflationary measures of up to 1 percent of GNP and by France to increase the budget deficit by about 0.5 percent of GNP, whereas Japan promised to secure a growth rate of GNP 1.5 percentage points higher than the year before by additional stimulation of domestic demand, if necessary. The United States, on the other hand, emphasized priority for anti-inflationary measures in fiscal policy. Its major contribution, however, was in energy conservation.

Although the action program included a number of newly announced measures, it is open to question whether this can be attributed to policy coordination, as there was a high probability of corresponding autonomous decisions. This holds for Germany, where economic policy was already about to strengthen the expansionary stance, and also for Japan, where following the "front-loading" of public investment in the first half of fiscal year 1978, supplementary expenditure was in the offing. In both cases, coordination efforts apparently supported the internal tendencies.

During the following years, after the second oil price hike had increased adjustment requirements dramatically and inflation surged worldwide, economic summit declarations reflected a shift from the concept of economic fine-tuning to the promotion of structural adjustment. Coordinated action was replaced by the principle of keeping one's own house in order. Obviously influenced by the turn to Reaganomics in the United States, demand policies gave way to supply considerations in the 1981 Ottawa Summit Declaration. Fighting inflation was addressed explicitly as a condition for higher investment and sustained growth. In this context, the required reduction of public borrowing was to be achieved by dampening public expenditure, monetary growth was to be low and stable, and the role of markets in the adjustment process was emphasized. The summit conference now provided a forum for a searching analysis of national policies.[10]

Ad hoc policy coordination via explicit measures by the major countries was not resumed before the mid-1980s, when the world economic situation, characterized by unsatisfactory growth and serious external disequilibria, resembled the situation in 1978. Evidence of coordinated action is to be found in the statements by finance ministers and central bank governors, who now regularly conducted "multilateral surveillance to make their best efforts to reach an understanding on appropriate remedial measures whenever there are significant deviations from an intended course" (1986 Tokyo Economic Declaration).

The turning point can be dated back to the Plaza Meeting of the Group of Five in September 1985. At that time, it was stated that "some further orderly appreciation of the main non-dollar currencies against the dollar is desirable," and that governments and central banks of the five participating countries "stand ready to cooperate more closely to encourage this." Strictly speaking, this was an agreement on an intermediate target, and with regard to macroeconomic policy this was tantamount to unspecified cooperation falling short of true coordination. "Agreed policy actions" represented a mere synopsis of current national policies.

After a substantial fall in the dollar exchange rate a fundamental change of strategy was precluded at the Louvre Meeting in February 1987, geared at stability of exchange rates "around current levels." Agreed policy undertakings again comprised a majority of national measures, resolved without international coordination. However, they were supplemented by commitments by Germany "to increase

---

[10]See Menil and Solomon (1983), p. 48.

the size of the tax reduction already enacted for 1988" and by Japan to prepare a "comprehensive economic programme . . . so as to stimulate domestic demand." Corresponding to these elements of announced policy coordination by surplus countries, U.S. policy was aimed at "reducing the fiscal 1988 deficit to 2.3 percent of GNP." Finally, the Statement of the Group of Seven in December 1987 contained additional commitments by the surplus countries. The Government of the Federal Republic of Germany stated that it "will not seek to offset the budget revenue losses arising from recent developments" and the Government of Japan that "in the FY 1988 budget the expenditure for general public works will not be less than that for the FY 1987 budget, including the July supplemental."

Compared with the explicit fiscal policy commitments in these statements, passages on monetary policy have been less elaborate and more vague. This is partly due to the important role of other institutions in this field, in particular of the monthly meetings of the central bank governors at the Bank of International Settlements (B1S) in Basle.

Effects of Macroeconomic Policy Coordination

The coincidence of national actions that take into account information obtained in the process of international cooperation, and of concerted actions in the framework of policy coordination, renders it impossible to separate the respective effects neatly. Apart from this fundamental restriction, the analysis of observed effects in the two periods of policy coordination cannot be expected to provide clear evidence, for different reasons. The effects of the 1978 Bonn Summit were obscured by the subsequent oil price shock. As for the recent approach, policy coordination is still under way; therefore, the investigation will be limited to examining the effects of announced coordinated policy measures on policy conduct and to commenting on actual economic performance with respect to the envisaged effects.

Bonn Summit

In order to comply with its commitments at the Bonn Summit the German Government in July 1978 decided on tax cuts and additional expenditure of about 1 percent of GNP in 1979 as well as in 1980. The Japanese Government in early September 1978 submitted a reflationary package, which comprised expenditure of 1.3 percent of GNP, distributed over two fiscal years. However, this expenditure was not additional to the original budget. The central government in Japan, which accounted for nearly half of the package, hardly raised budgeted expenditure figures, given savings stemming from lower-than-expected inflation.

According to a contemporary simulation using the OECD Linkage Model, the impact of the announced expansionary measures should have been marked, hinting at an increase in total output, compared with the baseline level, of 1.1 percent in 1979 and 1.4 percent in 1980 in Germany, and of 0.4 percent and 1.0 percent in Japan.[11] However, the external shock of the second oil price hike and the anti-inflationary response of monetary policy increasingly dominated economic developments. GNP growth began to slow in the second half of 1979 in Germany as well as in Japan, while inflation accelerated markedly. The resulting shift of the domestic demand differential between deficit and surplus countries sprang primarily from marked deceleration in the growth of domestic demand in the United States (see Table 1).

Given the strong impact of the oil price increase on economic developments and policies in industrial countries, any evaluation of the real effects of actions agreed at the 1978 Bonn Summit must be highly arbitrary. This supports the continuing division of opinions on the merits of the pursued "locomotive" or "convoy" approach to policy coordination. In any case, there is strong evidence that at the time of the summit meeting, expansion in Germany and Japan was about to accelerate on its own. Additional fiscal reflation (Table 2) met in both countries with accommodating monetary policy which had been aimed in 1977 and 1978 at slowing appreciation vis-à-vis the dollar. Thus, policy conditions favored the inflationary effects of increasing oil prices. Consequently stabilization and consolidation efforts in the following years turned out to be more costly in macroeconomic terms. These detrimental medium-term consequences must be emphasized in any critical assessment of the Bonn Summit policies,[12] rather than the size of possible output effects achieved in the short run. Obviously, negative evaluation is not so much directed at international policy coordination per se than on its capacity for fine tuning.

Coordination Since Plaza

Policy coordination following the Plaza Meeting in September 1985 was aimed at more balanced growth to reduce destabilizing external

---

[11]See OECD, *Economic Outlook* 24 (December 1978), p. 17. Gebert and Scheide (1980) point out that models did not reflect recent changes in important conditions connected, for example, with flexible exchange rates, and they supposed that the impact on production was overestimated.

[12]See Horne and Masson (1988), p. 274.

Table 1. Demand and Output in Industrial Countries, 1977–80
(Volume, annual change, in percent)

	1977	1978	1979	1980
United States				
Total domestic demand	5.5	4.9	1.5	−1.8
Final domestic demand	5.3	4.7	2.2	−1.2
Exports, goods and services	2.6	11.0	14.1	9.1
Imports, goods and services	11.1	7.0	4.1	−6.0
Change in foreign balance[1]	−0.9	+0.3	+1.0	+1.7
GNP	4.7	5.3	2.5	−0.2
Japan				
Total domestic demand	4.3	6.0	6.5	0.8
Final domestic demand	4.2	6.4	5.9	1.1
Exports, goods and services	10.7	−0.7	6.2	17.7
Imports, goods and services	3.2	5.1	13.4	−6.2
Change in foreign balance[1]	+0.9	−0.9	−1.4	+3.4
GNP	5.3	5.2	5.3	4.3
Germany, Fed. Rep. of				
Total domestic demand	2.7	3.6	5.5	1.1
Final domestic demand	3.5	4.0	4.4	1.9
Exports, goods and services	3.3	4.1	4.5	5.3
Imports, goods and services	3.6	5.5	10.5	3.7
Change in foreign balance[1]	−0.0	−0.3	−1.5	+0.4
GNP	2.7	3.3	4.0	1.5
Western Europe, total[2]				
Total domestic demand	1.6	2.4	4.2	1.5
Final domestic demand	2.1	2.9	3.3	1.6
Exports, goods and services[3]	4.7	5.0	6.1	2.3
Imports, goods and services[3]	2.3	3.0	9.6	2.1
Change in foreign balance[1]	+0.6	+0.5	−1.0	+0.0
GNP	2.3	2.9	3.3	1.5

Source: Organization for Economic Cooperation and Development, Quarterly National Accounts.
[1]Changes expressed as a percentage of GNP in the preceding period.
[2]OECD.
[3]Including intra-European trade in goods and services.

imbalances among major industrial countries without jeopardizing the moderate growth achieved. The first phase was marked by the statement that exchange rates should play a major role in adjusting imbalances, that is, that a depreciation of the dollar should shift competitive positions in order to foster adjustment. In fact, this approach was based in particular on corresponding policies by central banks, whereas fiscal policy was addressed only by a general admonition that deficits should be reduced in countries where the budget deficit was considered "too high."

The second phase, starting with the Louvre Meeting in February 1987, proclaimed exchange rate stability "around current levels" and

Table 2. General Government Financial Balances, 1977–80
(As a percentage of nominal GNP/GDP)

		Balance[1]	Change in Actual Balance	Change in Structural Balance[2]
United States	1977	−1.0	+1.2	+0.4
	1978	−0.0	+0.9	−0.1
	1979	0.5	+0.5	+0.5
	1980	−1.3	−1.7	−0.7
Japan	1977	−3.8	−0.2	−0.5
	1978	−5.5	−1.7	−2.0
	1979	−4.7	+0.7	+0.3
	1980	−4.4	+0.3	+0.2
Germany, Fed. Rep. of	1977	−2.4	+1.0	+0.9
	1978	−2.4	0.0	−0.5
	1979	−2.5	−0.1	−0.9
	1980	−2.9	−0.4	−0.1
United Kingdom	1977	−3.4	+1.5	+1.1
	1978	−4.2	−0.9	−2.0
	1979	−3.3	+1.0	+0.5
	1980	−3.5	−0.3	+1.7
France	1977	−0.8	−0.4	−0.3
	1978	−1.9	−1.0	−1.4
	1979	−0.7	+1.2	+1.1
	1980	−0.0	+0.7	+1.2
Italy	1977	−8.4	+1.1	+1.4
	1978	−10.3	−1.9	−1.8
	1979	−10.1	+0.2	−0.8
	1980	−8.5	+1.6	+1.0
Canada	1977	−2.4	−0.7	−0.4
	1978	−3.1	−0.8	−0.9
	1979	−2.0	+1.2	+1.0
	1980	−2.8	−0.8	−0.1
Average of six major countries (excluding United States)	1977	−3.4	+0.4	+0.2
	1978	−4.5	−1.1	−1.5
	1979	−3.9	+0.7	+0.2
	1980	−3.6	+0.2	+0.6
Average of seven major countries	1977	−2.3	+0.8	+0.3
	1978	−2.4	−0.1	−0.8
	1979	−1.8	+0.6	+0.3
	1980	−2.5	−0.7	−0.0

Source: Organization for Economic Cooperation and Development.

[1] Surplus (+) or deficit (−).

[2] OECD estimates. Reflects deliberate policy actions, fiscal drag, changes to debt service costs and variations in resource revenues. A positive sign indicates a move toward restriction (surplus); a negative sign indicates expansion (deficit).

implied a distinct change in the relative orientation of monetary policies. Beyond that, adjustment was now to be supported by ad hoc fiscal policy coordination among major industrial countries—hence, the agreement aimed at a coordinated shift of the policy mix among major countries.

Effects of Coordination on Monetary Policy

For years, summit meetings had been characterized by the "absence of any meaningful attempt to seriously address the problem of coordination of domestic monetary policies, or the international consequences of divergent monetary policies."[13] This was traced back to the independence of leading central banks from governments, the prior need to coordinate domestic monetary policy with domestic fiscal policy, and important differences in the formulation and conduct of monetary policy in the different countries. Beyond that, the often discreet character of monetary policy obviously renders it unsuitable for the conspicuous procedures of economic summits. Instead, monetary cooperation is discussed in the framework of the Fund, the BIS, and the European Community; of these, the monthly meetings of the central bank governors at the BIS are pivotal for policy coordination. Examples of ad hoc action were the discount rate cuts by the central banks of the United States, Japan, and Germany in March 1986, or the concerted action by a number of European central banks in November 1987. However, quite often coordination and the phenomenon of leadership and followership in monetary policy cannot be clearly separated.

Although monetary policy per se continued to play a minor role in recent summit declarations and Group statements, policy conduct has been markedly influenced by the agreements on exchange rate objectives, as in surplus countries the emphasis shifted, at least temporarily, from money supply as an intermediate target to the stabilization of exchange rates.[14] However, commitments still remained vague: this holds for commonly accepted exchange rate targets, as the discussion on the pace of the dollar depreciation during the period between the Plaza and the Louvre Meetings and on the existence of unpublished target zones for exchange rates since then has shown; and for instruments, in particular for the timing and amount of intervention on the exchange markets. This vagueness can be partly accounted for by the endeavor of governments and central banks to keep away as far as

---

[13]See Menil and Solomon (1983), p. 50.
[14]See Pöhl (1987), Section IV.

possible from the problems typical of a fixed-rate regime. But there was partly a real lack of consensus on fixing common targets or on the evaluation of instruments and their effects.

Indeed, depreciation of the dollar took place in 1986 without true coordination of monetary policies between major industrial countries. The Federal Reserve Board of the United States continued its previous expansionary stance and the pronounced weakness of the dollar in the course of 1986 also induced the central banks of surplus countries to adhere to expansionary policies. This period was characterized by recurrent conflict on appropriate levels of interest rates in the major countries.

Indications of cooperative conduct in monetary policy appeared after the Louvre Meeting, when stabilization "around current levels" was agreed as a new exchange rate objective. The essential monetary policy change was a gradual tightening in the United States, though the central bank discount rate was not raised before early September 1987. The contribution by the central banks of surplus countries to the coordination of monetary policies showed up in a progressive widening of short-term interest differentials in 1987 (see Table 3 and Chart 1). In Japan and Germany this happened at the expense of adherence to their respective money supply projection or target. The strategy was supported by substantial exchange market interventions, in particular by non-U.S. central banks. However, reconciling the support of the exchange rate of the dollar with internal policy objectives in the United States and in the surplus countries increasingly posed problems. The exchange-rate-oriented coordination of monetary policies apparently reached its limits last autumn, obviously because the Louvre level of exchange rates was out of line with determinants, apart from monetary policy considerations.

The analysis of monetary developments since the Plaza Meeting leaves room for doubt that true policy coordination existed among the major countries—in the sense that it led to policies that were different from those implemented in interdependent economies without international cooperation. This problem is closely related to the factual leadership of the United States in monetary policy, which, in its turn, was obviously governed primarily by internal priorities. Thus, the change of orientation from intended depreciation of the dollar to dollar-supporting policies at the time of the Louvre Meeting clearly went along with a shift from one-sided demand stimulation to the prevention of rising inflation in the United States.[15]

---

[15]See Monetary Policy Report to the Congress, submitted on February 19, 1987.

Table 3. Quarterly Monetary Indicators

	1985				1986				1987				1988
	I	II	III	IV	I	II	III	IV	I	II	III	IV	I
Money[2]	*(Percent change over 12 months[1])*												
United States	6.5	7.6	10.4	12.0	11.5	12.9	13.6	15.2	16.5	13.9	9.4	5.8	3.9
Japan	6.6	4.9	4.1	3.0	2.7	5.8	8.7	12.3	11.2	11.7	9.0	4.5	9.8[5]
Germany, Fed. Rep. of	3.6	2.7	4.5	5.7	6.7	9.5	9.6	9.1	9.0	9.5	10.0	9.5	9.9
United Kingdom	14.9	14.4	17.1	16.4	20.3	21.4	23.4	23.3	23.1	24.0	22.7	23.3	
Money plus quasi-money													
United States	9.4	9.5	10.5	9.8	8.4	8.6	8.5	8.8	8.9	7.4	5.6	4.3	4.2[5]
Japan	7.6	7.6	7.3	8.8	8.4	8.5	9.8	9.6	8.9	10.7	10.1	11.2	13.0[5]
Germany, Fed. Rep. of[3]	5.0	5.0	4.9	6.7	5.2	5.1	6.0	5.3	7.4	7.8	6.9	6.1	6.0
United Kingdom[3,4]	11.9	11.8	14.1	13.4	16.9	18.9	18.0	18.7	19.2	19.9	21.3	22.5	
Interest rates, money market	*(Quarterly average, in percent per annum)*												
United States	8.5	7.9	7.9	8.1	7.8	6.9	6.2	6.3	6.2	6.7	6.8	6.9	6.7
Japan	6.3	6.1	6.3	7.3	6.1	4.4	4.6	4.1	4.0	3.3	3.3	3.5	3.5
Germany, Fed. Rep. of	5.7	5.6	4.8	4.6	4.7	4.5	4.5	4.6	4.0	3.7	3.7	3.5	3.2
United Kingdom	11.0	10.1	11.3	10.8	12.2	9.4	10.2	10.9	10.5	9.1	9.8	9.2	9.0
Interest rates, government bonds													
United States	11.6	10.8	10.3	9.8	8.6	7.6	7.3	7.3	7.2	8.3	8.9	9.1	8.4
Japan	6.6	6.4	6.1	6.3	5.2	4.9	4.9	4.7	4.0	3.6	4.8	4.5	4.1
Germany, Fed. Rep. of	7.4	7.1	6.5	6.5	6.1	5.7	5.8	6.0	5.7	5.5	6.0	6.2	5.8
United Kingdom	11.0	10.8	10.4	10.4	10.2	9.0	9.6	10.7	9.7	9.0	9.7	9.6	9.5[5]

Source: International Monetary Fund, *International Financial Statistics* (partly supplemented from national sources).
[1] Quarterly average of monthly rates.
[2] M1.
[3] M3.
[4] Last month of period until 1986, II.
[5] January/February.

Effects of Coordination on Fiscal Policy and on Policy Mix

The discretion peculiar to monetary policy was not applied to the coordination of fiscal policy. To some extent this was due to the desire of governments to improve their reputation by demonstrating the success of international negotiations. Beyond that, however, the coordination of demand management by fiscal policy was obviously given a high degree of credit by several governments.

Fiscal measures announced in 1987 have been executed or are under way. Thus, the May 1987 fiscal package in Japan included tax cuts of 0.3 percent of GNP and public investment expenditure of 1.5 percent of GNP, distributed over two fiscal years. In Germany, tax cuts for 1988 were raised from 0.4 percent to 0.7 percent of GNP. Complying with the commitment of the Group of Seven Statement of December 1987, the German budget deficit has increased markedly. The general government deficit will come close to 2½ percent of GNP in 1988—twice as large as two years before.

Chart 1. Exchange Rates and Interest Rate Differentials, 1985–87

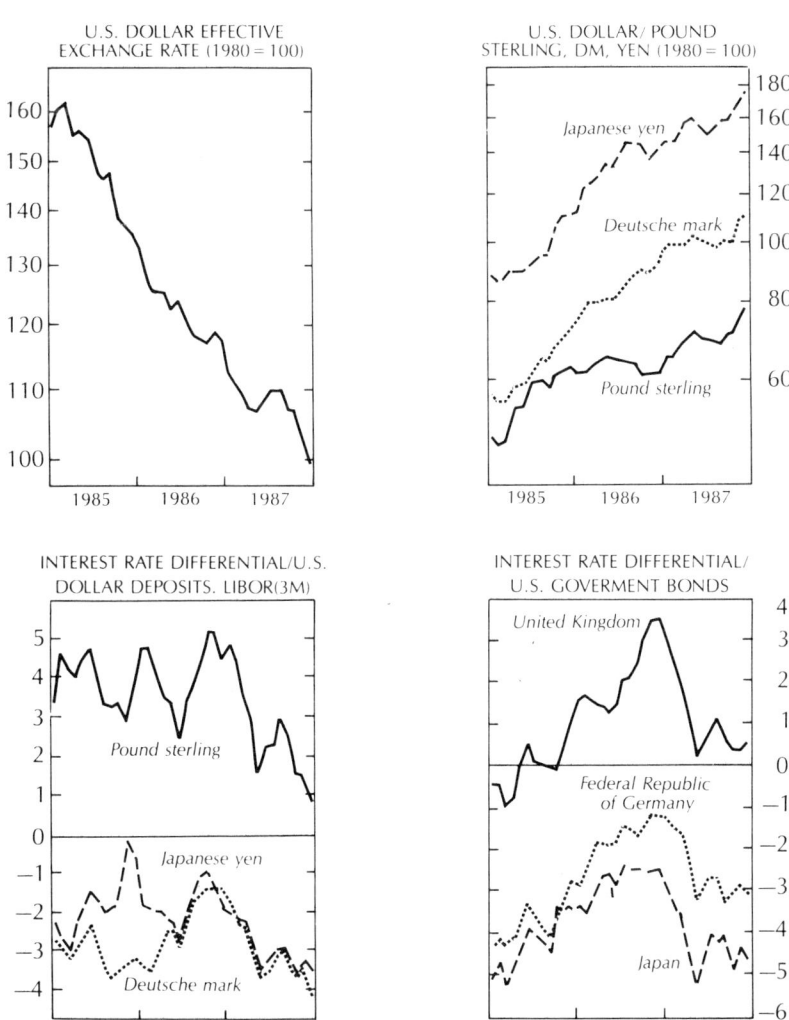

Source: International Monetary Fund, *International Financial Statistics*.

Corresponding to expansionary measures by the surplus countries, the United States has enacted consolidation measures. However, the reduction of the deficit will fall short of the announcement of the Louvre Accord, which envisaged a deficit of 2.3 percent of GNP in fiscal year 1988. After a subsequent revision of targets, the expected outcome is now about 1 percentage point higher. Indeed, the figure in the Louvre Accord corresponding to legislated deficit targets lacked credibility from the beginning. This experience points to the limits of identifying published "agreed undertakings" with policy coordination.

As the influence of coordination efforts on the formation of national policies cannot be separated from that of coincident autonomous decisions in the framework of international interdependence, an evaluation of recent developments will be confined to the question whether the fiscal policy conduct in major industrial countries has, on the whole, worked toward realizing commonly declared objectives.

As to the envisaged promotion of sustained growth, some progress was achieved by the reduction of the aggregate general fiscal deficit of industrial countries in 1987 and the consequent improvement of conditions for lower real interest rates in the world.[16] The short-term impact of relative changes in the fiscal policy stance of major countries indeed supported the envisaged reduction of external imbalances, if changes in public sector deficits are taken as a yardstick. Whereas the expansionary stance in the United States climaxed in 1986 and was followed by a tendency toward consolidation, fiscal policy stance has shifted from deflationary to about neutral in Japan since 1985,[17] and from deflationary to expansionary in Germany (see Table 4).

The difficulties of evaluating the impact of policy coordination on effective policy conduct since the Plaza Meeting are compounded in the assessment of the mix of monetary and fiscal policy. In the United States, however, where both fiscal and monetary policy were to be termed expansionary in 1985 and 1986, and rather deflationary in 1987, national decision making was obviously dominant. In the surplus countries, on the other hand, coordination may have had some influence, at least on the timing of policy actions. This holds for Germany, where the mix of deflationary fiscal policy and broadly neutral monetary policy in 1985 has made way for a rather expansionary stance in both fields since 1986, and also for Japan, where similar

---

[16]For the crucial role of fiscal policies for the world interest level as well as for dealing with current account imbalances see Genberg and Swoboda (1987b). Mansur (1988) also takes into account the relation to private sector savings.

[17]The interpretation of observed changes in government financial balances is difficult because of influences from special factors.

Table 4. General Government Financial Balances, 1984–87
(As a percentage of nominal GNP/GDP)

		Balance[1]	Change in Actual Balance	Change in Structural Balance[2]
United States	1984	−2.8	+1.0	−0.7
	1985	−3.3	−0.5	−0.8
	1986	−3.5	−0.2	−0.4
	1987	−2.5	+1.0	+0.8
Japan	1984	−2.1	+1.6	+1.1
	1985	−0.8	+1.3	+0.9
	1986	−1.1	−0.3	+0.1
	1987	−0.3	+0.8	+0.6
Germany, Fed. Rep. of	1984	−1.9	+0.6	+0.0
	1985	−1.1	+0.8	+0.8
	1986	−1.2	−0.1	−0.3
	1987	−1.7	−0.5	−0.3
United Kingdom	1984	−3.9	−0.5	−0.7
	1985	−2.9	+1.0	+0.3
	1986	−2.6	+0.2	−0.4
	1987	−1.7	+1.0	−0.0
France	1984	−2.7	+0.4	+0.8
	1985	−2.9	−0.2	+0.1
	1986	−2.9	−0.1	−0.1
	1987	−2.3	+0.7	+0.7
Italy	1984	−11.5	−0.8	−1.5
	1985	−12.3	−0.8	−1.1
	1986	−11.3	+1.1	+0.7
	1987	−10.8	+0.5	−0.0
Canada	1984	−6.6	+0.3	−1.2
	1985	−7.0	−0.4	−1.0
	1986	−5.5	+1.5	+1.3
	1987	−4.4	+1.1	+0.7
Average of six major countries (excluding the United States)	1984	−3.9	+0.5	+0.1
	1985	−3.4	+0.5	+0.3
	1986	−3.2	+0.2	+0.1
	1987	−2.6	+0.6	+0.3
Average of seven major countries	1984	−3.4	+0.7	−0.3
	1985	−3.3	+0.0	−0.2
	1986	−3.3	+0.0	−0.1
	1987	−2.6	+0.8	+0.5

Source: Organization for Economic Cooperation and Development.
[1] Surplus (+) or deficit (−).
[2] OECD estimates. Reflects deliberate policy actions, fiscal drag, changes to debt service costs and variations in resource revenues. A positive sign indicates a move toward restriction (surplus); a negative sign indicates expansion (deficit).

change materialized. On the whole, the shift in relative policy mixes in these three countries starting in 1986 seems to have supported the different domestic demand trends called for by the need to diminish external imbalances. At the same time, however, limitations to this approach were seen by surplus countries with regard to the general objective of ensuring conditions for noninflationary growth.

Empirical Evidence of Effects of Coordinated Policies on Economic Performance

The difficulties of distinguishing uncoordinated national policy undertakings from coordinated efforts impede any attempt to show the impact of coordinated policies on the economic performance of participating countries. This is true even without the external shocks that were experienced after the 1978 Bonn Economic Summit. In these circumstances, actual international policy discussion disregards specific relationships between realized measures and their impact. It centers instead on the comparison of envisaged economic developments with effective performance or with forecast figures in the case of current periods.

Given that policy coordination since the 1985 Plaza Statement was aimed primarily at more balanced growth and a reduction in external disequilibria, progress in major industrial countries is showing up in real developments. Though aggregate GNP growth of the major industrial countries held close to the 3 percent figure of 1985 and obviously came up to expectations of governments, Western Europe, especially Germany, lagged. But this pattern was markedly influenced by the progress in external adjustment, as net exports were a retarding force in Western Europe and in Japan from 1986 onward, and a stimulating force in the United States from 1987 (see Table 5). Against that, the growth differential of real domestic demand shifted in line with respective policy differentiation between major surplus and deficit countries. Taking 1985 as a base year, figures for 1987 show a distinct acceleration in Germany as well as in Japan, against deceleration in the United States. This demand differential will continue in 1988. Progress in real adjustment will be reflected increasingly in nominal balances, as J-curve effects will abate.

It must be kept in mind, however, that the realization of the envisaged differentiation of demand trends between the United States and the surplus countries are specific evidence of coordinated policy actions. The case of fiscal coordination measures in Japan illustrates this point. There, the remarkable fiscal package of May 1987 made up for an otherwise considerable contractionary impulse, and the net

Table 5. Demand and Output in Industrial Countries, 1984–89
(Volume, annual change, in percent)

	1984	1985	1986	1987	1988	1989
United States						
Total domestic demand	8.7	3.6	3.9	2.5	1.7	2.2
Final domestic demand	6.6	5.3	3.7	1.8	2.4	2.1
Exports, goods and services	6.8	−1.7	3.3	12.8	...	...
Imports, goods and services	23.8	3.9	10.5	7.3	...	...
Change in foreign balance[1]	−2.0	−0.7	−1.0	+0.3	+1.1	+0.5
GNP	6.8	3.0	2.9	2.9	2.9	2.7
Japan						
Total domestic demand	3.8	4.0	4.0	5.1	5.6	4.4
Final domestic demand	3.4	3.6	4.6	5.2	5.2	4.1
Exports, goods and services	17.5	5.6	−5.2	3.5	...	...
Imports, goods and services	11.1	−0.1	2.8	9.1	...	...
Change in foreign balance[1]	1.3	1.1	−1.4	−0.7	−1.3	−0.6
GNP	5.1	4.9	2.4	4.2	4.1	3.8
Germany, Fed. Rep. of						
Total domestic demand	2.0	0.9	3.8	2.9	2.7	2.0
Final domestic demand	1.6	1.4	3.6	2.5	2.7	2.0
Exports, goods and services[2]	9.0	6.7	−0.2	0.8	...	...
Imports, goods and services[2]	5.3	3.7	3.7	4.8	...	...
Change in foreign balance[1]	1.3	1.1	−1.1	−1.1	−0.9	−0.3
GNP	3.3	2.0	2.5	1.7	1.7	1.7
Western Europe, total[3]						
Total domestic demand	2.1	2.5	4.0	3.5	2.6	2.2
Final domestic demand	1.6	2.4	3.7	3.0	2.7	2.3
Exports, goods and services	7.9	5.1	1.5	4.0	...	...
Imports, goods and services	6.3	4.9	5.8	7.0	...	...
Change in foreign balance[1]	0.6	0.2	−1.3	−1.0	−0.6	−0.3
GNP	2.7	2.6	2.7	2.5	2.0	2.0

Sources: Calculated from national figures, Western Europe: OECD, Quarterly National Accounts; International Monetary Fund forecasts for 1988 and 1989.
[1] Changes expressed as a percentage of GNP in the preceding period.
[2] Including intra-European trade in goods and services.
[3] OECD. 1987 partly estimated.

fiscal stance is estimated now to be broadly neutral in 1987 and 1988.[18] Taking this into account, the vigorous increase of domestic demand must be attributed mainly to factors apart from fiscal policy; among these, the highly flexible adjustment of the economy to the earlier dollar shock seems to have been of crucial importance. On the contrary, in Germany where fiscal stimulus has occurred in 1987 and 1988, slow growth points to structural impediments for adjustment as being more important than in Japan.

---

[18] See *OECD Economic Outlook 42* (December 1987), p. 89.

Table 6. Foreign Balances of the United States, Japan, and the Federal Republic of Germany, 1984–89

	1984	1985	1986	1987	1988	1989
Balance of payments on current accounts	(In billions of dollars)					
United States	−107.0	−116.4	−141.4	−160.7	−141.1	−133.8
Japan	35.0	49.2	85.8	86.7	77.8	75.4
Germany, Fed. Rep. of	9.8	16.4	39.1	44.8	41.4	40.7
	(In percentage of GNP)					
United States	−2.8	−2.9	−3.3	−3.6	−3.0	−2.6
Japan	2.8	3.7	4.4	3.6	2.7	2.5
Germany, Fed. Rep. of	1.6	2.6	4.4	4.0	3.3	3.1
Foreign balance, goods and services	(At current prices, in percentage of GNP)					
United States	−1.6	−2.0	−2.5	−2.7	...	...
Japan	2.9	3.8	4.4	4.1	...	...
Germany, Fed. Rep. of	3.1	4.3	5.7	5.4	...	...
	(At constant prices,[1] in percentage of GNP)					
United States	−2.4	−3.0	−3.9	−3.5	−2.4	−1.8
Japan	3.4	4.3	2.8	2.0	0.6	0.0
Germany, Fed. Rep. of	4.3	5.3	4.1	2.9	2.0	1.6

Sources: Calculations based on national figures and on forecasts by the International Monetary Fund for 1988 and 1989.

[1] United States: 1982; Japan, Federal Republic of Germany: 1980. Forecast figures based on annual percentage changes of foreign balances and GNP.

Empirical Evidence from International Macroeconomic Models

All in all, ad hoc policy coordination has not only been rare up to now, but, when accomplished, the observed effects were far from clear. This experience continues to support the search for empirical evidence based on econometric simulations. The most extensive exercise of predicting the external and the domestic effects of specified policy changes in this way was organized by the Brookings Institution in 1986 on the basis of twelve leading international macroeconomic models. The following discussion focuses on the effects of a sustained increase of government spending equal to 1 percent of GNP, separately for the United States and for non-U.S. OECD, and likewise of an increase in money supply of 4 percent of GNP (see Table 7). On average, predictions for the second year of the policy change showed a marked concentration of GNP effects on the region where policy was changed.[19] The effect of fiscal stimulus on foreign GNP is somewhat

---

[19] However, the results may be reversed in the medium term. See, for example, the results of the Federal Reserve Board's Multi-Country-Model for the impact of fiscal expansion over six years, shown by Tanzi (1988), p. 41, from Edison and Tryon (1986).

Table 7. Simulation Effects of Monetary and Fiscal Policy Changes[1]

International Model	Monetary Expansion[2]								Fiscal Expansion[3]							
	In U.S.				In non-U.S. OECD				In U.S.				In non-U.S. OECD			
	GNP effect (In percent)		CA effect (In billions of dollars)		GNP effect (In percent)		CA effect (In billions of dollars)		GNP effect (In percent)		CA effect (In billions of dollars)		GNP effect (In percent)		CA effect (In billions of dollars)	
	D	F	D	F	D	F	D	F	D	F	D	F	D	F	D	F
MCM	+1.5	−0.7	−3.1	−3.5	+1.5	−0.0	+3.5	+0.1	+1.8	+0.7	−16.5	+8.9	+1.4	+0.5	−7.2	+7.9
EEC	+1.0	+0.2	−2.8	+1.2	+0.8	+0.1	−5.2	+1.9	+1.2	+0.3	−11.6	+6.6	+1.3	+0.2	−9.3	+3.0
EPA	+1.2	−0.4	−1.6	−10.1	+0.8	+0.1	−0.1	+0.1	+1.7	+0.9	−20.5	+9.3	+2.3	+0.3	−13.1	+4.7
LINK	+1.0	−0.1	−5.9	+1.5	+0.0	+0.0	−1.4	+3.5	+1.2	+0.1	−6.4	+1.9	+1.2	+0.2	−6.1	+6.3
LIVERPOOL	+0.1	−0.0	−13.0	+0.1	+0.8	+0.1	+7.1	−8.2	+0.6	−0.0	−7.0	+3.4	+0.3	−0.5	−17.2	+11.9
MSG	+0.3	+0.4	+2.6	−4.4	+0.4	+0.3	−15.9	+12.0	+0.9	+0.3	−21.6	+22.7	+1.1	+0.4	−5.3	+10.5
MINIMOD	+1.0	−0.2	+2.8	−4.7	+0.8	−0.3	+3.6	−1.4	+1.0	+0.3	−8.5	+5.5	+1.6	+0.1	−2.2	+3.2
VAR	+3.0	+0.4	+4.9	−5.1	+0.8	+1.2	+5.2	−10.0	+0.4	−0.0	−0.5	−0.2	+0.5	+0.3	+1.7	−2.6
OECD	+1.6	+0.3	−8.4	+3.1	+0.8	+0.1	−1.6	+2.3	+1.1	+0.4	−14.2	+11.4	+1.5	+0.1	−6.9	+3.3
Taylor	+0.6	−0.2	...	...	+0.8	−0.1	...	...	+0.6	+0.4	...	...	+1.6	+0.6	...	...
Wharton	+0.7	−0.4	−5.1	+5.3	+0.2	−0.1	+2.6	+0.5	+1.4	+0.2	−15.4	+5.3	+3.2	+0.0	−5.5	+4.7
DRI	+1.8	−0.6	−1.4	+14.5	+0.0	+0.0	...	...	+2.1	+0.7	−22.0	+0.8	+0.0	+0.0	...	...
Average[4]	+1.2	−0.0	−2.8	+0.7	+0.6	+0.3	−0.2	+0.1	+1.2	+0.4	−13.1	+6.9	+1.5	+0.2	−7.1	+5.3

Source: Simulation effects as reported by Frankel and Rockett (1986) for the second year of policy change. Participating models were MCM, Federal Reserve Board; EEC, European Commission; EPA, Japanese Economic Planning Agency; LINK, Project Link; LIVERPOOL, Patrick Minford; MSG, McKibbin-Sachs; MINIMOD, Haas-Masson (International Monetary Fund); VAR, Sims-Litterman; OECD, Interlink; Taylor, Stanford; Wharton; DRI, Data Resources.

[1] Effects on gross national product (GNP) and on current account (CA) of respective domestic (D) and foreign (F) economies.
[2] Increase in money supply of 4 percent.
[3] Increase in government expenditure equal to 1 percent of GNP.
[4] Average of reporting models.

more pronounced when the policy is implemented by the United States rather than by non-U.S. OECD. The effects of fiscal stimulus on current balances in either case showed a distinct deterioration of the own balance and an improvement of foreign balances. Against that the consequences of an increase of money supply on current balances were on average negligible in the case of action by non-U.S. OECD, whereas in the case of action by the United States the impulse was negative for its own balance and only slightly positive for the balance of the non-U.S. OECD. The latter points to interaction with non-OECD, often neglected in discussion of the effects of policy coordination. However, the average figures[20] are generated from predictions of the twelve models that vary widely in magnitude and also in sign.[21] Taking into account the different properties of the models, such disagreements came as no surprise, and they point to the limits of empirical evidence of externalities derived even from respected models.

A specific approach is needed for predicting not only the effects of singular policy action, but of policy coordination per se. There have been relatively few empirical studies in this field, an overview of which was presented in the paper of Horne and Masson (1988). These comparisons of a cooperative solution with a noncooperative equilibrium are based on essential assumptions concerning, for example, the models of the decision makers in the exercise, the availability and use made of information, and the objectives of governments. The respective characteristics of simulations are quite different, and the outcome is highly dependent on the assumptions made. However, if it is assumed that information on other national policies is available and also taken into account by governments in uncoordinated national policies, evidence from simulation in general shows only small gains from coordination.[22]

Recent discussion among governments of major industrial countries pointing to disagreement "on how the world actually works"[23] drew special attention to the assumption of consensus on a "true"

The cumulative impact of a permanent increase of U.S. real government expenditure of 1 percent is estimated at 1.8 percent of U.S. GNP in the second year, falling to 0.1 percent in the sixth year, whereas the cumulative impact on foreign GNP rises from 0.7 percent to 1.0 percent.
[20]Further average changes were calculated by Fischer (1987) for consumer price indices, interest rates, and exchange rates.
[21]See Frankel and Rockett (1986) and Frankel (1987).
[22]The evaluation took into consideration studies of Oudis and Sachs (1984), McKibbin and Sachs (1985, 1986), Taylor (1985), and Canzoneri and Minford (1986). See Horne and Masson (1988), pp. 286–87.
[23]See Cooper (1986), p. 9.

model. A study of Frankel and Rockett (1986), on the consequences of disagreements among policymakers on the model, used the results of econometric models of the world economy that participated in the parallel simulation arranged by the Brookings Institution. Under the assumption that each model might qualify as the true model, 512 possible combinations of different models of policymakers and of models representing reality were analysed. The investigation in the outcome of international coordination of monetary policy then resulted in welfare gains for the United States in 56 percent of cases, as against losses in 40 percent, with no effects found in a few cases. For non-U.S. OECD countries the respective figures were 58 percent against 39 percent. International coordination of fiscal and monetary policy together resulted in gains for the United States in 55 percent of cases, and in losses in 45 percent, whereas in non-U.S. OECD countries 55 percent stood against 43 percent. According to this simulation, the likelihood of improvement by policy coordination comes out slightly higher, on average, than that of deterioration.

To be sure, empirical evidence for the effects of policy coordination derived from existing econometric models for the world economy cannot claim to form an image of true relationships and effects, as restrictions arising from imperfections of the models, from inevitable simplifications and assumptions made in the exercise are important for the outcome.[24] The lack of distinctiveness leaves ample room for approaches trying to improve knowledge on the externalities of policy action and on the working of policy coordination by using simple models. Often, results from such exercises are less ambiguous, but they cannot pass for empirical evidence.

Summary

As the analysis has shown, empirical evidence for the effects of policy coordination among major industrial countries is still scarce, and often not very reliable. This partly reflects the general problem of separating the specific impact of macroeconomic policy from other determinants of economic developments. Beyond that, it is difficult in reality to distinguish policy coordination from less intensive international cooperation and from autonomous national policies, which take into account generally available information on the policy of foreign

---

[24]Levine and Curry (1987) point to the influence of assumptions on the credibility of governments vis-à-vis their private sectors. Ghosh and Masson (1988) focus on the question whether policymakers take account of the presence of model uncertainty in choosing their optimal plans. If they do, gains from coordination are expected to increase considerably.

countries. Identified cases of ad hoc macroeconomic policy coordination are confined to the 1978 Bonn Economic Summit and to the most recent period since the 1985 Plaza Meeting. They offer little evidence of discernible effects, whereas the outcome of simulation by existing models for the world economy obviously comes up against essential restrictions.

There is a number of causes for the observed scarcity of policy coordination. Notwithstanding the existence of a commonly emphasized main target, mainly "inflation-free sustainable growth," evidence has repeatedly shown that priorities are different from country to country in short-term conflicts and in the way risks are weighed. Apart from divergent preferences, influenced by specific historical experience or, at times, by political orientation, there are also objective reasons. Thus the role of the deutsche mark as a minor reserve currency in fact creates stronger stability constraints for the German economy than the dollar does for the U.S. economy.[25]

A more important impediment to the transformation of readiness for cooperation into effective coordination was differing views on how economies work, and correspondingly, on appropriate action. Sometimes these divergences seemed to be determined by different time horizons, also related to election dates, but often underlying schools of thought were apparently distinct. If, as a consequence of this, the monetary policy stance, for example, was measured by the money supply in one country, and by the level of interest rates in another, sustained monetary policy coordination was hardly possible. Agreement on fiscal policy coordination was impeded primarily by lack of consensus in weighing the short-term impact on demand against longer-term effects on growth. Apart from this, the limits for ad hoc fiscal coordination arising from internal political constraints for national decision making were apparent, in particular in the United States.

Divergences of opinion were accentuated in the 1980s by rather quick changes of concepts and policies in the United States. This has complicated the role of economic leadership. Doubts in this respect, together with the ability of the *économie dominante* to demonstrate long lasting benign neglect of external imbalances tended to reduce the credibility of coordination announcements. This amounts to scaling down possible reduction of uncertainties on foreign economic policies.

The few cases of ad hoc macroeconomic policy coordination were aimed primarily at short-term effects. Even tax cuts that were part of supply-oriented strategies were timed according to their immediate

---

[25]See Matthes (1987), p. 309.

effects on demand. However, internationally coordinated fine tuning is subject to the many restrictions that are well known at the national level. Occurrence of ad hoc macroeconomic policy coordination was favored, therefore, by the appearance of a common feasibility illusion or of a feasibility illusion of the *économie dominante* at least.

Whereas the possible effects of policy coordination at the end of the 1970s were concealed by the effects of the second oil price hike, coordination in the second phase starting with the Plaza Statement is still under way. Apart from new dislocations caused by the oil price shock in 1986, though with the opposite sign to the two former price hikes, the effects of policy coordination cannot be separated even approximately from the effects of other determinants. Therefore, recent misfortunes of policy coordination on the common targeting of the dollar exchange rate cannot be safely attributed to single causes. However, it appears that an adequate contribution of fiscal policy coordination among major industrial countries to the adjustment process meant too heavy a load on monetary policy inside and outside the United States.

The source of the rising demand for macroeconomic policy coordination is the obvious misfortune of noncoordinated national policies and the disturbing consequences of disregarding externalities. Widespread belief in coordination gains seems to be derived from a comparison of these experienced shortcomings with the expected advantages of a theoretical approach based on assumed common knowledge of future trends, of true economic relationships, and of appropriate policies. In all respects, however, recent experience warns us to be modest and thereby confirms the hesitation derived from simulations of coordinated policies using existing models. In these circumstances, the merits of international economic cooperation among major industrial countries are to be expected rather in the field of an increasing awareness of the externalities of national policies, in improving the international exchange of information on economic trends and policies, and in taking all this into due consideration when conceiving national economic policies.

REFERENCES

Bean, Charles R., "Macroeconomic Policy Coordination: Theory and Evidence." *Recherches Economiques de Louvain* (Louvain), Vol. 51 (No. 3/4, 1985), pp. 267–83.

Cooper, Richard N. "Economic Interdependence and Coordination of Economic Policies," in Ronald W. Jones, and Peter B. Kenen, eds., *Handbook of International Economics*, Vol. 2 (Amsterdam: North-Holland, 1984), pp. 1195–1234.

———, "International Economic Cooperation: Overview and a Glimpse of the Future," paper presented at the OECD 25th Anniversary Symposium on "Opportunities and Risks for the World Economy: The Challenge of Increasing Complexity," Paris, October 21–22, 1986.

De Grauwe, Paul, "Fiscal Policies in the EMS: A Strategic Analysis," Katholieke Universiteit te Leuven, Centrum voor Economishe Studien, International Economic Research Paper No. 53 (Louvain, October 1986).

Fischer, Stanley, "International Macroeconomic Policy Coordination," NBER Working Paper No. 2244 (Washington, National Bureau of Economic Research, May 1987).

Frankel, Jeffrey A., "Obstacles to International Macroeconomic Policy Coordination," International Monetary Fund Working Paper WP/87/29 (Washington, April 1987).

———, and Katharine A. Rockett,"International Macroeconomic Policy Coordination when Policy-Makers Disagree on the Model," NBER Working Paper No. 2059 (Washington, National Bureau of Economic Research, October 1986).

Gebert, Dietmar, and Joachim Scheide, *Die Lokomotiven-Strategie als Wirtschaftspolitisches Konzept* (Kiel: Institut für Weltwirtschaft, 1980).

Genberg, Hans, and Alexander K. Swoboda (1987a), "Policy and Current Account Determination under Floating Exchange Rates," International Monetary Fund Working Paper WP/87/69 (Washington, October).

———, and ——— (1987b), "The Current Account and the Policy Mix Under Flexible Exchange Rates," International Monetary Fund Working Paper WP/87/70 (Washington, October).

Ghosh, Atish R., and Paul R. Masson, "International Policy Coordination in a World with Model Uncertainty," *Staff Papers*, International Monetary Fund (Washington), Vol. 35 (June 1988), pp. 230–58.

Horne, Jocelyn, and Paul R. Masson, "Scope and Limits of International Economic Cooperation and Policy Coordination," *Staff Papers*, International Monetary Fund (Washington), Vol. 35 (June 1988), pp. 259–96.

Levine, Paul, and David Currie, "Does International Macroeconomic Policy Coordination Pay and Is It Sustainable?: A Two Country Analysis," *Oxford Economic Papers* (Oxford), Vol. 39 (March 1987), pp. 38–74.

Mansur, Ahsan, "Fiscal-Monetary Mix and Exchange Rate Movements in the Major Industrial Countries, 1980–84," International Monetary Fund Working Paper WP/88/3 (Washington, January 1988).

Marris, Stephen, *Defizite und der Dollar. Die Weltwirtschaft in Gefahr* (Hamburg: Verlag Weltarchiv, 1986).

Masson, Paul R., and Malcolm Knight, "International Transmission of Fiscal Policies in Major Industrial Countries," *Staff Papers*, International Monetary Fund (Washington), Vol. 33 (September 1986), pp. 387–438.

Matthes, Heinrich, "Koordinierung der Wirtschaftspolitik innerhalb der EG," *Wirtschaftsdienst* (Hamburg), Vol. 67 (May 1987), pp. 247–60.

McKibbin, Warwick J., and Jeffrey D. Sachs, "Coordination of Monetary and Fiscal Policies in the OECD," NBER Working Paper No. 1800 (Washington, National Bureau of Economic Research, January 1986).

Menil, George de, and Anthony M. Solomon, *Economic Summitry* (New York: Council on Foreign Relations, 1983).
Oudis, Gilles, and Jeffrey Sachs, "Macroeconomic Policy Coordination Among the Industrial Economies," *Brookings Papers on Economic Activity: I* (1984), The Brookings Institution (Washington), pp. 1–75.
Pelkmans, Jacques, "Collective Management and Economic Cooperation," in Cesare Merlini, ed., *Economic Summits and Western Decision-Making* (New York: St. Martin's Press, 1984).
Pöhl, Karl O., "Cooperation—a Keystone for the Stability of the International Monetary System," First Arthur Burns Memorial Lecture at the American Council on Germany (New York, November 1987).
Putnam, Robert D., and Nicholas Bayne, *Weltwirtschaftsgipfel im Wandel* (Bonn: Europaunion, 1985).
Scheide, Joachim, and Stefan Sinn, "Internationale Kooperation der Wirtschaftspolitik: Pro und Contra," Kiel Discussion Papers (Kiel, November 1987).
Schlesinger, Helmut, "Fiscal and Monetary Policy—Elements of International Cooperation," Lecture at the 43rd Congress and Semicentennial of the International Institute of Public Finance (Paris, August 1987).
Solomon, Robert, "Forums for Intergovernmental Consultations about Macroeconomic Policies," Brookings Discussion Papers in International Economics No. 15 (Washington, The Brookings Institution, April 1984).
Tanzi, Vito, "Fiscal Policy and International Coordination: Current and Future Issues," Paper presented at the Conference on Fiscal Policy, Economic Adjustment and Financial Markets (Milan, January 1988).
Ungerer, Horst, Owen Evans, Thomas Mayer, and Philip Young, "The European Monetary System: Recent Developments," International Monetary Fund Occasional Paper No. 48 (Washington: IMF, December 1986).
Vaubel, Roland, "International Collusion or Competition for Macroeconomic Policy Coordination? A Restatement," *Recherches Economiques de Louvain* (Louvain), Vol. 51 (No. 3/4 1985), pp. 223–40.
Wegner, Manfred, "Scope and Limits of International Economic Policy Coordination," *World Economy* (London), Vol. 10 (September 1987), pp. 283–305.

Comment

Hans Tietmeyer

For a large part of my professional career I have been closely involved in international policy cooperation, including the preparation of summit meetings, and since 1982—as the sherpa of Chancellor Kohl—I have been charged directly with the preparation of the summit conferences. I am, therefore, extremely interested in the topic of coordination. Having the advantage of insider knowledge, I will try to bring into this discussion my own experience with policy coordination among the major industrial countries. As a participant I am not at best equipped to have a clear judgment on the empirical evidence. So I will take the liberty to make some general remarks on policy cooperation. (I prefer cooperation to coordination, because cooperation has a broader meaning, while coordination has more the taste of an ambitious international demand management.)

In the course of the last few years, policy cooperation among these countries has developed into a dense network of mutual consultations and policy commitments, of which the summits and Group of Five or Seven meetings were the most important part. Evaluating the impact of this form of policy cooperation, one has to be aware that it means much more than mere coordination of macroeconomic policies in the fiscal and monetary fields. It means cooperation between sovereign nations on all important economic issues such as trade, development and debt, energy and structural policy, and coordination through international organizations such as the Fund, the General Agreement on Tariffs and Trade (GATT), and the Organization for Economic Cooperation and Development (OECD).

In addition, over the years since Rambouillet there has been no single and agreed economic summit philosophy. The communiqués rather reflect changing priorities in national policies and divergent theories on how the economy works and accordingly what strategy should be pursued. So one should not speak of economic coordination as though it were well defined.

The main motive and the objective of the first summit in Rambouillet was to overcome the impact of the oil price hikes on the world economy and to find a new framework for cooperation on exchange rate matters after the breakdown of the Bretton Woods System.

The industrial countries had reacted to these challenges with divergent policies which in turn produced growing inflation differentials and current account disequilibria. The main issue on the agenda was better coordination of macroeconomic policies, even if the other topics—the commitments to free trade and the formalization of the existing monetary system—gained more public attention in the press. The agreed policy approach to this situation was a discretionary international coordination of the Keynesian demand-oriented national policies already underway in the participating countries. Despite some differences in the concept, this summit philosophy of coordinated demand management prevailed until the Bonn Summit in 1978, where—as described in the preceding paper by Günter

Großer—a detailed fine-tuned quantitative program to stimulate the economies was launched. But one can dispute whether, for example, the German decision would not have been taken without the summit.

With the Reagan Administration coming into office in 1980, the summit philosophy and thus the economic strategies shifted from demand management to more supply-side policies. The following Summits of Ottawa, Versailles and especially that of Williamsburg, tried to reach a common understanding on a more lasting improvement of the conditions for economic growth by supply-side measures, free markets, free floating, and strict monetary targeting.

The concept of economic policy competition on the basis of agreed principles instead of macroeconomic policy coordination gained ground—at least on the U.S. side the attitude of benign neglect vis-à-vis exchange rate movements of the U.S. dollar prevailed. At that time the course of macroeconomic policy and especially the policy mix of fiscal and monetary policy in the United States was quite different from that in the other industrial countries. And despite many efforts on the sidelines of the summits, in reality there was no chance of a change at that time. Had a consensus in fact materialized then, our current problems would no doubt be much less serious. But things took a different turn.

Since the middle of the 1980s the pendulum has swung back again to more concrete forms of economic policy coordination. The unbalanced policy mix in the United States, the different growth performance in the United States, Japan, and Europe, and the resulting distortions in the exchange and current account pattern called for a new coordinated policy approach between the major industrial countries.

At the Bonn Summit in 1985, the participating countries committed themselves to a more detailed program of action and specific priorities for national policy to sustain noninflationary growth and higher employment. This agreement in Bonn was the starting point for the Plaza Accord launched in September 1985. The situation in Bonn in 1985 appeared to resemble that in 1978. However there were substantial differences in the objectives and the concept. The main thrust of economic policy commitments of the Bonn Summit of 1985 remained directed toward the supply side by following a prudent fiscal and monetary policy, reducing—where excessive—the share of public spending in GNP and removing obstacles to economic growth. There was no return to ambitious fine tuning in demand management and no program of specific quantitative targets.

Over the years, not only philosophies and economic concepts have

changed; the summits also reflected the changing priorities that heads of state attached to the other topics of international policy cooperation. To illustrate:
- In the second half of the 1970s, energy policy was at the center. Summit countries pledged to conserve energy and to increase and diversify energy production in order to reduce the dependence of industrial countries on oil and other imported energy to less than 50 percent. They even agreed on the need to increase nuclear energy production—an impasse as we now know.
- In the early 1980s, more emphasis was put on development aid and on the north-south dialogue. The question of how to deal with the dramatic increase of external debt of a number of developing countries became increasingly important and will—no doubt—remain on the agenda in the coming years.
- From 1983 onwards, environmental policy, and, since Tokyo, agricultural policy have become major issues on the agenda.
- The most important topic at all summits—besides the coordination of fiscal and monetary policies—was the trade issue. All participants were convinced right from the beginning that protectionism does not solve problems but creates them, even if in reality they all are sinners in one way or another.

This brief reminder of the economic issues discussed at the summits and of the changes in economic theories and priorities over time makes it sufficiently clear, I believe, how difficult it would be to give any quantitative assessment of the impact of coordination. It would, therefore, fail to do justice to the complex process of this form of economic cooperation if one were to distinguish—as suggested in the paper—between unspecified cooperation and identified cases of policy cooperation like the 1978 Bonn Summit. It is not surprising, therefore, that the numerous theoretical approaches to measuring the advantages or disadvantages of international cooperation are highly controversial.

Before giving my own assessment of the effects of the summit meetings I should briefly describe the role of the summits as I see it. The summits are not decision making forums. Each year they take stock of all relevant areas of national and international policy and provide an opportunity to frame economic guidelines. This gives the heads of state, who deal mainly with national policies in their day-to-day work, once a year a comprehensive overview of the most urgent international economic problems, the areas of interdependence in the world economy, and the risks involved for their national economies. This has certainly contributed to making them aware of their long-term self-interest.

In addition, the summits provide heads of state with the unique opportunity to get to know different economic "models" and policy concepts and the different decision making processes in the participating countries. For the United States, Canada, and Japan, the economic summits are the only international forum for economic policy discussion at the highest level, whereas the heads of state of the European countries have been involved in this process since the establishment of the European Economic Community.

From my experience in these discussions, there seems to be not so much a lack of willingness to cooperate, but more often disagreements and misunderstandings on how to cooperate. This concerns not only the different policy principles and theories, but especially the differences in constitutional competences and traditions. Judgments of the so-called " lack of political will" should, therefore, be made with care. Even the heads of state and governments have limited and—what might be more important—different powers to commit countries to a specific policy.

Empirical evidence of the effects of this summit cooperation could primarily be expected from quantitative programs of the type agreed at Bonn in 1978. However—as Großer's paper points out—even the effects of this quantitative policy coordination cannot be separated from the effects of other determinants. When evaluating the general impact of policy cooperation among the major industrial countries, one should therefore rather ask what has been avoided by the summits, and what impulses have been given.

One of the most concrete achievements—in my view—has been the worldwide resistance to direct protectionism in trade; the summits have given new impulses to our liberal trade system (such as the Tokyo and Uruguay Rounds). Another result has been the initiatives to alleviate the debt burden, specially of the poorest countries. Looking back to the 1970s, I would say that the summits have contributed greatly to preventing misdirected policy prescriptions to counter the energy shocks. Furthermore, the very sensitive issue of agricultural policy has now been put on the agenda of the summits and thus will come under worldwide surveillance. The same is true of environmental policy. The indirect economic effects of the summit meetings at national and international levels are of course impossible to qualify.

The absence of major disturbances in the world economy over the past years cannot be attributed alone to the stronger cooperative efforts, but I am convinced that these efforts have been a significant contributing factor.

Could the summit procedure be improved? When Giscard d'Estaing and Helmut Schmidt initiated the first summit, they were inspired by the intimate atmosphere of their meetings in the Library Club as Ministers of Finance. The attempt to transfer this atmosphere to the meetings of the heads of state of the seven countries turned out to be an illusion. Summits bringing together the heads of state and governments of the seven major countries will always be a major public event, for home consumption as well.

There is, however, room to make this form of cooperation more efficient. I only want to mention a few points:
- heads of state must have enough time for comprehensive discussion on major policy issues and should not quarrel over pre-prepared communiqués;
- economic summits should avoid short-term orientation of their objectives and should stick more to long-term strategies;
- the summit countries should resist building up a "summit bureaucracy";
- discussions about political issues without direct economic relevance, like terrorism or drugs, should be kept to a minimum at economic summit meetings, although they cannot be avoided completely at this level.

The other main forums for economic policy coordination—also mentioned in Großer's paper—are the meetings of the ministers of finance and the central bank governors of the summit countries. In substance they are more important than the summits. The cooperative policy approach introduced with the 1985 Plaza Agreement and further developed in the 1987 Louvre Accord and the renewal of that Accord in December last year aimed to defuse the dangerous and acute tensions resulting from the erratic exchange rate movements of the U.S. dollar and the imbalances in current accounts by more conspicuous operational measures in the field of fiscal, interest rate, and intervention policy.

This cooperation (which besides the formal meetings of the ministers includes a regular exchange of views among the ministers, governors, and deputies) represents the extent of cooperation that can now be realistically achieved in the macroeconomic sector between the major industrial countries. It is a pragmatic type of cooperation, that attempts to bring economic policies closer into line and, by doing so, contributes toward greater stability in the exchange rate system. It would be wrong—in my view—to focus too much on exchange rates, even if exchange rates can be of high importance in certain situations. The main focus has, of course, to be on underlying policies. But cooperation can involve in certain situations taking a position on the appropriateness of a given pattern of exchange rates and giving coordinated signals to the markets or resisting short-term disruptive or disorderly movements in exchange rates by coordinated intervention. In this context, the use of a selected list of indicators can also be useful for better coordination of policies. It is, however, clear that these indicators can only serve as an analytical tool. They cannot replace the exercise of judgment, nor should they be used as "triggers" for policy decisions.

As to the evaluation of this more concrete form of cooperation, I think there is now widespread agreement, both among the participants and the general public, that this coordinated policy approach has been all in all advantageous. The recent stance of policies in the major industrial countries has been clearly influenced by the Louvre Accord of last year.

- Fiscal policy in the respective countries has now begun to play a more important role in the adjustment process. Divergences in fiscal stance among industrial countries tend to be reversed.
- Monetary and intervention policy in the exchange markets are being more closely coordinated and more effectively used to stabilize exchange rates without risking new worldwide inflationary pressures.
- Structural and trade policies are no longer excluded from the adjustment process and will become a major issue in future discussions.

The adjustment process to achieve a better balance of payments pattern, the most important objective of this form of cooperation, is now clearly under way.

The fact that the dollar has stood the test during recent months and has been quite stable since the beginning of the year, that central banks have intervened only temporarily, and that interest rate differentials have remained relatively unchanged is—in my view—sufficient empirical evidence that this coordination has been effective.

Of course, economic summits and meetings of the ministers of the Groups of Five and Seven cannot solve all the problems the world economy is facing. But they can and they have provided efficient tools for the containment of conflicts. These conflicts would have escalated and unilateral decisions with negative side effects would have been taken more often if they had not been channeled through this rather dense network of consultation procedures.

The present degree of global economic integration, which is likely to intensify in the future, calls for enhanced cooperation on economic policy. Such cooperation can only be successful in the long term, however, if it is based upon market forces and caters to the legitimate interests of all sides. It has to be built on the long-term self interest of the countries concerned.

Comment

Manuel Guitián[1]

In this paper, Günter Großer has provided us with a broad, well-reasoned and interesting examination of the record of economic policy coordination among major industrial countries since the mid–1970s. After a brief summary of the existing forums for policy coordination and the scope of the various economic summit meetings, the paper focuses on an analysis of the evidence of macroeconomic policy coordination, beginning with the oft-examined Bonn Summit Meeting of 1978 (see Putnam and Henning (1986), Bryant (1987), and Fischer (1987), for example) and continuing with the experience that has become available since the Plaza Agreement of September 22, 1985. The paper discusses the actual record of coordination on the conduct and mix of fiscal and monetary policies and, in addition, it examines the evidence that has been derived on the basis of econometric simulations from a variety of models conducted under the auspices of the Brookings Institution.

The analysis and the broad assessment of policy coordination contained in the paper are balanced and, accordingly, they lead to conclusions that are measured and, as such, easy to agree with. In my comments, therefore, rather than focusing on specific country experiences, I will highlight certain issues raised in the paper that I believe are critical to achieve further progress in the investigation of the merits and demerits of policy coordination at the international level.

In the analysis of issues of policy coordination, there are a number of taxonomic and methodological questions to be addressed at the outset. On the taxonomy front, there is a need to distinguish clearly the meaning and scope given to the term "coordination" within a spectrum of possible interpretations, that before reaching the level of what is normally understood by coordination, encompasses consultation, cooperation, and harmonization—to use Henry Wallich's terminology (Wallich (1984); see also Bryant (1987)). Großer is well aware of these issues, as is shown by his conclusion with regard to the difficulty of distinguishing policy coordination from less intensive modalities of cooperation and even from autonomous policymaking.

In the area of methodology, there arise the well-known issues of the appropriate standards of measurement that can be applied to the empirical evidence available on policy coordination. Should coordina-

---

[1] The views expressed in the paper are those of the author and not necessarily those of the International Monetary Fund.

tion be evaluated by comparisons of experiences "before and after" its introduction (*what is versus what was*)? Or should it be assessed by relating the results to the objectives of coordination (*what is versus what should be*)? Or should it be focused instead on a comparison between the outcomes of a specific instance of policy coordination and those that would obtain either in its absence (*what is versus what would have been*), or in the presence of other possible instances of coordinated policy action (*what is versus what could have been*)?

The issues posed by these methodological quandaries and taxonomic difficulties are thorny and the paper under discussion (as well as the increasing number of articles which are appearing on the subject of coordination) provides evidence to this effect when it states, for example, that the observed effects between two periods "cannot be expected to provide clear evidence" on policy coordination for a variety of reasons (p. 116). Among these reasons, the paper points to the difficulty of distinguishing the effects of an independent national policy action that is based on information available on other countries' policy stances from those that would result from explicitly coordinated actions. The paper also notes the complications that arise in this regard on account of the absence of ceteris paribus conditions, which tends to mar the identification of the direct consequences of policy measures. The former difficulty focuses on the need to separate independent (though informed) action from coordinated action and, therefore, it concerns the possibility of identifying unambiguously instances of policy coordination. The latter complication centers instead on problems that relate to the standard of measurement of empirical evidence. The paper uses mainly one of the standards discussed above, that is, the yardstick that compares actual economic performance (results) with that which had been envisaged (objectives) at the time the coordinated policy decisions were made (see in particular the section on the effects of macroeconomic policy coordination). But there are also instances of comparisons of a conjectural nature that relate outcomes from coordinated actions to a presumption of what would have happened in their absence. This is clear, for example, in the statement that outcomes typically associated with actions agreed at the 1978 Bonn Summit would have taken place even in the absence of those actions (pp. 116–117).

Given the shortcomings of these various comparisons, it is acknowledged explicitly in the paper that the actual evidence that is available cannot be interpreted unambiguously; in the author's own words, "ad hoc policy coordination has not only been rare up to now but, when accomplished, the observed effects were far from clear" (p. 128). Therefore, the paper also examines evidence derived from econometric model simulations conducted under the sponsorship of the Brookings Institution (see Bryant and others (1988)). In analogy with other studies that had considered this evidence earlier, the paper remarks that the simulations show that the effects of policy interactions appear to be relatively small (see, in this context, Fischer (1987)) or that they are possibly too varied in magnitude and even in sign to provide a basis for coordinated action (see Tanzi (1988)).

At present, therefore, perhaps a position of agnosticism on the record of policy coordination may be the appropriate one to adopt. This has also been a conclusion reached recently (though with some reluctance) by Ralph Bryant when he wrote: "While acknowledging that agnosticism is the only defensible conclusion for the moment, I thus still incline somewhat toward the view that the gains potentially realizable through cooperation (consultation *and* coordination) are worth writing home about" (Bryant (1987)). But then, we need to be specific about what we mean by coordination. Clearly exchange of information and consultation among countries are important elements for the process of national policy formulation, as properly stressed in the conclusions of Großer's paper. That there are "trade" gains to be derived from information flows is generally well recognized.

But should coordination go beyond the stage of consultation and exchange of information? In particular, should countries be asked or expected to adapt their domestic policies in response to objectives agreed with other countries or, more broadly, to move toward joint policy implementation to attain those agreed aims? Views vary widely on these questions. Arguments against going too far in this direction have been advanced on a variety of grounds: as already noted, it has been contended that the smallness of the gains likely to be obtained through coordination is hardly worth the effort; it has also been said that coordination is improbable as long as differences of view prevail regarding the transmission mechanism from policy instruments to policy aims (or, as the paper puts it (p. 130), as long as there is "disagreement on how the world actually works") as well as differences on the policy objectives to be pursued; and it has been pointed out that the cost of negotiating and policing coordinated actions may exceed their benefit. Against all these arguments, the fundamental proposition remains that the presence of externalities establishes a presumption in favor of cooperative decisions, a presumption that is behind many of the cases made in favor of policy coordination.

Differences of views also characterize the growing number of assessments of summit outcomes. Perhaps the clearest example yet is provided by the 1978 Bonn Summit and the so-called locomotive approach to international policy coordination, although it could be said that the more recent Louvre Accord is providing some competition in this respect. In common with conceptual arguments, differences in empirical assessments of coordination are not amenable to single or categorical solutions. To some observers, the 1978 Bonn Summit is an illustration of constructive coordinated action (see, for example, Bryant (1987)). For many others, however, this summit was clear evidence of the shortcomings of "fine tuning" as an approach to macroeconomic management at the international level (see, for instance, Haberler (1987)). In this context it must be noted that, as Großer points out in his paper, criticisms of this sort seem to be directed more to such an approach to macroeconomic policy than to the concept of policy coordination per se.

Here again, the various interpretations given to the sequence of events that followed the 1978 Bonn Summit underscore the validity of Großer's findings concerning the difficulties of distinguishing policy coordination from less intensive forms of cooperation—or even, I would say, from well-informed national policymaking—as well as those that arise from the scarcity and limited reliability of the information yet available to assess the effects of policy coordination. Some of the general issues that are raised in the paper are nevertheless fundamental, if only because some measure of *coordination* is inevitable in any *interdependent system* consisting of *independent components*.

On the international economic sphere, an important measure of (commonly agreed, or indeed should we say coordinated?) progress has been made for several decades now to open up and integrate national economies into a global system. As a result, the system at large has become closely interdependent and self-contained; therefore, it confronts an "nth country problem," the resolution of which calls either for clear rules, or for an exercise of discretion, or for a regime that balances rules and discretion so as to make the system compatible or internally consistent (Horne and Masson (1988)).

Illustrations of "rule-based" systems are, of course, the Bretton Woods par value regime that prevailed until the early 1970s and, presently, the European Monetary System (see Guitián (1988)). Such systems are to a large extent self-enforcing in nature so that policy coordination becomes endogenous, so to speak, because when policies become incompatible with the operation of the system, the rules typically point in a relatively unambiguous manner to the need for policy adaptation. This basic characteristic is stressed in Großer's paper where, in the context of the EMS, it is noted that "international monetary rules can work as a substitute for coordination of economic policies" (p. 113).

The flexible exchange rate arrangements that currently characterize the international monetary regime fall more within the pattern of "discretion-based" systems, a context in which both calls for and impetus toward policy coordination inevitably surface. This is also clearly acknowledged by Großer when he writes: "The rise of international policy coordination as a new instrument was promoted by the transition to a regime of flexible exchange rates" (p. 111). As he argues, the broader scope for discretionary national actions, by increasing uncertainty and the likelihood of inconsistencies, contributed to the demand for coordination.

The analysis and the evidence discussed in the paper suggest that there are themes in discussions of national economic policymaking that should find more of an echo at the international level. One of them has already been referred to in the context of the 1978 Bonn Summit, that is, the appropriateness (or lack thereof) of fine tuning as an approach to macroeconomic policy; in this regard, I think that Großer's general warning that such an approach at the international level is subject to as many pitfalls as at the national level, cannot be more opportune. Another related theme concerns the dimensions of policy that are desirable to emphasize at a particular time. For example, should policies be predictable or should they be adaptable? Rule-based systems—which focus on interdependence—stress predictability; in contrast, discretion-based systems—which are concerned with independence—emphasize adaptability. Where is the balance to be drawn? Either extreme is clearly inadvisable: predictability cannot be taken to mean total policy immobility regardless of circumstances; but neither can adaptability be taken to the point where policy direction loses its meaning.

The basic question lies around the balance to be given to national and international considerations in domestic policymaking. A concrete illustration of this question is provided in the paper's discussion (pp. 126–27) of the dominant factors behind policy decisions in the last two years or so, where national considerations are described as the policy movers in the United States while the requirements of coordination (international considerations) are seen as the factors behind the policy actions in surplus countries (the Federal Republic of Germany and Japan). The likelihood of attaining a proper balance on these issues increases with the availability of information; hence, the general agreement on the desirability of exchange of views and consultations at the international level. But balance will also require a measure of consensus on objectives and priorities which obtains only rarely; hence, the divergence of views on the desirability of policy coordination.

As in many other economic policy areas, I believe the issues here involve intertemporal choices nationally as well as internationally. The choices are rarely straightforward and in their evaluation it is important to acknowledge at the outset the limitations that characterize policy coordination as well as those that confine policy autonomy. After all, pursuit of global economic objectives, even if they have been internationally agreed, cannot be expected to persist if it conflicts with or runs counter to domestic aims and priorities; correspondingly, the pursuit of domestic objectives that run counter to or conflict with those sought elsewhere cannot be sustained indefinitely. From this dual perspective, the choice is not whether or not to coordinate but, rather, how to do so. Clearly it would be unrealistic to expect coordination to be based solely on what a country can do for others. On the contrary, the argument should center instead on the areas of coincidence between national and international interest, which are often broader than generally thought. This said, however, perhaps we should take a sequential view of coordination along the following lines. First, attainment of the "Fischer standard" (Fischer (1987))—that is, let each country do its best "to keep its own economy in shape." This stage would permit governments to establish a reputation with respect to their ability to coordinate economic policies domestically, this being in itself no mean endeavor. Within this general desideratum, a basis can then be established to set up a system whereby intertemporal choices can be clarified so that a global set of objectives and priorities can be determined as a commonly agreed aim for internationally coordinated policy action, that is, establish a basis from which reputations for domestic policy coordination can acquire an international dimension. In this respect, it must be stressed that coordination is no substitute for appropriate national policies.

Papers like Großer's, by clarifying choices and examining policy impacts, lay down stepping stones in the road toward international cooperation. They thus provide grounds for further progress to be made toward policy coordination based on an enlightened balance of national and international considerations.

REFERENCES

Bryant, Ralph, "Inter-Governmental Coordination of Economic Policies: An Interim Stocktaking," in *International Monetary Cooperation: Essays in Honor of Henry C. Wallich*, Essays in International Finance No. 169 (Princeton, New Jersey: Princeton University, December 1987).

———, and others, eds., *Empirical Macroeconomics for Interdependent Economies* (Washington: The Brookings Institution, 1988).

Fischer, Stanley, "International Macroeconomic Policy Coordination," NBER Working Paper No. 2244 (Cambridge, Massachusetts: National Bureau of Economic Research, May 1987).

Guitián Manuel, Massimo Russo, and Giuseppe Tullio, *Policy Coordination in the European Monetary System*, International Monetary Fund Occasional Paper No. 61 (Washington: IMF, forthcoming, 1988).

Haberler, Gottfried, "Further Thoughts on International Policy Coordination," in *International Monetary Cooperation: Essays in Honor of Henry C. Wallich*, Essays in International Finance No. 169 (Princeton, New Jersey: Princeton University, December 1987).

Horne, Jocelyn, and Paul R. Masson: "Scope and Limits of International Economic Cooperation and Policy Coordination," *Staff Papers*, International Monetary Fund (Washington), Vol. 35 (June 1988), pp. 259–96.

Putnam, Robert D., and C. Randall Henning, "The Bonn Summit of 1978: How Does International Economic Policy Coordination Actually Work?," Brookings Discussion Papers in International Economics No. 53 (Washington, The Brookings Institution, October 1986).

Tanzi, Vito, "Fiscal Policy and International Coordination: Current and Future Issues," Paper presented at a conference on *Fiscal Policy, Economic Adjustment and Financial Markets* (Milan, 1988).

Wallich, Henry C., "Institutional Cooperation in the World Economy," in Jacob A. Frenkel, and Michael L. Mussa, eds., *The World Economic System: Performance and Prospects* (Chicago: University of Chicago Press, 1984).

Chapter 4

International Coordination of Economic Policies: Scope, Methods, and Effects

Jacob A. Frenkel, Morris Goldstein, and Paul R. Masson[1]

> "Coordination of macroeconomic policies is certainly not easy; maybe it is impossible. But in its absence, I suspect nationalistic solutions will be sought—trade barriers, capital controls, and dual exchange-rate systems. War among nations with these weapons is likely to be mutually destructive. Eventually, they, too, would evoke agitation for international coordination."
> James Tobin (1987), p.68

> "... I believe that many of the claimed advantages of cooperation and coordination are wrong, that there are substantial risks and disadvantages to the types of coordination that are envisioned, and that an emphasis on international coordination can distract attention from the necessary changes in domestic policy."
> Martin Feldstein (1988), p.3

This paper discusses the scope, methods, and effects of international coordination of economic policies. Coordination is defined here, following Wallich (1984, p. 85), as "... a significant modification of national policies in recognition of international economic interdependence." The existence of a number of comprehensive surveys of the literature on coordination makes the task easier.[2] This discussion can, therefore, be selective and focus on a number of key issues that impinge on the advisability and practicality of strengthening policy coordination among the larger industrial countries. The purpose is to

---
[1] The views expressed are the authors' alone and do not represent the views of the International Monetary Fund. In addition to colleagues in the Research Department, the authors are indebted to Hali Edison, Martin Feldstein, Peter Korteweg, and Jacques Melitz for helpful comments on an earlier draft.
[2] See the surveys by Artis and Ostry (1986), Cooper (1985), Fischer (1987), Hamada (1979), Horne and Masson (1988), Kenen (1987), Polak (1981), and Wallich (1984).

identify and evaluate factors that merit attention in any serious examination of the subject.

The paper is organized as follows. Section I covers economic policy coordination in the widest sense and addresses various dimensions of the *scope* for and of coordination. The terrain covered includes the applicability of the "invisible hand" paradigm to decentralized economic policy decisions, barriers to coordination, the range and specificity of policies to be coordinated, the frequency of coordination, and the number of participants to be included in the coordination exercise. Section II narrows the discussion to monetary and fiscal policies and turns to the *methods* of coordination. The emphasis here is on the broad issues of rules versus discretion, single-indicator versus multiple-indicator approaches, and hegemonic versus more symmetric systems.

Section III is still more specific and confronts the problem of how to infer the *effects* of coordination. In an attempt to shed some light on how the world economy might be affected by different rule-based proposals for coordination, some simulations are presented of a global macroeconomic model (MULTIMOD) developed in the International Monetary Fund. The simulations considered range from "smoothing" rules for monetary and fiscal policy that imply only minimum international coordination, to more activist "target zone" proposals that place greater restrictions on national authorities in the conduct of monetary and/or fiscal policies. The results of the simulations are compared to the actual evolution of the world economy over the 1974–87 period.

Scope For and Of Coordination

The most logical starting point is to ask why international policy coordination would be beneficial in the first place. After all, if in the domestic economy the working of the invisible hand under pure competition translates independent decentralized decisions into a social optimum, why should the same principle not apply to policy decisions by countries in the world economy?

The answer is that economic policy actions, particularly those of larger countries, create quantitatively significant *spillover effects* or *externalities* for other countries, and that a global optimum requires that such externalities be taken into account in the decision making calculus.[3] Coordination is then best seen as a facilitating mechanism for *internalizing* these externalities.

This conclusion can perhaps be better appreciated by emphasizing

---

[3]Evidence on the size of spillover effects from policy actions by the major industrial countries is discussed in the latter part of this section and in Table 1.

the departures from the competitive model in today's global economy. Cooper (1987) has identified several such departures, and his analysis merits some extension here.

Unlike the atomistic economic agents of the competitive model who base their consumption and production decisions on prices that are beyond their control, larger countries exercise a certain degree of *influence over prices,* including the real exchange rate. This of course raises the specter that they will manipulate such prices to their own advantage and at the expense of others. Two examples are frequently cited—one dealing with inflation, and the other with real output and employment. Under floating rates, a Mundellian (1971) policy mix of tight monetary and loose fiscal policy allows an appreciated currency to enhance a country's disinflationary policy strategy—but at the cost of making it harder for trading partners to realize their own disinflation targets. Similarly, under conditions of high capital mobility and sticky nominal wages, a monetary expansion under floating rates leads to a real depreciation and to an expansion of output and employment at home. But the flip side of the coin is that output and employment contract abroad.[4] Seen in this light, the role of coordination is to prevent—or to minimize—such intentional as well as unintentional "beggar-thy-neighbor" practices. Most international monetary constitutions have injunctions against "manipulating" exchange rates or international reserves.

The existence of *public goods*—and their role in the resolution of inconsistencies among policy targets—constitute a second important point of departure from the competitive model. When there are n currencies, there can be only n–1 independent exchange rate targets. Similarly, not all countries can achieve independently set targets for current account surpluses.

Adherents of decentralized policymaking—sometimes rather inappropriately labelled the "German school"—argue that such inconsistencies provide no justification for intervention.[5] Much as in the

---

[4]The conclusion that a monetary expansion under floating rates affects real output in opposite directions at home and abroad is associated with the Mundell (1971)-Fleming (1962) model. For a recent evaluation of this model, see Frenkel and Razin (1987a); a broader survey of the international transmission mechanism can be found in Frenkel and Mussa (1985). Econometric models are more divided on whether a monetary expansion under floating rates has negative transmission effects on real output abroad; see Helliwell and Padmore (1985) and Bryant and others (1988).

[5]We regard the label as inappropriate, both because the proponents of decentralized macroeconomic policymaking—including Corden (1983), (1986), Feldstein (1988), Niehans (1988), Stein (1987), and Vaubel (1985)—are geographically quite diverse, and because some prominent German economists, such as Poehl (1987), have stressed the importance of coordination.

competitive model, the economic system will generate signals—in the form of changes in exchange rates, interest rates, prices, and incomes —that will lead to an adjustment of targets such that they eventually become consistent. If, however, the path to consistency involves large swings in real exchange rates, or, even more problematically, the imposition of restrictions on trade and capital flows, then reliance on decentralized policymaking may not be globally optimal. Implicit in this conclusion is the notion that a certain degree of stability in real exchange rates and an open international trading and financial system are valued in and of themselves, that is, they are public goods. (In contrast, the market signals that resolve supply/demand inconsistencies in the competitive model are not regarded as public goods.) If that is accepted, there is a positive role for coordination, both to identify target inconsistencies at an early stage and to resolve them in ways that do not produce *too little* of the public good(s).[6] It is of course possible for groups of countries who value the public good highly to attempt to obtain more of it by setting up "regional" zones of exchange rate stability or of free trade, and some have done just that (including the establishment of the European Monetary System (EMS)).[7] But the essence of a public good is that it will tend to be *under*supplied so long as some large suppliers or users act in a decentralized fashion.

Once the realm of atomistic competitors is left and that of nontrivial spillovers of policies is entered—be it via goods, assets, or labor markets—the possibility arises that choices made independently by national governments would not be as effective in achieving their objectives as policies that are coordinated with other governments.[8] A popular example suffices to illustrate the point. Whereas any single country acting alone may be reluctant to follow expansionary policies designed to counter a global deflationary shock for fear of unduly worsening its external balance, coordinated expansion by many countries will loosen the external constraint and permit each country to move closer to internal balance.

---

[6] Corden (1986) has recently argued that there may be a case for asking large countries to slow their speed of adjustment to desired policy targets so as to dampen movements in real exchange rates that could cause difficulties for others (see Section IV).

[7] Another constraint on regional attempts to create more of the public good is that they may divert or discourage its production outside the region; the argument here is analogous to the concepts of "trade creation" and "trade diversion" in the customs-union literature.

[8] To reach this conclusion, it is necessary to assume that each player does not have sufficient policy instruments to achieve all its policy targets simultaneously, and that coordination alters the tradeoffs among policy targets; see Gavin (1986). Without those assumptions, the motivation for coordination would disappear.

All of this establishes a *presumption* that there can be valid reasons for deviating from the tradition of decentralized decision making when it comes to economic policy, that is, that there is scope for coordination. This presumption is reinforced by two empirical observations. The first is that the world economy of 1988 is considerably more open and integrated than that of 1950, or 1960, or even of 1970. Not only have simple ratios of imports or exports to GNP increased but also—and probably more fundamentally—global capital markets are more integrated.[9] With larger spillovers, there is more at stake in how one manages interdependence. Second, there is by now widespread recognition that the insulating properties of floating exchange rates are more modest than was suspected prior to their introduction in 1973.[10]

But a presumption that cooperation could be beneficial is not the same as a guarantee—nor does it preclude the existence of sometimes formidable *obstacles* to its implementation.

Suppose national policymakers have a predilection for inflationary policies but are restrained from implementing them by the concern that relatively expansionary monetary policy will bring on a devaluation (or depreciation). Yet, as outlined by Rogoff (1985), if all countries pursue such inflationary policies simultaneously, none has to worry about the threat of devaluation. Here, coordination may actually weaken discipline by easing the balance of payments constraint. In a similar vein, as noted by Feldstein (1988), there is the potential risk that a coordinated attempt to stabilize a pattern of nominal or real exchange rates could take place at an inappropriately high aggregate rate of inflation. The proposals put forward by U.S. Treasury Secretary Baker and U.K. Chancellor Lawson, at the 1987 Annual Meetings of the Fund and the World Bank, for a *commodity-price-basket* indicator as a potential "early-warning" signal of emerging aggregate price developments, addresses just such a concern.[11] Equally troublesome would be a coordination of fiscal policies that yielded an aggregate fiscal deficit for the larger countries that put undue upward pressure on world interest rates. The basic point is straightforward: there is nothing in the coordination process in and of itself that reduces the importance of sound macroeconomic policies.[12] There can be coordi-

---

[9] See Fischer (1987) and Frenkel (1983, 1986).

[10] See Goldstein (1984). This is not to say that the insulating properties of floating rates are inferior to those of alternative regimes. Indeed, it is hard to see any other exchange rate regime surviving the shocks of the 1970s without widespread controls on trade and capital.

[11] On the possible use of commodity price indicators in the conduct of monetary policy, see Heller (1987).

[12] See Bocklemann (1988) for a similar conclusion.

nation around *good* policies and coordination around *bad* ones—just as with the exchange rate regime, where there are good fixes and bad fixes, and good floats and bad floats.[13] Welfare improvements are not automatic.

It is only realistic, too, to acknowledge that there are barriers to the exercise of coordination. Four of the more prominent ones are worth mentioning.[14] *First,* international policy bargains that involve shared objectives can be frustrated if some policy instruments are treated as objectives in themselves. Schultze (1988), for example, offers the view that it would have been difficult to have reached a bargain on target zones for exchange rates in the early 1980s given President Reagan's twin commitments to increased defense spending and cutting taxes. In some other countries, the constraints on policy instruments may lie in different areas—including structural policies—but the implications are the same.

Second, there can at times be sharp disagreements among countries about the effects that policy changes have on policy targets. In some cases, these differences may extend beyond the size to even the sign of various policy-impact multipliers.[15] The harder it is to agree on how the world works, the harder it is to reach agreement on a jointly designed set of policies.

Third, while most countries have experienced a marked increase in openness over the past few decades, there remain huge cross-country differences in the degree of interdependence. Large countries—the United States being the classic case in point—are generally less affected by other countries' policies than small ones. Coordination—as Bryant (1987) has recently emphasized—is not a matter of altruism. It is rather the manifestation of mutual self interest. To the extent that large countries are less beset by spillovers and feedbacks than small ones, the former's incentive to coordinate on a continuous basis may be lower.[16] In this regard, the high degree of trade interdependence shared by members of the EMS can be seen as a positive factor in reinforcing incentives to coordinate in that group.

Finally, as Polak (1981) has reminded us, international bargaining

---

[13]See Frenkel (1985).

[14]Another barrier is disagreement over forecasts for key economic variables over the medium term; on this point, see Tanzi (1988).

[15]See Bryant and others (1988) and Helliwell and Padmore (1985) for a comparison of open-economy multipliers from different global econometric models. Frankel and Rockett (1986) illustrate the sensitivity of welfare effects of coordination to the selection of the "right" versus the "wrong" economic model.

[16]See Fischer (1987). Dini (1988) goes further to argue that when the incentives to coordinate differ widely among group members, there may be a tendency for *bilateral* bargains to take place among those who have the most to trade.

typically comes after domestic bargaining. More specifically, the compromise of growth and inflation objectives at the national level may leave little room for further compromise on demand measures at the international level.

These barriers to coordination should not be overestimated: one of the clearest examples of true coordination—the Bonn Economic Summit of 1978—occurred just when domestic bargaining over the same issues was most intense;[17] the growing integration of capital markets —of which the global stock market crash of October 1987 is but one reminder—has brought the implications of interdependence home to even large countries; and continued empirical work on multicountry models should be able progressively to whittle down the margin of disagreement on the effects of policies. Still, as readers of Sherlock Holmes will be aware, sometimes the most telling clue is that the hounds *didn't* bark. If the scope for coordination is to expand beyond the efforts of the past, these obstacles will need to be overcome.

Turning from the scope *for* to the scope *of* coordination, a key issue concerns the appropriate *range* and *depth* of policies to be coordinated.

The case for supporting a wide-ranging, multi-issue approach to coordination is that it increases the probability of concluding some policy bargains that benefit all parties,[18] that favorable spillover effects are generated across negotiating issues, and that improved economic performance today depends as much on trade and structural policies as on exchange rate and demand policies. Exhibit A is the Bonn Economic Summit of 1978 where commitments to accelerate growth by Japan and the Federal Republic of Germany were exchanged for a commitment by the United States to come to grips with its inflation and oil problems, and where agreement on macroeconomic and energy policies has been credited with reinforcing progress on the Tokyo Round of Multilateral Trade Negotiations.[19]

The defense of a narrower approach to coordination rests on the arguments that negotiation costs rise rapidly within the spread of issues under consideration,[20] that prospects for implementation of agreements dim as the number of jurisdictional spheres expands (that is, finance ministers can negotiate agreements but fiscal policy is typically the responsibility of legislatures, while monetary policy is the province of independent central banks); and that heated disputes

---

[17]See Putnam and Bayne (1984). At the same time, the Bonn Summit is regarded in some quarters as illustrative of the pitfalls of coordinating macroeconomic policies when the economic outlook is changing rapidly.

[18]See Putnam and Bayne (1984).

[19]Putnam and Henning (1986).

[20]Artis and Ostry (1986).

on some issues (such as the stance of monetary and fiscal policies) can frustrate the chance for agreements in other areas (like defense and foreign assistance) where coordination might be more fruitful.[21] In addition, a case could be made that coordination is only likely in areas where there is a consensus about the effects of common policies.[22]

In view of these conflicting considerations, it is hard to fault present institutional practices on the range of coordination. Those practices entail high-frequency coordination on narrow issues in a multitude of forums (such as the International Monetary Fund, the Organization of Economic Cooperation and Development (OECD), the Bank of International Settlements (BIS), and the General Agreement on Tariffs and Trade (GATT));[23] less frequent (say, biannual) and wider coordination at a higher level in more limited forums such as the Fund's Interim Committee, or the Group of Seven major industrial countries); and even less frequent (annual), wider-yet coordination at the highest level (heads of state and of governments at the economic summits). Thus, there are occasional opportunities for multi-issue bargaining, but without the exponential increase in negotiation costs that might ensue if this were the order of the day. All in all, probably not a bad compromise.

The "depth" of coordination covers the degree of specificity and disaggregation within a given policy area. Here, two issues arise—one dealing with fiscal policy, and the other with structural policies. A strong implication of recent research is that aggregate measures, such as the central or general government fiscal deficit, are not likely to be a good guide to the effects of *fiscal policies* on macroeconomic variables such as the current account, the exchange rate, and the rate of interest.[24] The reason is that such effects depend on *how* the deficit is altered: that is, taxes versus expenditures, expenditures on tradables versus nontradables, taxes on investment versus those on saving, fiscal action by a country with a current account surplus versus a deficit, and anticipated versus unanticipated policies. This suggests that more specificity in coordination—quite apart from its positive effect on the ability to monitor the implementation of agreed-on policies—would be desirable. It is notable that the Louvre Accord of February 1987 among the Group of Seven specified not only quantita-

---

[21] Feldstein (1988).
[22] Cooper (1988).
[23] Another example of high-frequency coordination is that among central banks of the largest countries on exchange-market intervention tactics.
[24] See Frenkel and Razin (1987b).

tive targets for budget deficits but also some quantitative guidelines of how these overall fiscal targets were to be achieved.[25]

In the area of *structural policies*, a good case can also be made for specificity—but on somewhat different grounds. Here, coordination may often best be interpreted not as the simultaneous application of the same policy instrument in different doses or directions across countries, but rather as the simultaneous application of different policy instruments[26]—with each country adopting the policy best tailored to its particular structural weakness.[27] In some cases, this may imply reducing impediments to labor mobility or to market-determined wages; in others, it may mean increasing incentives for private investment relative to those for private saving; and in still others, it may mean changes in the trade and distribution system. The simultaneous application of the policy measures across countries may be necessary to overcome the blocking tactics of domestic pressure groups and to enhance the credibility of the exercise. Again, the depth or specificity of coordination can be as relevant as the range.

Another salient issue concerns the question of *when* to coordinate. There has been, and continues to be, wide variation in the frequency of coordination across different forums—ranging from one-of-a-kind meetings like the 1971 Smithsonian Conference on exchange rates to the near continuous discussion and decision making at the Executive Boards of the Fund and the World Bank.

One position is that, given the constraints, true coordination cannot be expected to be more than an episodic, regime-preserving effort.[28] Dini (1988) has recently argued that international considerations still

---

[25]For example, the Louvre Communiqué states that: "The United States Government will pursue policies wth a view to reducing the fiscal 1988 deficit to 2.3 percent of GNP from its estimated level of 3.9 percent in fiscal 1987. For this purpose, the growth in government expenditures will be held to less than 1 percent in fiscal 1988 as part of the continuing program to reduce the share of government in GNP from its current level of 23 percent"; see International Monetary Fund (1987).

[26]Because coordination of structural policies typically involves different policy instruments, individual country actions cannot—unlike coordination of fiscal policies—be evaluated with reference to an aggregate policy indicator that would be desirable from a global perspective.

[27]This is not to deny the helpful role that *harmonization* of structural policies—ranging from adopting similar tax provisions to implementing common regulations concerning movements of goods, labor, and capital—could play in certain circumstances.

[28]Those who hold the view that international factors have minimal influence on policymaking sometimes also argue that countries' policy commitments in coordination agreements represent policies that would have occurred even in the absence of such agreements. Under this view, coordination affects only the timing of policy announcements, with countries delaying such announcements until coordination meetings so that they can present a dowry to the others.

play only a small factor in policymaking, and that only at times of crisis is a common interest in coordinated action clearly recognized. Some might even go farther and argue that the reservoir of international compromise should be conserved for situations when there is a high probability of a policy deal and when failure to reach an agreement would carry a high cost.

Our view is that both the likelihood and effectiveness of coordination will be enhanced when it is a regular, ongoing *process*—and for at least three reasons. *First*, the potential for multiperiod bargaining expands the opportunities for policy bargains (by facilitating, for example, phasing of policy measures). What should count in assessing the gains to coordination is the present discounted value of welfare-improving policy agreements over an extended period—not the welfare change in a single period. *Second*, as suggested in the game-theoretic literature, the existence of repeated bargaining strengthens the role of *reputational* considerations in coordination.[29] In contrast, when coordination is a once-and-for-all or episodic exercise there is a higher risk that agreed policies will never be implemented because of the much-discussed problem of time-inconsistency, that is, the temptation to renege on earlier policy commitments when it later becomes advantageous to do so.[30] To be effective, coordination agreements need to pass through the market filter of credibility, and credibility is more likely if sticking to the agreement enhances reputation, which in turn allows profitable bargains to be struck in the future. *Third*, once coordination is established as a routine ongoing process, there is apt to be more freedom of policy maneuver for all participants than when negotiations are conducted in a crisis atmosphere and when disagreements—which after all are inevitable—may be inappropriately seen as signaling the collapse of coordination itself.[31]

As any good newspaper reporter knows, the three W's of *why*, *what*, and *when* are not sufficient for writing a story. One also has to bring in the fourth W, namely *who* should coordinate. Again, existing practice does not provide a definitive answer. Among the industrial countries, we have the Group of Seven and the Group of Ten. For the developing countries, there are the Group of Twenty-Four and the Group of Seventy-Seven. And in the Executive Board of the Fund—

---

[29]See the papers in Buiter and Marston (1985).

[30]The classic references are Kydland and Prescott (1977) and Calvo (1978).

[31]As Poehl (1987, pp. 19–20) notes: " . . . international cooperation does not necessarily imply that all parties must agree on all details at all times. It is important that we regard it as a process of maintaining stability in our increasingly interrelated world economy . . . The process of international cooperation may be difficult and burdensome, even frustrating at times, but there is no alternative to it."

where industrial and developing countries alike are represented—there are twenty-two representatives of various country groupings—a Group of Twenty-Two.

Among the factors that should influence the size of the coordinating group, three would seem to stand out. *First*, to the extent that the raison d'être of coordination is the internalization of externalities, the group should include those countries whose policies generate the largest externalities. This argues for including the largest industrial countries. *Second*, there is the general proposition that the costs of negotiation, and conflicts that might endanger the continuity of the exercise, increase significantly with the number of players. This argues for a relatively small group. *Third*, and pointing in the opposite direction, a small group runs the risk of concluding policy agreements which are beneficial to the direct participants—but which are not satisfactory to those countries not sitting at the coordination table.[32]

In light of these considerations, it is worth mentioning two features of recent coordination efforts by the Group of Seven. One of them, proposed at the Venice Economic Summit in 1987 and incorporated in subsequent coordination meetings, is the addition of *aggregate indicators* for the Group of Seven as a whole to the list of individual-country indicators. Aggregate indicators for the group may include such variables as the growth rate of real GNP and of domestic demand, the interest rate, the current account position, and the real exchange rate. A strong motivation for such aggregate indicators is that they can be helpful in gauging the impact of coordination agreements and actions among the Group of Seven on the rest of the world, with particular reference to the developing countries. For example, it has been estimated that each 1 percent change in real GNP in the industrial countries is associated, ceteris paribus, with approximately a 3 percent change (in the same direction) of export earnings in developing countries. Similarly, a 1 percent change in "world" interest rates implies roughly a $3–4 billion change in net interest payments by capital importing developing countries. In short, aggregate indicators can be seen as an analytical instrument for helping to evaluate whether a given policy package for the larger countries is also in the interest of others.

A second notable feature is that the Managing Director of the Fund participates in these Group of Seven coordination meetings. Since the Fund's membership includes not only the larger industrial countries but also the smaller industrial countries, as well as most of the developing countries, one rationale for the Managing Director's par-

---

[32]It is precisely because of the risk of "collusion" among the coordinating countries that Vaubel (1985) favors decentralized decision making.

ticipation is that it provides a *systemic* perspective and evaluation on proposed policy agreements—while still keeping the meeting small enough for administrative efficiency.

Methods of Coordination

This section shifts the focus from whether to coordinate to *how* to coordinate. More specifically, the advantages and disadvantages of alternative *methods* of coordination are discussed, with particular attention to the issues of rules versus discretion, single versus multi-indicator approaches, and hegemonic versus symmetric systems.

It is not surprising that many of the issues that emerged during the long and continuing debate on the relative merits of *rules* versus *discretion* in domestic economic policy should have resurfaced in the dialogue on international economic policy coordination. After all, the present system of managed floating, even as it has evolved since the Plaza Agreement of September 1985, is much closer to a pure discretion than to a pure rules model. In this regard, the gold standard with its automatic specie flow mechanism, the adjustable peg system with its clear implications for the subordination of domestic monetary policy to the exchange rate (except during fundamental disequilibria), the EMS with its parity grid and divergence indicator, target zone proposals with their trigger for coordination discussions whenever the actual exchange rate threatens to breach the zone, and pure floating with its complete prohibition on all official intervention in the exchange market—all can be considered less discretionary than the present exchange rate system. The debate is thus not about what is, but rather about what *should be*.

Those who support a more rule-based approach to international economic policy rest their case on essentially four arguments. *First*, the most promising route to eliminating any excess demand for coordination in the world economy is not by increasing the supply, but rather by decreasing the *demand* (or the need) for coordination.[33] That decrease in demand, in turn, can best be brought about by the application of simple policy rules, such as the maintenance of a fixed exchange rate. In the process, one would eliminate—so the argument goes—most of the negotiation costs and burden-sharing conflicts that are intrinsic to more discretionary systems. *Second*, rules are regarded as the only viable mechanism for imposing discipline on economic policymakers who might otherwise manipulate the instruments of policy for their own objectives.[34] *Third*, rules are regarded as enhanc-

---

[33]See Polak (1981) and Kenen (1987).

[34]It is in this context that the problems of time inconsistency and moral hazard often surface.

ing the predictability of policy actions and thereby improving the private sector's ability to make informed resource allocation decisions.[35] *Fourth*, rules are championed as providing protection against the lack of knowledge about how the economy operates by preempting destabilizing fine tuning.

The main counter-arguments in favor of a discretionary approach are the following. *First*, rule-based adjustment systems often turn out to be less automatic in practice than in theory. For example, the automaticity of the specie-flow mechanism under the historical gold standard was often undermined by the proclivity of authorities to offset or sterilize the effect of gold flows.[36]

Second, rules will impart discipline to the conduct of macroeconomic policy only to the extent that the penalties for breaking the rules are significant enough to ensure that the rules are followed. The Bretton Woods rule that countries should consult with the Fund once there was a cumulative parity change of 10 percent or more, while complied with in a technical sense, fell short in a substantive sense of its original purpose. The discussion surrounding the revision of the original Gramm-Rudman deficit-reduction targets in the United States is a more recent case in point. History could in fact be seen as just as kind to the proposition that the policy regime adjusts to the amount of discipline that countries want to have as to the reverse.[37] Also, care needs to be taken to separate the effects of policy rules on economic outcomes from other influences. In this connection, the oft-made argument that the EMS was a major determinant of the 1979–85 disinflation in Europe would seem to be based on shaky ground.[38]

Third, it is by no means clear that rules are necessary to obtain the benefits of greater predictability of policy. For example, the practice of pre-announcing money supply targets—sometimes accompanied by announcements of public sector borrowing requirements—provides the markets with information on the authorities' policy intentions, but

---

[35] Advocates of rules also argue that once the public knows better what the authorities will do, markets will demand less of a risk premium to hold the authorities' financial obligations.

[36] See Cooper (1982) and U.S. Congress (1982).

[37] Goldstein (1980), (1984), Frenkel (1982), and Frenkel and Goldstein (1986).

[38] Kenen (1987) cites a regression of the *change* in the inflation rate between 1979 and 1985 on the *level* of the inflation rate in 1979 and a zero-one dummy variable denoting participation in the exchange rate mechanism of the EMS. The sample was comprised of 22 industrial countries. The EMS dummy variable was *not* statistically significant, whereas the level of the inflation rate in 1979 was. Note that this finding does not preclude a helpful role of the EMS in disinflation since participation could still have reduced the output *cost* of disinflation (see, for example, Giavazzi and Giovannini (1988)); but this is a different story.

stops well short of a rigid rule.

Finally, while rules diminish the risk emanating from fine tuning, they increase the risk stemming from lack of adaptability to changes in the operating environment.[39] The idea of a "crawling-peg" rule based on inflation differentials drew quite a few supporters in the 1960s as the right antidote for sticky nominal exchange rates. Yet its neglect of the need for *real* exchange rate changes now seems more serious in light of the real economic disturbances of the early 1970s.[40] More recently, the crumbling of the link between narrow monetary aggregates and the ultimate targets of monetary policy in the face of large-scale financial innovation and institutional change has reminded us anew of the limitations of policy rules.

In light of all this, there may not be any attractive alternative to conducting economic policy coordination in a *judgmental* way.

Even after the choice is made about coordinating via rules or discretion, there remains the decision of whether to coordinate around a *single indicator* or a *set of indicators*. A regime of fixed exchange rates or target zones is an example of the former approach, while the ongoing Group of Seven coordination exercise is an example of the latter.

There are two main considerations that are typically advanced to support the single-indicator approach. One is that it avoids *overcoordination* of policies by preserving for each country freedom of action over those policies not used to reach the single target variable. Thus, for example, if the exchange rate is the focus of coordination, monetary policy will be constrained, but other policies will be less affected. Implicit in this line of argument is the view that attempts to place many policies under international coordination will ultimately prove self defeating and may even induce national authorities to compensate by exercising greater independence in *un*coordinated policy instruments, such as trade policy.[41]

The second, and probably more important, defense of a single-indicator approach is that it sends a *clear signal* to markets about the course of future policy. If, for example, the monetary authorities commit themselves to maintaining a fixed exchange rate within a given band, then movements of the exchange rate provide an unambiguous guide for monetary policy. A similar message would derive

---

[39] As developed in Polak (1988), the need for rules to guard against the dangers of fine tuning has receded in any case since economic policy in most industrial countries is now oriented much more toward the medium term. Fischer (1987) makes the complementary point that the state of our knowledge about the effects of monetary and fiscal policy is too rudimentary to justify policy rules. Niehans (1988) expresses doubts that rules could be relied upon to reduce international disturbances.

[40] On the limitations of purchasing power parity rules, see Frenkel (1981).

[41] See Frenkel (1975).

from a nominal income target for monetary or fiscal policy, with the exchange rate left to determination of the market. In contrast, a multi-indicator approach increases the authorities' scope for discretion since they can appeal to the conflicting messages coming from different indicators. In cases where the authorities' past record of policy performance has been weak and where a single objective of policy is predominant (such as disinflation), a single-indicator framework for coordination can carry significant advantages in the battle to restore credibility to policy.

But relying on a single policy indicator can also carry substantial risks. Perhaps the most serious one is that the single indicator can send weak—or even *false*—*signals* about the need for changes in other policies that are not being coordinated. This is perhaps best illustrated by considering the problem of errant fiscal policy under a regime of fixed exchange rates or of target zones.

First, consider *fixed rates*. With high capital mobility, a fiscal expansion will yield an incipient positive interest rate differential, a capital inflow, and an overall balance of payments surplus—not a deficit. Here, exchange rate fixity helps to finance—and by no means disciplines—irresponsible fiscal policy.[42] Only if and when the markets expect fiscal deficits to be monetized will they force the authorities to choose between fiscal policy adjustments and devaluation.[43] The better the reputation of the authorities, the longer in coming will be the discipline of markets—the exchange rate will provide only a weak and late signal for policy adjustment. In this connection, it is worth observing that whereas the EMS has produced a notable convergence of monetary policy, convergence of fiscal policy has not taken place.[44]

Next, rerun the same fiscal expansion under a *target zone regime*, where the zones are to be defended by monetary policy. In such a scenario, the appreciation of the currency induced by the fiscal action will prompt a loosening of monetary policy to keep the rate from breaching the zone. Here, coordination around a single indicator, namely, the exchange rate, will have exacerbated—not corrected—the basic cause of the problems.[45] The single indicator would have sent the *wrong* signal for policy adjustment.

---

[42]Frenkel and Goldstein (1988).
[43]The literature on "speculative attacks" deals with just this phenomenon; see, for example, Flood and Garber (1980).
[44]Tanzi and Ter-Minassian (1987) and Holtham and others (1987).
[45]See Frenkel and Goldstein (1986). This missing link between exchange rate movements and fiscal policy under target zones is being increasingly recognized. Whereas first-generation target zone proposals spoke only of monetary policy, second-generation proposals have added a policy rule or guideline for fiscal policy; contrast Williamson (1985) with Williamson and Miller (1987).

In contrast, a multi-indicator approach to coordination—assuming that the list of indicators included monetary and fiscal policy variables—would not be susceptible to this weak- or false-signal problem.[46] This is because such an approach goes directly to the basic stance of fiscal and monetary policies, rather than passing through the medium of the exchange rate. If, for example, the impetus for coordination was a misalignment of exchange rates, and if the root cause of the misalignment was an inappropriate stance and/or mix of monetary and fiscal policies, the multi-indicator approach would be appealing.

But all is not a bed of roses here either. While all effective approaches to coordination require a consistency of policy instruments and targets within and across countries, this requirement of *consistency* or compatibility can take an added prominence when authorities make public a set of targets and intended courses for policy instruments.[47]

Two aspects merit explicit mention. *One* is that exchange rate targets—or even concerted views on the existing pattern of exchange rates—must be consistent with the announced course of monetary and fiscal policies. Without that consistency, attempts to provide the market with an anchor for medium-term exchange rate expectations are likely to prove fruitless.

The *second* point is that the credibility of multiple policy targets also hinges on the *constraints* on policy instruments. Two such constraints are the striking *in*flexibility of fiscal policy in almost all industrial countries,[48] and the limited ability of sterilized exchange market intervention to affect the level of the exchange rate over the medium term (unless of course it provides a signal about the future course of policies).[49] A relevant concern is that limitations on other policy instruments may wind up with *monetary policy* being asked to carry too heavy a burden—with primary responsibility for maintaining internal and external balance. In such a case, any contribution that a multi-indicator approach to coordination could make to enhancing the predictability of policies would also be diminished. This is so because a shock to the system—such as the October 1987 global stock market crash—might raise the question in minds of market partici-

---

[46]The list of indicators noted in the Communiqué of the Tokyo Economic Summit included growth rates of gross national product, interest rates, inflation rates, unemployment rates, ratios of fiscal deficits to GNP, current account and trade balances, money growth rates, international reserve holdings, and exchange rates.

[47]There is also the question of the proper *assignment* of policy instruments to policy targets. This issue is touched on in the next section.

[48]See Tanzi (1988).

[49]See Mussa (1981) and the Jurgensen Report (1983).

pants of whether monetary policy would serve its internal or external master.

Yet another key methodological issue associated with coordination—particularly when it involves joint decision making—is whether one country should, by common consent, have a predominant voice on the course of policies, or alternatively, whether that influence should be shared more equally. In this respect, the historical gold standard, the Bretton Woods System, and the EMS are all often regarded as *hegemonic* systems, while the ongoing Group of Seven coordination process would qualify as a more *symmetric* exercise.[50]

Hegemonic exchange rate systems have typically operated under what might be called an *"implicit contract"* between the leader and the satellite countries.[51] Under Bretton Woods, the leader (that is, the United States) carried the obligation to conduct prudent macroeconomic policies—perhaps best summarized by a steady, low rate of inflation. This obligation was reinforced by the leader's commitment to peg some nominal price—in that case, the price of gold. Since there can be only n-1 exchange rates among n countries, the leader was passive about its exchange rate. The satellite countries committed to peg their exchange rates within agreed margins to the leader. As a reaction to the competitive depreciation of the 1930s, cumulative exchange rate adjustments greater than 10 percent were to be placed under international supervision and were to be taken only under conditions of "fundamental disequilibrium." By virtue of their exchange rate obligations, the satellites sacrificed independence in their monetary policies but expected to import stability from the leader.

With the benefit of hindsight, this implicit contract came under strain from two main directions (in addition to Triffin's (1960) well-known "confidence problem"). One was the breakdown (after the mid-l960s) of discipline by the leader such that the satellites came to see it as exporting inflation rather than stability. The response was for the satellites to sever their formal links with the leader (in the early 1970s) and thereafter to seek stability via other mechanisms, including national money supply targeting and regional exchange rate arrangements. The second strain was an excessive rigidity of nominal exchange rates in the face of fundamental disequilibrium that produced a misalignment of the leader's *real* exchange rate in the late l960s. The leader then abandoned the commitment to be passive about its exchange rate.

---

[50]This characterization is not universally shared. Williamson and Miller (1987), for example, regard the gold standard and Bretton Woods as more symmetric systems.
[51]See Frenkel and Goldstein (1988).

The implicit contract in the EMS is similar in many ways to that under Bretton Woods. While there is no formal leader, most observers regard the Federal Republic of Germany (and its Bundesbank) as the de facto or acknowledged leader.[52] Germany follows macroeconomic policies that export price stability and anti-inflationary credibility to the others. It is noteworthy that while there have to date been 11 realignments in the EMS, none of them has resulted in a revaluation relative to the deutsche mark, thus leaving Germany's reputation as an exporter of stability intact. Other members of the exchange rate mechanism of the EMS can be characterized as "tying their hands" on domestic monetary policy so as to make credible both their exchange rate obligations and their inflation objectives.[53] Exchange rate adjustments are placed under common supervision. When realignments do take place, they do not always provide full compensation for past inflation differentials. In this way, the resulting real appreciation for high-inflation countries can act as a disincentive to inflation (by penalizing exports, output, and employment), while the leader receives a gain in competitiveness that provides some quid-pro-quo for its export of anti-inflationary credibility.[54] Monetary policy in Germany is typically regarded as the anchor and is considered so disciplined as to do away with the need to peg to some "outside" nominal price.

While there have clearly been periods when large countries have exerted a stabilizing influence on the system, it is hard to accept that hegemony is a necessary characteristic of a well-functioning system of international economic policy coordination. There are several reasons. *First*, careful study of alleged hegemonic systems, including the gold standard, reveals that the amount of coordination needed for smooth functioning was substantial.[55] The coordinated interest rate actions of September 1987 in the EMS when Germany and the Netherlands lowered their rates, and France raised its rate, are a recent example of such cooperation. *Second*, much of what passes for the stabilizing influence of hegemony can also reflect common objectives. Again, the EMS serves as a useful laboratory. In the early 1980s, disinflation was the top priority in virtually all EMS countries. Since Germany had the best reputation for price stability, there was a

---

[52]See Giavazzi and Giovannini (1986).

[53]In practice, high-inflation countries have sometimes resorted to capital controls during exchange rate crises so as to avoid the choice of having to give up either monetary independence or the exchange rate target.

[54]To the extent that the EMS produces greater stability and predictability of exchange rates, all members also share any efficiency gains associated with moving closer to a single currency.

[55]Eichengreen (1987).

commonality of interests in trying to converge to the German inflation rate. Now, however, some observers argue that given both the progress already made with inflation and the high unemployment rates prevailing in some EMS (and potential EMS) countries, it is time to give greater weight to objectives other than inflation.[56] *If* such a decision were taken, it would probably result in a more symmetric EMS—and this quite apart from shifts among members in relative economic size or reputation.[57] *Third*, attempts to reinstate a hegemonic approach to coordination when economic realities no longer support it could be counterproductive. In the present context, there appears to be no obvious candidate that *combines* an unblemished record for economic stability, a dominant position in international trade and finance (relative to other members of the coordination group), and a willingness to accept the requisite responsibilities.

Effects of Coordination

Identifying key issues related to the scope and methods of economic policy coordination is one thing; attempting to infer its *effects* is quite another. The latter is obviously an empirical question that requires for analysis some type of quantitative economic model.

Earlier efforts to gauge the effects of international economic policy coordination or of alternative international monetary arrangements fall into two categories. One strand of the literature compares the value of a welfare function where each country maximizes welfare independently with that where the countries maximize a *joint* welfare function. Two controversial findings are that the gains from coordination are likely to be "small" for the largest countries and that the gains can even be negative if countries coordinate using the "wrong" model of the world economy.[58]

These findings should not be used as an indictment of coordination —for at least five reasons. *First*, a comparison of optimal uncoordinated with optimal coordinated policies may not be generalizable to the more relevant comparison of *sub*optimal uncoordinated with *sub*optimal coordinated policies. In particular, the link between pressures for protectionism on the one hand, and recession and exchange rates on the other, could result in quite a different "counterfactual"

---

[56]See Dornbusch (1988).

[57]Holtham and others (1987). See the proposals on the EMS put forward to the European Community Monetary Committee last fall by Minister Balladur of France as prefacing such a symmetric development of the EMS.

[58]See Oudiz and Sachs (1984), McKibbin and Sachs (1988), and Taylor (1985) for evidence on the size of the gains, and Frankel and Rockett (1986) for the effects of using the "wrong" model.

(that is, what would happen in the absence of coordination) from that assumed in these studies.[59] *Second*, some of the gains from coordination may be unobservable (unwritten pledges to alter policies in the future), or difficult to separate from less ambitious forms of cooperation (exchange of information across countries), or extend beyond the realm of macroeconomic policy (joint measures to combat terrorism, to harmonize international fare schedules for air travel, and so on). *Third*, a judgment that gains from coordination are small presupposes some standard of comparison. Would the gains from international coordination be small relative to the gains from coordination of policies across different economic agencies within a national government? *Fourth*, empirical estimates of gains from coordination have typically compared policies that do not exploit the incentive governments have to adhere to agreements in order to enhance their reputation for consistency. Currie, Levine, and Vidalis (1987) argue, in contrast, that comparison of "reputational" policies shows large gains. *Fifth*, the danger that coordination may reduce welfare because policymakers use the wrong model(s) is greatest if they ignore model uncertainty. If, however, policymakers recognize that they do not know the true model and take this uncertainty into account, policy may be set in a more cautious fashion, with positive effects on the gains from coordination.[60]

The second strain of the empirical literature attempts to quantify the effects of specific policy proposals (such as the introduction of target zones) by comparing them either with a baseline that describes the current policy stance, or with historical values for the macroeconomic variables of interest. This typically involves the simulation of a global econometric model. Such an application of models is still in its infancy. To date, most attention has been paid to rule-based proposals for policy coordination that focus on real effective exchange rates. Two examples of such studies are Edison, Miller, and Williamson (1987) and Currie and Wren-Lewis (1987). They compare simulated outcomes of cooperative policy rules to recent historical experience. Both of these studies, however, are open to the classic Lucas (1976) critique that, due to the endogeneity of expectations of economic agents, as well as other endogenous responses to the policy regime, estimates of "structural parameters" will differ under different policy regimes; in these studies, expectations are formed in a mechanistic fashion—independent of the policy regime.

---

[59]See Schultze (1987) and Bryant and others (1988). As an example of the difficulties associated wth identifying the "counterfactual," contrast Feldstein's (1987) appraisal of the likely evaluation of exchange rates in the absence of the Plaza Agreement with that of Lamfalussy (1987).

[60]See Ghosh and Masson (1988).

This chapter reports some initial rule-based simulations from a global macroeconomic model developed in the Research Department of the Fund, called MULTIMOD. Two questions are addressed: *first*, would a smoother path of monetary and fiscal policies have produced a smoother path for real exchange rates, real output, and inflation than that observed historically; and *second*, what would be the variability of policy instruments under a simple or extended "target zone" scheme where the real effective exchange rate is treated as an intermediate target?[61] The "effects" of coordination are generated by comparing the counterfactual simulations to a baseline simulation where MULTIMOD is constrained to replicate the historical data over 1974–87 by including the appropriate residuals in each equation. These same residuals are also used in the counterfactual simulations, each of which postulates that policy would have been different in some way from its historical stance.

By virtue of using MULTIMOD for the simulations, this approach differs from earlier work in two important respects. One is that expectations are *forward looking* and reflect the stance of policy. This permits expectations to differ across different policy regimes.[62] For instance, if it is known that the monetary authorities will resist movements away from an "equilibrium" level for the exchange rate, then this will condition the value expected for the exchange rate in the future. In this sense, the results are less subject to the Lucas critique than previous work.[63] In a related vein, the model attributes complete credibility to the government's policy stance and assumes that the private sector forms its expectations in a fashion that turns out to be correct ex post. Thus, it gives a potentially powerful influence to changes in present and future policies. Second, although this section concentrates on the larger industrial countries, MULTIMOD contains a fully specified developing-country block.

---

[61] See Williamson (1985) and Williamson and Miller (1987).

[62] Another recent paper, Taylor (1986), considers different exchange rate arrangements in a rational expectations model; however, only completely fixed and freely floating exchange rates are compared, and the model is limited to the seven major industrial countries.

[63] The model simulations do not, however, allow for two other ways in which private sector behavior may be affected by changes in policy regimes. First, the variance of output, prices, or exchange rates may be different, leading to different degrees of substitutability among goods or assets. For example, it has been argued that the greater variability of exchange rates has led to a lower level of international trade than would have prevailed under fixed rates. Second, expectations may contain "speculative bubbles" in some circumstances, and hence may not solely reflect economic fundamentals. For example, the rise of the U.S. dollar early in 1985 despite declining interest rate differentials in favor of dollar-denominated assets is hard to explain.

Before proceeding to a capsule summary of MULTIMOD and to the simulations themselves, it is worth emphasizing a caveat. This paper is the first attempt to apply MULTIMOD to policy coordination issues. The results should, therefore, be considered tentative, preliminary, and relevant only to a few rule-based proposals. Much more will need to be learned over time about which aspects of the simulation are quite model specific, about the sensitivity of the conclusions to particular parameter values and historical periods, and about the effects of alternative coordination proposals—including those that rely on *judgmental* or *discretionary* application of policies.

MULTIMOD is documented fully elsewhere and we will therefore limit ourselves here to describing its main features.[64] The model contains submodels for the three largest industrial countries separately—that is, for the United States, Japan, and the Federal Republic of Germany—for the remaining four Group of Seven countries as a group (France, the United Kingdom, Italy, and Canada), and for the remaining smaller industrial countries as a group. Developing countries (excluding the high-income oil exporters) are modeled as one region, but with some industrial disaggregation. Each of the country or regional submodels has equations explaining the components of aggregate demand as well as the supply of the various goods produced. The submodels are linked through trade and financial flows. The parameters of the behavioral equations are in most part estimated using annual data available since the early 1960s.

In the case of industrial countries, financial markets are assumed to exhibit both perfect capital mobility and perfect substitutability between assets denominated in different currencies.[65] Consequently, arbitrage conditions link the returns on long- and short-term bonds and on domestic and foreign bonds. Moreover, as suggested earlier, expectations are assumed to be forward looking, and to be consistent with the model's solution in future periods. Thus interest parity holds both ex ante and ex post in model simulations where future variables

---

[64]See Masson and others (1988).

[65]In contrast to the industrial countries, developing countries are not assumed to face perfect capital markets. Instead, the availability of financing reflects their ability to service debt, as measured by a ratio of their inflation-adjusted interest payments to the value of their exports. It is assumed that there is an upper limit to this ratio, beyond which the risk of nonrepayment becomes high, and consequently creditors would refuse to grant further new lending. As a result of the financing constraint, imports by developing countries are also constrained, tending to reduce both consumption and investment. The constraint on financing is, however, not solely based on current developments, but also reflects an assessment of future export prospects of developing countries; expected future exports are made to be consistent with the model's solution for those future exports.

Table 1. Spillovers from Changes in Fiscal and Monetary Policies in MULTIMOD
(First and third year, domestic and foreign effects)

Government Spending Increase of 1 Percent of GNP in 1988
(Temporary; each successive year is 70 percent of previous year's)

Country Taking Action		Real GDP in:[1]				Current balance of:[2]				Real effective exchange rate[1]			
		United States	Japan	Germany	Other G-7 Countries	United States	Japan	Germany	Other G-7 Countries	United States	Japan	Germany	Other G-7 Countries
United States	First year	1.2	0.5	−0.1	0.2	−13	3	−1	3	1.5	−0.3	−0.1	−0.5
	Third year	0.6	0.1	0.1	0.6	−18	6	—	7	1.8	−0.2	−0.4	−0.6
Japan	First year	—	1.5	−0.1	0.1	1	−5	—	2	0.1	0.5	0.1	−0.3
	Third year	0.1	0.6	—	0.3	1	−8	1	4	−0.1	0.9	—	−0.4
Germany, Fed. Rep. of	First year	0.1	0.1	0.8	0.2	—	1	−6	2	−0.3	−0.2	0.7	−0.2
	Third year	0.1	0.2	0.3	0.2	2	—	−5	3	−0.4	−0.3	0.9	−0.2

Increase in Money Supply Target by 5 Percent Relative to Baseline

Country Taking Action		Real GDP in:[1]				Current balance of:[2]				Real effective exchange rate[1]			
		United States	Japan	Germany	Other G-7 Countries	United States	Japan	Germany	Other G-7 Countries	United States	Japan	Germany	Other G-7 Countries
United States	First year	1.2	−0.1	−0.3	−0.1	6	5	5	—	−3.8	0.6	1.4	0.6
	Third year	0.8	−0.1	−0.1	−0.1	6	5	6	−1	−2.1	0.3	1.0	0.3
Japan	First year	−0.1	1.1	−0.1	−0.3	−1	3	—	−1	0.4	−2.2	0.3	0.6
	Third year	−0.1	1.0	−0.1	−0.3	−1	6	−1	−4	0.3	−1.2	—	0.4
Germany, Fed. Rep. of	First year	−0.1	—	2.1	—	−1	—	—	1	1.2	0.8	−3.5	1.0
	Third year	−0.1	−0.1	1.1	−0.2	−1	−1	−1	−1	0.7	0.5	−1.8	0.5

[1] Percentage deviation from baseline.
[2] Deviation from baseline, in billions of dollars.

are correctly anticipated—that is, where there are no "surprises."[66] As a result, the change in the exchange rate between two currencies from one period to the next is determined by their interest differential prevailing in the first period.

Similarly, expected long-term bond rates and rates of inflation are also consistent with the model's solutions for future periods in the absence of further shocks. The rate of inflation—unlike prices in financial markets—is not assumed perfectly flexible. Instead, rigidities in wage and product markets make for persistent effects on output as a result of purely monetary shocks; only in the medium to long run will full employment result.[67] Thus, both monetary and fiscal policies of the industrial countries have significant and persistent effects on real variables, both in the country undertaking the policy change and in other countries.

In order to provide some feel for the properties of MULTIMOD, Table 1 shows the effects of monetary and fiscal policies in each of the three major countries on itself, on the other three major countries, and on the remaining Group of Seven countries. These policy changes are assumed to be *un*anticipated at the time of initiation. Two comments are in order about the results. *First*, and not surprisingly, policy actions taken by the United States have much larger spillover effects than those undertaken in Japan or in the Federal Republic of Germany. This reflects the large size of the U.S. economy and the fact that, while a relatively closed economy to imports, a relatively large share of its imports come from other Group of Seven countries. Japan is only roughly half as large (in terms of GNP) and obtains more of its imports from outside the Group sources. Germany is the most open but is smaller than Japan; the spillovers of its actions primarily affect other European countries. *Second*, while both monetary and fiscal policies have strong effects on domestic real output over the medium term, fiscal policy has a much larger own effect on the current account than does monetary policy.[68] This is because the output and relative price effects go in the *same* direction for a fiscal policy change, whereas they *offset* each other in the case of monetary policy. A fiscal expan-

---

[66]This is a feature that will be relaxed in future work—in particular, by imposing shocks to residuals in successive periods.

[67]Labor markets do not appear explicitly in the model, but features of wage bargaining, such as those due to overlapping multiperiod contracts, are reflected in the equation estimated for inflation.

[68]One strong implication of this empirical regularity is that any "assignment rule" that assigns monetary policy to the current account—for example, Williamson and Miller's (1987) blueprint—is going to face problems; on this point, see Genberg and Swoboda (1987) and Boughton (1988).

Chart 1. Money Growth Rates: Actual Values
(Percent change)

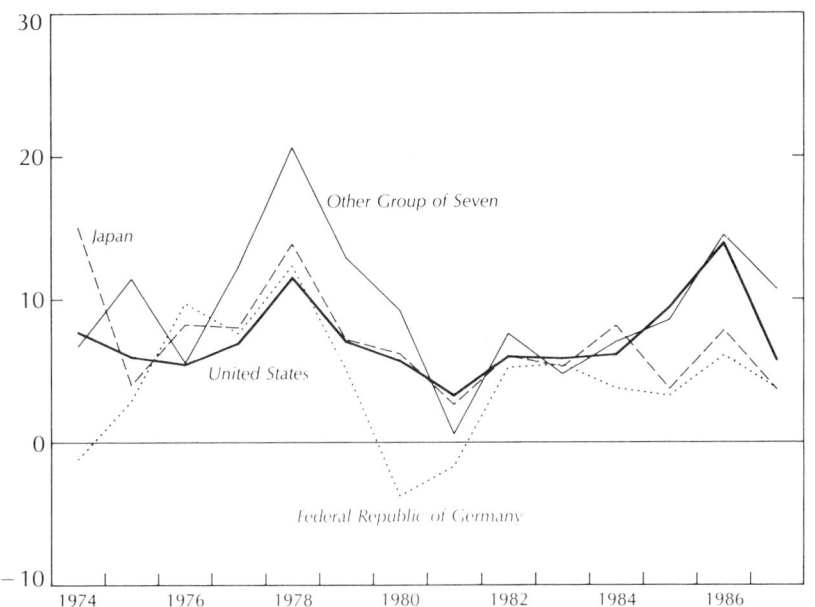

sion, for example, induces an appreciation of the real exchange rate and an increase in domestic demand—both of which lead to a fall in net exports.[69] In contrast, a monetary expansion yields a depreciation of the real exchange rate—which promotes net exports—and an increase in domestic demand—which penalizes them; because the relative-price effect dominates and the result is a small improvement in the current account—at least in the case of the United States and Japan.

One rather minimalist interpretation of coordination is that large countries should use their monetary and fiscal policies in a largely independent decentralized way but should avoid sharp changes in policy stance that would, in turn, generate sharp changes in real exchange rates. Such a concession to internalizing externalities would not affect the ultimate size of the stock adjustment of actual to desired policies but would constrain the *speed* of adjustment—much in the same spirit that speed limits in boat marinas discourage large boats

---

[69]It is assumed here that fiscal expansion is *not* accommodated by an increase in money growth. Current account effects also reflect the impact of interest rate changes on net investment income.

Chart 2. Government Spending Share: Actual Values
(Percent change)

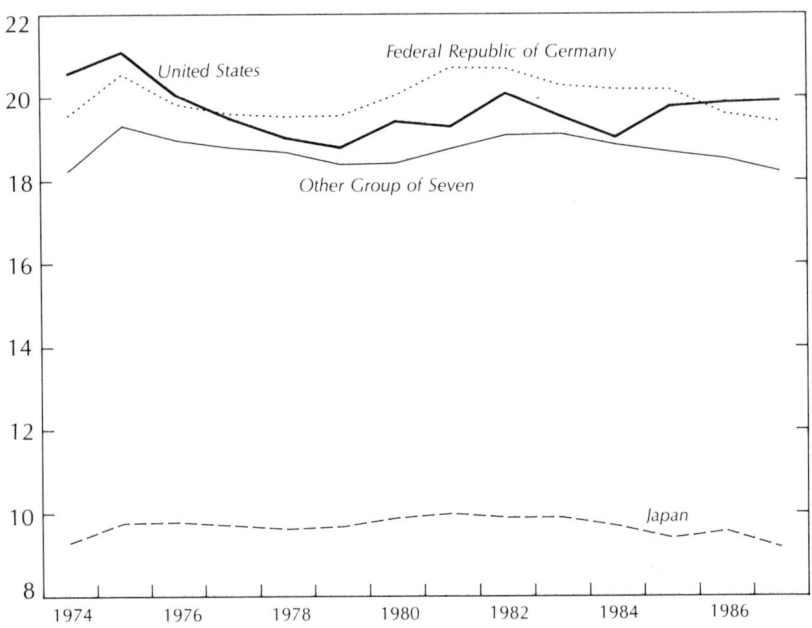

from producing wakes that would topple smaller boats. One exponent of "smoothing" guidelines is Corden (1986, p. 431), who states:[70]

> "If we accept that the spillover effects of a foreign fiscal policy change can be defined as the adverse effects of the destabilization of the real exchange rate, two implications follow.
> The most important implication is that each country benefits the other by maintaining relatively stable policies, meaning policies which will minimize real exchange-rate changes in either direction. Coordination consists essentially of a reciprocal agreement to modify policies that generate real exchange-rate instability."

Charts 1 to 3 summarize developments for some indicators of policy stance since the first full year of generalized floating (1974), while

---

[70]Niehans (1988, p. 215) also stresses the importance of steady policies: "The first, and most promising, step to reducing international disturbances must surely be the avoidance of the policy shifts that produce them. Especially for the dominant economy, the United States, the most important part of cooperation is steadiness."

Chart 3. Tax Rates: Actual Values
(In percent)

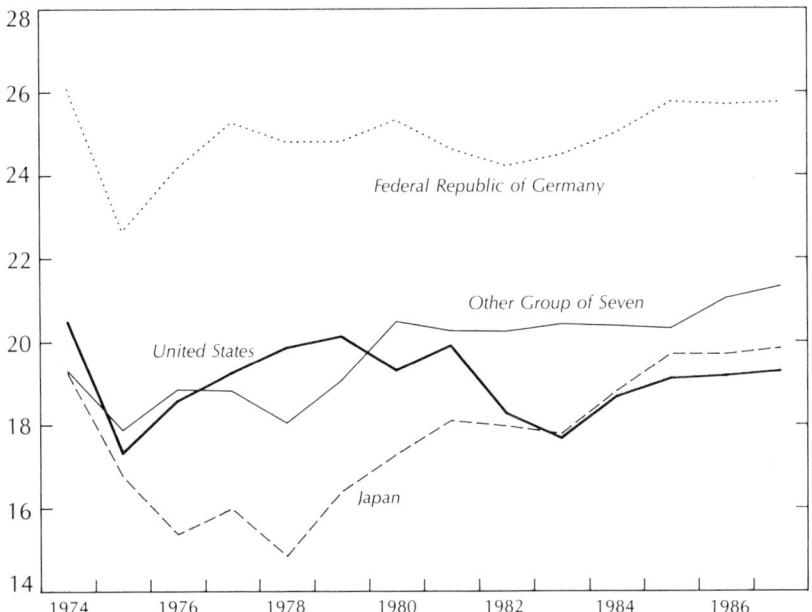

Chart 4 gives a measure of real effective exchange rates for the Group of Seven countries.[71] There are well-known difficulties in getting good policy indicators, including the problem that each of the series—money growth, the share of government purchases on goods and services in GNP, and the ratio of tax receipts less noninterest transfer payments to net national product and interest receipts—are all endogenous to some extent. It should also be emphasized that this historical period contains several different policy regimes, ranging from targeting of monetary aggregates over much of the earlier part of the period, to the strengthening of international economic policy coordination since the Plaza Agreement of September 1985.

Nevertheless, some useful stylized facts emerge from an examination of historical data. *First*, money growth rates are quite volatile and appear to be positively correlated across economies. *Second*, taxes net of transfers seem to exhibit more variation than government spending; evidence of fiscal stimulus in the United States in 1983 is clear.

---

[71]The measure of real effective exchange rate is the country's manufactured export price, divided by a weighted average export price of its competitors, including developing countries. Thus, an increase indicates appreciation.

Chart 4. Real Effective Exchange Rates: Actual Values
(Percentage deviation from 1980 value)

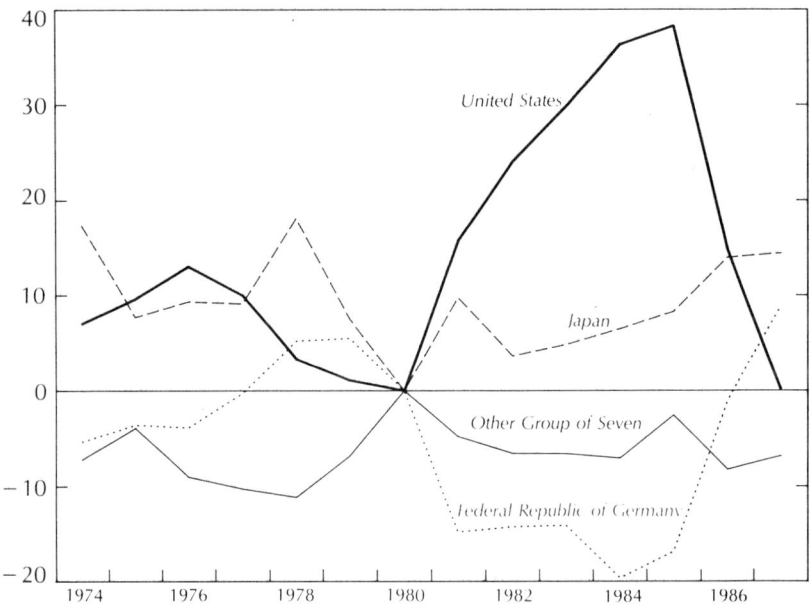

Finally, real exchange rates exhibit large fluctuations, especially for the United States.

To estimate the effects of "smoother" policies, each of the variables in Charts 1 to 3 was replaced by its five-year moving average. Those values then were input as exogenous variables into MULTIMOD and the values of endogenous variables were calculated.

Table 2 presents the mean and standard deviation of several macroeconomic indicators, comparing their historical values with those resulting from a simulation of smoother policies. Interestingly enough, smoothing of policy variables is nowhere near sufficient to produce smooth values for major macroeconomic variables. On the contrary, such a *simple* smoothing rule tends to accentuate some of the fluctuations in the historical data. For example, though the average growth of real gross domestic product is about the same as in the historical data, its standard deviation is higher in the policy smoothing simulation. Real effective exchange rates are somewhat less variable with smoothing, but real short-term interest rates are considerably more variable.

Table 2. MULTIMOD Simulations: Comparisons of Historical Policy Stance (1) with Values of Endogenous Variables when Money Growth, Tax Rates, and Stance of Government Spending in GDP are Smoothed (2)

Variable	Mean Values, 1974–87		Standard Deviations, 1974–87	
	(1)	(2)	(1)	(2)
Growth rate of real GDP				
United States	2.5	2.6	2.8	4.6
Japan	3.7	3.8	1.8	2.9
Germany, Fed. Rep. of	1.9	2.0	1.9	3.6
Other Group of Seven	2.2	2.4	1.4	3.0
Rate of inflation				
United States	6.5	7.4	3.0	3.0
Japan	5.0	6.5	6.0	5.9
Germany, Fed. Rep. of	3.9	4.5	2.1	.9
Other Group of Seven	10.2	11.4	5.4	6.1
Real effective exchange rate (1980 = 0)				
United States	14.6	16.3	12.9	11.7
Japan	9.4	9.3	5.2	5.1
Germany, Fed. Rep. of	−5.4	−5.1	9.1	8.9
Other Group of Seven	−6.6	−8.6	3.0	3.1
Real short-term interest rate				
United States	2.1	2.5	3.6	4.4
Japan	2.7	2.5	3.5	4.6
Germany, Fed. Rep. of	2.9	2.7	2.4	3.1
Other Group of Seven	2.3	2.4	5.7	6.8

This simulation illustrates that smoothing policy instruments may lead to less, not more, smoothness in target variables. Other variables exogenous to the model are also a source of variation in output and exchange rates. The model simulation suggests that the random shocks over the historical period, including changes in nonpolicy variables such as oil production, have had a greater influence in producing swings in exchange rates and in economic activity than economic policy variables. The role of policy has been to accommodate partially those shocks. For instance, money growth rates were increased initially after the first and second oil price shocks, but a permanent increase was resisted. The basic point is that the variability of policy instruments has to a large degree been a *response* to shocks, rather than an exogenous source of instability;[72] put in other words, the historical period already contains considerable smoothing—albeit of a discretionary rather than rule-based variety—and therefore attempts to impose additional smoothing on top of it do not produce salutary effects.

Note also that real effective exchange rates take on values in this simulation that are very similar to the historical data, though they are somewhat less volatile when policy is smoothed. There seems to be little support here for the notion that exchange rate stability can be achieved *solely* through the application of simple mechanistic smoothing rules. Recall, however, that the smoothing simulation has only considered a change in the *path* of policy variables—leaving their end points unchanged—rather than a permanent change in those variables. A permanent increase in the rate of money growth or in the shares of taxes or government spending in output might have more powerful effects.

A more activist approach to the coordination of economic policies would go beyond smoothing. One such approach would be to postulate that monetary authorities resist movements of an intermediate variable—in particular the real effective exchange rate—from their long-run equilibrium levels. A system of *target zones* for exchange rates has been proposed by Williamson (1983 and 1985), and extended by Williamson and Miller (1987). The original proposal calculated "fundamental equilibrium exchange rates," and advocated the use of monetary policies to resist movements away from those rates. As explained by Williamson (1983, p. 56):

> "The basic focus of exchange rate management should be on estimating an appropriate value for the exchange rate and seeking to limit deviations from that value beyond a reasonable range (p. 47). . . . While other techniques, like sterilized intervention, may be able to give limited assistance, a serious commitment to exchange rate management leaves no realistic alternative to a willingness to direct monetary policy at least in part toward an exchange rate target."

More recently, Williamson and Miller (1987, p. 7) supplement the prescription that monetary policies be used to target real effective

---

[72]Corden (1986, p. 431) recognizes this to some extent: "[Coordination] means, incidentally, that if private investment in a country declines there should be some compensating increase in its fiscal deficit to modify the current account effect. It does not necessarily mean that a fiscal policy stance should be stable."

exchange rates with the assignment of fiscal policies to targets for the growth in domestic demand for the Group of Seven countries:

> "The basic argument is that a nominal income target fulfills the same function as a money supply rule, providing a 'nominal anchor' to prevent inflation from taking off and a guide to expectations, while avoiding the shocks to demand that come from variations in velocity. . . ."

In addition, the proposal, or "blueprint," specifies (p. 2) that:

> ". . . the average level of world (real) short-term interest rates should be revised up (down) if aggregated growth of nominal income is threatening to exceed (fall short of) the sum of the target growth of nominal demand for the participating countries."

Earlier simulation studies of target zones have been undertaken by Williamson and Miller (1987, Appendix C), based on Edison and others (1987). Those studies employed the Federal Board's multi-country model (MCM), which is characterized by adaptive expectations. As emphasized earlier, MULTIMOD uses model-consistent forward looking expectations—a difference that should produce different—and we would argue, more firmly grounded—answers.

Two simulations were performed—one for the original target zone proposal (labeled "target zones"), and one for target zones augmented by a rule for fiscal policy (labeled "blueprint"). The attempt was made to stay close to the spirit of the original proposals while still making a few minor modifications.

Much of the action in a target zone scheme centers around the *monetary reaction function* since it is monetary policy that is typically assigned to the exchange rate. In the standard version of MULTIMOD, the reaction function for short-term interest rates involves resisting movements away from an exogenous target for base money. The demand for base money, in turn, is assumed to depend on real GNP and on its deflator, with elasticities close to unity. When the effects of target zones are simulated, this term is retained but with a much lower weight than normal.[73] The "target zone" element in the reaction function is represented by the assumption that the short-term

---

[73]The role of this variable is to give a nominal anchor to the system. The inclusion of this term is also consistent with the intent of the blueprint proposal to make the level of interest rates depend (in an unspecified fashion) on the growth of aggregate GNP.

Chart 5. Real Effective Exchange Rates: Actual and Simulated Values
(Percentage deviation from 1980 value)

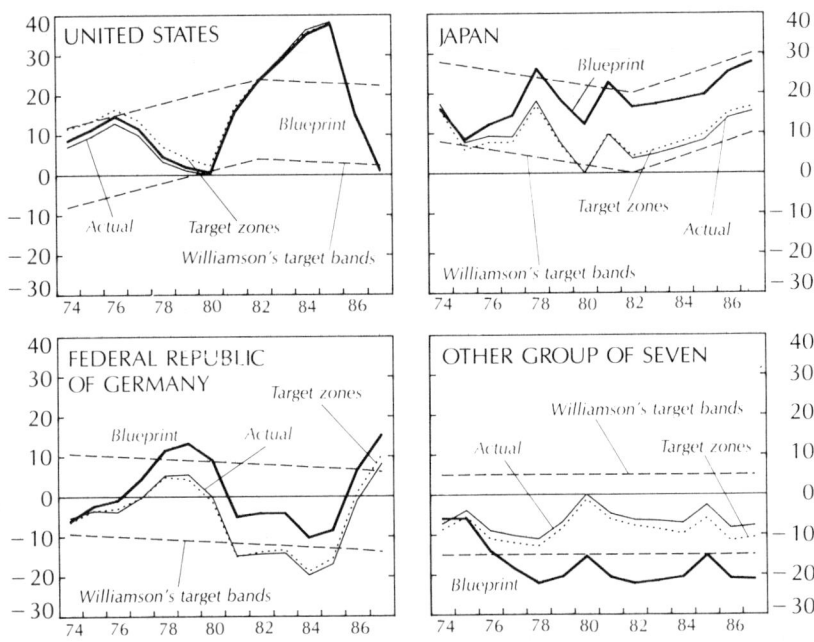

interest rate deviates from the baseline depending on the cube of the deviation of the real effective exchange rate from its target value.[74] Thus, the monetary policy rule used in both the target zone and blueprint simulations takes the following algebraic form:

(1) $r - r^b = [(c-\bar{c})/n]^3 + a\,[\bar{m}-m]$,

where, as in Edison and others (1987), r is the short-term rate, r^b is its baseline value, c is the log of the real effective exchange rate, $\bar{c}$ its target value, and n is half the width of the target zone, (namely, 10 percent). Then $\bar{m}$ is the target for the monetary base, m the long-run demand for the monetary base with baseline interest rates but simulated output and prices, and a is a negative constant.[75]

Targets for the real effective exchange rate were taken from Wil-

---

[74] Edison and others (1987, p.97).

[75] In implementing the rule, the value given by Edison and others (1987) to n, 10 percent, was initially tried, but the model either would not solve or gave negative nominal interest rates. Consequently a higher value, 20 percent, was used, implying a lower feedback of exchange rate misalignments on interest rates.

Chart 6. Rate of Growth of GNP: Actual and Simulated Values
(Percent change)

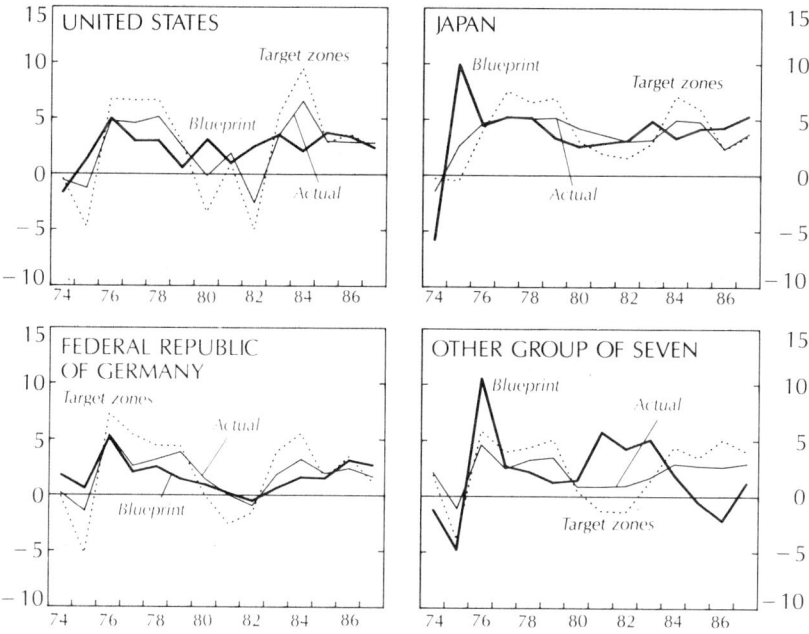

liamson (1985).[76] As in Edison and others (1987), an adjustment to the level of the target real effective rate is made to keep it compatible with the definition used in the model, but the constraint is imposed that the translated target exchange rate variable follow the same *path* as in Williamson (1985).[77]

As mentioned earlier, the "blueprint" proposes that fiscal policy follow a rule targeted on nominal domestic demand growth. As such, the equations in MULTIMOD for real government spending on goods and services had to be endogenized along such lines. The target paths for nominal domestic demand growth were taken from Williamson

---

[76] Again, we adopt Williamson's (1985) estimates of target or equilibrium real effective exchange rates merely to stay as close as possible to the original proposals. There should be no implication that we agree or disagree with those estimates.

[77] It should also be noted that MULTIMOD's definition of real effective exchange rates is wider than most measures, since it allows for competition from manufactures produced in developing countries.

and Miller (1987) for the period 1980–87; outside that period, we used their formula to calculate targets.

The main *results* of interest are portrayed in Charts 5 – 8, where actual (historical) values are compared to simulated values for the target zone proposal and for the blueprint proposal. The charts cover real effective exchange rates, real GNP growth rates, rates of inflation, and current account balances. Bands of 10 percent on each side of Williamson's fundamental equilibrium exchange rates have been drawn on Chart 5.

Several interesting—albeit tentative—conclusions emerge from the simulations.

First, there is surprisingly little success in limiting real exchange rate movements away from their targets, especially for the United States.[78] This is apparent for both the more limited assignment of monetary policy to target exchange rates and the case where fiscal policy is made endogenous, though not specifically for exchange rate targeting. Also, the cost of resisting exchange rate movements in terms of greater variability of nominal interest rates appears to be quite high in the model. In 1985, the short-term rate in the United States is 370 basis points below its baseline value in the target zones simulation, and 260 basis points above in the Federal Republic of Germany. An attempt to increase the feedback onto interest rates of real exchange rates produced explosive behavior in the model, and negative nominal interest rates. Why is the movement in real effective exchange rates so small? In the model, this is the result of the long-run neutrality of real variables with respect to monetary policy, and of the fact that monetary policy changes are *anticipated* in advance. A nominal depreciation resulting from anticipated monetary expansion leads quite soon to increases in import prices and domestic inflation, reducing the amount of real depreciation. Such a scenario has been discussed by Feldstein (1987, pp. 11–12) in the following terms:

> ". . . if the United States had agreed in 1983 to the demands of the French and others who wanted us to stop the dollar's rise . . . [it would have come about through] easier monetary policy [which] would have produced inflation and the inflation would have caused the dollar's nominal value to decline. In the end, there would have been no change in the real exchange rate or the trade deficit but a higher price level and a higher rate of inflation."

---

[78]It is also the case in Edison and others (1987) that real exchange rates under a target zone regime differ little from their historical values.

Chart 7. Rate of Inflation: Actual and Simulated Values
(Percent change)

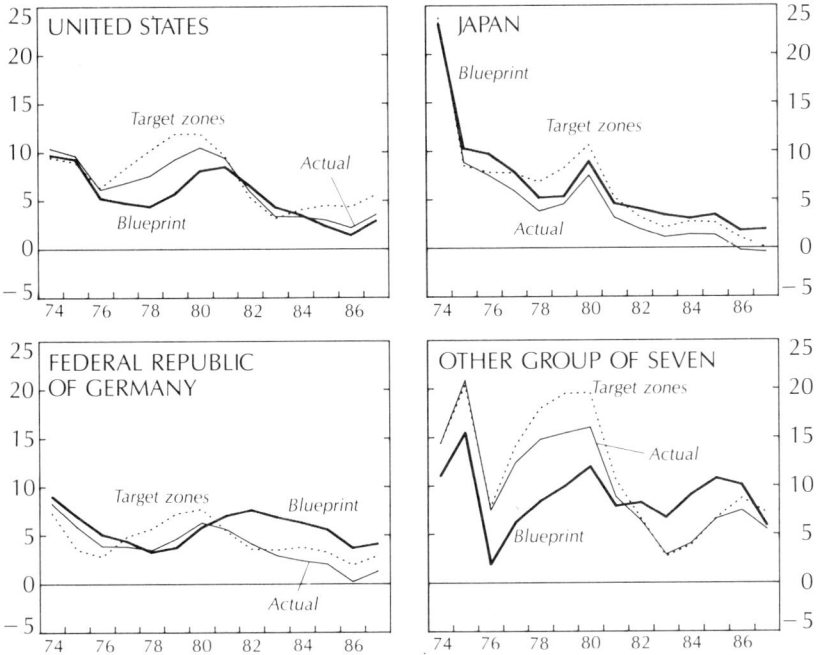

With perfect foresight of policy changes, the required movements in monetary policy may be quite large for even small, and transitory, real exchange rate changes. It can be seen from Chart 5 that the dollar's real effective exchange rate is judged by Williamson and Miller (1987) to be undervalued in 1978–80, but overvalued from 1982–85. Thus, interest rates have to rise in the earlier period but fall in the latter (relative to baseline). With perfect foresight, the amount they must rise in the earlier period is amplified because it is known that they will be lower later.[79] Note that monetary policy is effective in the model in

---

[79]Suppose there are three time periods, and that interest parity relates interest rates and exchange rates. Suppose also that the exchange rate is unchanged in the third period. In each period, the interest rate differential is equal to the appreciation that is expected (and actually occurs) next period. Thus, in terms of deviations from baseline, $d_t = e_{t+1} - e_t$, where $e_3 = 0$. Then in the second period, the interest differential will have to be equal to the desired change in the exchange rate; if it is overvalued by 5 percent, interest rates will have to be 5 percentage points lower. If in the first period the exchange rate is undervalued by 5 percent, then interest rates will have to be not 5, but 10 percentage points, higher.

the short run, provided that the money supply change is *un*anticipated. Table 1 indicates that an increase in the money supply of 5 percent causes a real effective depreciation in the first year ranging from 2 percent in the case of Germany to 4 percent in the United States; by the second-year, the depreciation has been reduced to 1 – 2 percent. If anticipated beforehand, the extent of the depreciation is further reduced.

In future work, we intend to relax the assumption that the shocks of the 1980s—as well as the policy reactions—are correctly anticipated when the simulation begins. Specifically, we plan to do an experiment where the values of exogenous variables are projected using information then available, and where in each period a drawing is made from the random errors in both policy reaction functions and in relationships describing private behavior. Expectations of future variables would thus be successively updated. This alternative method of simulation is discussed more fully below. It will be interesting to see whether this alternative expectations structure, which provides market participants with less information than assumed here, produces a significantly different outcome for exchange rate behavior under target zone proposals.

A *second* conclusion is that the use of monetary policy alone to maintain target zones—keeping the same stance of fiscal policy as in the baseline—seems to exacerbate the *inflationary* pressures of the late 1970s and early 1980s, and to lead to more variable inflation rates; see Chart 7. In this simulation, the United States eases monetary policy to prevent the dollar's appreciation in the 1980–85 period; with perfect foresight of such a policy stance, inflation rises somewhat in the late 1970s in anticipation. Conversely, the dollar's undervaluation in 1987 (according to the calculated fundamental equilibrium exchange rate) requires a tightening of policy, which tends to lower inflation rates in the mid-1980s below baseline levels.

The substantial effects on real variables in the blueprint simulation appear to be the result mainly of the fiscal rule. In the blueprint simulation, GNP growth is smoothed considerably in the United States and the Federal Republic of Germany; see Chart 6. The recession of 1982 and the high growth of domestic demand in the United States in 1984 are both smoothed out; U.S. GNP growth in 1984 is only 2.7 percent, compared to 7.2 percent historically, while the United States no longer experiences a recession in 1982. Moderation of sharp GNP movements is however not so evident for Japan and the other Group of Seven countries. Indeed, the non-U.S. Group of Seven countries experience large output variations in 1975–76 in the blueprint simulations. This may be a result of a mechanical application of

Chart 8. Current Balance as Ratio to GNP: Actual and Simulated Values
(Percent change)

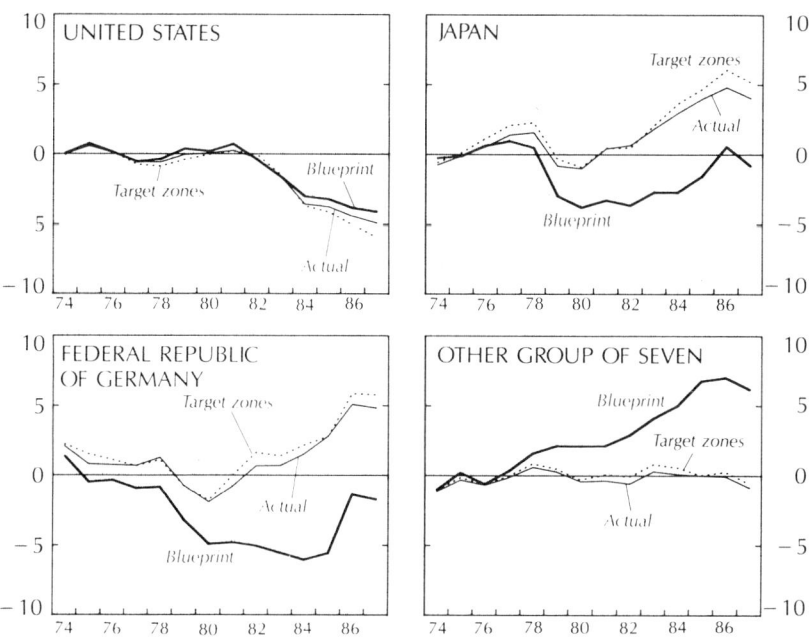

the Williamson-Miller formula for calculating nominal demand targets; if adjusted in an ad hoc fashion (as is done in Williamson and Miller (1987) for the second oil shock), a more reasonable path might result.

Third, current account imbalances are reduced for the major three countries in the blueprint simulation, in the sense of being closer to zero; see Chart 8. Most of the effects again come as a result of the changes in fiscal stance. In particular, targets for domestic demand growth in Germany and Japan are consistently *above* the historical values, and this leads to a much more stimulative fiscal policy in these countries (see Williamson and Miller (1987), Charts 4 and 5). But again, there is a cost. General government fiscal deficits reach 10 percent of GNP in Germany and 8 percent in Japan in the early 1980s! By the same token, it is the fiscal stimulus—rather than the monetary policy change—that is the cause of the sizable appreciation of the yen and deutsche mark in the 1980s relative to baseline. Clearly, such large deficits would be neither desirable—nor tolerable politically. It is also noteworthy that the counterpart to the smaller current account surpluses in Germany and Japan is larger surpluses in the other Group of Seven countries, rather than a reduction of U.S. deficits. This occurs because a weighted average of domestic demand targets for France, the United Kingdom, Italy, and Canada in Williamson and Miller (1987) is consistently *lower* than actual demand over the period 1974–87.

In concluding this discussion, we reiterate that it is important *not* to read too much into these preliminary simulation results—for at least three reasons.

To begin with, and harking back to our earlier discussion about the *quality* of coordination, it would be inappropriate to generalize about the effects of more *judgmental* discretionary approaches to coordination from simulations of more mechanical rule-based coordination proposals.

Second, we need to obtain more information on the robustness of our preliminary findings with respect to alternative assumptions about the relationship between interest rates and exchange rates, and to alternative targets for real effective exchange rates and nominal domestic demand growth. In a similar vein, it would be useful to employ MULTIMOD to draw out the implications of alternative coordination proposals for the *developing countries*.

Finally, *the method* of simulating alternative policies itself requires further study. It is sufficient here to note just two of the avenues that might be explored in further work.

Instead of recreating history by using the same residuals as in the historical data, it could be revealing to do many simulations based on different drawings from the distribution of the error terms present in the historical data. Such repeated *stochastic* simulations avoid the criticism that a policy rule may be appropriate only to a particular historical episode, rather than to fundamental features of the economy.

A second avenue is to delve more deeply into the nature of policy guidelines and rules, and how these relate to historical experience. One way to tackle this problem would be to assume that actual policy over the historical period could be described by an estimated reaction function, with a systematic part (that is a function of observable variables) and a random part. In one set of simulations, the systematic part of the policy rule (that is, the "feedback rule," including the variables targeted and their coefficients) would be changed but the random part would be left unchanged. The argument here would be that the random part represents either a component of discretionary behavior or errors in implementing policy, and that this random element would remain under all policy regimes. In a second set of simulations, one would alternatively assume that any new policy rule would be implemented without error so that the random part is identically zero. The latter set of simulations could be viewed as too favorable to a new policy rule, while the first set would perhaps not be favorable enough. The two alternatives may therefore give reasonable bounds to the effects of new policies and may help us distinguish expectational errors from shocks to structural equations.

REFERENCES

Artis, Michael, and Sylvia Ostry, *International Economic Policy Coordination*, Chatham House Papers, No. 30, Royal Institute of International Affairs (London: Routledge and Kegan Paul, 1986).

Bockelmann, H., "The Need for Worldwide Coordination of Economic Policies." Paper presented at conference on "Financing the World Economy in the Nineties," School for Banking and Finance, Tilburg University, Tilburg, March 1988.

Boughton, James, "Policy Assignment Strategies with Somewhat Flexible Exchange Rates," International Monetary Fund Working Paper, 1988, forthcoming.

Bryant, Ralph, and others, eds., *Empirical Macroeconomics for Interdependent Economies* (Washington: The Brookings Institution, 1988).

Bryant, Ralph, and Richard Portes, eds., *Global Macroeconomics: Policy Conflict and Cooperation* (London: Macmillan, 1987).

Buiter, Willem H., and Richard C. Marston, eds., *International Economic Policy Coordination* (New York: Cambridge University Press, 1985).

Calvo, Guillermo A., "On the Time Consistency of Optimal Policy in a Monetary Economy," *Econometrica* (Evanston, Illinois), No. 46 (November 1978), pp. 1411–28.

Cooper, Richard N., "The Gold Standard: Historical Facts and Future Prospects," *Brookings Papers on Economic Activity: 1* (1982), The Brookings Institution (Washington), pp. 1–45.

———, "Economic Interdependence and Coordination of Economic Policies," in Ronald Jones and Peter Kenen, eds., *Handbook of International Economics* (Amsterdam: North-Holland, 1984) Vol. 2, Chapter 23, pp. 1194–1234.

———, "International Economic Cooperation: Is It Desirable? Is It Likely?," Lecture presented at International Monetary Fund, October 1987.

———, "U.S. Macroeconomic Policy, 1986–88: Are the Models Useful?," in Bryant and others (1988), pp. 255–66.

Corden, W. Max., "The Logic of the International Monetary Non-System," in Fritz Machlup and others, eds., *Reflections on a Troubled World Economy*, Essays in Honour of Herbert Giersch (London: Macmillan, 1983), pp. 59–74.

_____ , "Fiscal Policies, Current Accounts and Real Exchange Rates: In Search of a Logic of International Policy Coordination," *Weltwirtschaftliches Archiv* (Tübingen), Vol. 122, No. 3 (1986), pp. 423–38.

Currie, David, Paul Levine, and Nicholas Vidalis, "Cooperative and Non-Cooperative Rules for Monetary and Fiscal Policy in an Empirical Two-Bloc Model,"in Bryant and Portes (1987).

_____ , and Simon Wren-Lewis, "Conflict and Cooperation in International Macroeconomic Policymaking: The Past Decade and Future Prospects"(unpublished, International Monetary Fund, December 1987).

Dini, Lamberto, "Cooperation and Conflict in Monetary and Trade Policies," International Management and Development Institute, U.S.-European Top Management Roundtable, Milan, February 19, 1988.

Edison, Hali J., Marcus H. Miller, and John Williamson, "On Evaluating and Extending the Target Zone Proposal," *Journal of Policy Modelling* (New York), No. 1 (Spring 1987), pp. 199–224.

Eichengreen, Barry, "Hegemonic Stability Theories of the International Monetary System," Discussion Paper No. 193, Centre for Economic Policy Research, London, July 1987.

Feldstein, Martin, "Distinguished Lecture on Economics in Government: Thinking about International Economic Coordination," *The Journal of Economic Perspectives* (Nashville, Tennessee), Vol. 2 (Spring 1988).

Fischer, Stanley, "International Macroeconomic Policy Coordination," NBER Working Paper No. 2224 (Cambridge, Massachusetts: National Bureau of Economic Research, May 1987).

Fleming, J. Marcus, "Domestic Financial Policies Under Fixed and Under Floating Exchange Rates," *Staff Papers*, International Monetary Fund (Washington), Vol. 9 (November 1962), pp. 369–79.

Flood, Robert, and Peter Garber, "Market Fundamentals Versus Price Level Bubbles: The First Tests," *Journal of Political Economy* (Chicago), Vol. 88 (August 1980), p. 745.

Frankel, Jeffrey, "Obstacles to International Macroeconomic Policy Coordination," International Monetary Fund Working Paper No. WP/87/29 (April 1987).

Frankel, Jacob A., "Current Problems of the International Monetary System: Reflections on European Monetary Integration," *Weltwirtschaftliches Archiv* (Tübingen), Vol. 3, No. 2 (1975), pp. 216–21.

_____ , "The Collapse of Purchasing Power Parities During the 1970's," *European Economic Review* (Amsterdam), Vol. 16 (May 1981), pp. 145–65.

_____ , *Turbulence in the Market for Foreign Exchange and Macroeconomic Policies*, The Henry Thornton Lecture, City University Centre for Banking and International Finance, London 1982.

_____ , "International Liquidity and Monetary Control," in George M. von Furstenberg, ed., *International Money and Credit: The Policy Roles* (Washington: International Monetary Fund, 1983).

_____ , "A Note on 'the Good Fix' and 'the Bad Fix'," *European Economic Review* (New York), Vol. 1–2 (June-July 1985).

―――――, "International Interdependence and the Constraints on Macroeconomic Policies," *Weltwirtschaftliches Archiv* (Tübingen), Vol. 122, No. 4 (1986).

―――――, and Morris Goldstein, "A Guide to Target Zones," *Staff Papers*, International Monetary Fund (Washington), Vol. 33 (December 1986), pp. 633–670.

―――――, and ―――――, "The International Monetary System: Developments and Prospects," Paper Presented to Cato Institute Conference, February 1988 (also *Cato Journal*, Fall 1988, forthcoming).

―――――, and Michael Mussa, "Asset Markets, Exchange Rates and the Balance of Payments," in Ronald W. Jones and Peter B. Kenen, eds., *Handbook of International Economics*, Vol. II (Amsterdam: North-Holland, 1984).

―――――, and Assaf Razin (1987a), "The Mundell-Fleming Model: A Quarter Century Later," *Staff Papers*, International Monetary Fund (Washington), Vol. 34, (December).

―――――, and ―――――, (1987b) *Fiscal Policies and the World Economy* (Cambridge: MIT Press).

Gavin, Michael, "Macroeconomic Policy Coordination under Alternative Exchange Rate Regimes" (unpublished, Federal Reserve Board, September 1986).

Genberg, Hans, and Alexander Swoboda, "The Current Account and the Policy Mix Under Flexible Exchange Rates," International Monetary Fund Working Paper No. WP/87/70, October 1987.

Ghosh, Atish R., and Paul R. Masson, "International Policy Coordination in a World with Model Uncertainty," *Staff Papers*, International Monetary Fund (Washington), Vol. 35 (June 1988), pp. 230–58.

Giavazzi, Francesco, and Alberto Giovannini, "The EMS and the Dollar," *Economic Policy Review* (April 1986), pp. 455–73.

―――――, and ―――――, "Interpreting the European Disinflation: The Role of the Exchange Rate Regime," *Información Comercial Española* (forthcoming, 1988).

Goldstein, Morris, *Have Flexible Exchange Rates Handicapped Macroeconomic Policy?*, Special Papers in International Economics No. 14, Princeton University (Princeton, New Jersey: Princeton University Press, June 1980).

―――――, *The Exchange Rate System: Lessons of the Past and Options for the Future*, IMF Occasional Paper No. 30 (Washington: International Monetary Fund, July 1984).

Gotur, Padma, "Effects of Exchange Rate Variability on Trade: Some Further Evidence," *Staff Papers*, International Monetary Fund (Washington), Vol. 32 (September 1985), pp. 475–512.

Hamada, Koichi, "Macroeconomic Strategy and Coordination Under Alternative Exchange Rates," in Rudiger Dornbusch and Jacob A. Frenkel, eds., *International Economic Policy: Theory and Evidence* (Baltimore: Johns Hopkins University Press, 1979), pp. 292–324.

Heller, H. Robert, Address before the International Economic Working Group in Washington, D.C., March 24, 1987.

Helliwell, John F., and Tim Padmore, "Empirical Studies of Macroeconomic Interdependence," in Ronald Jones and Peter Kenen, eds., *Handbook of International Economics* (Amsterdam: North-Holland, 1984), Vol. 2, Chapter 21, pp. 1107–51.

Holtham, Gerald, Giles Keating, and Peter Spencer, *EMS: Advance or Face Retreat* (London: Credit Suisse First Boston Ltd., 1987).

Horne, Jocelyn, and Paul R. Masson, "Scope and Limits of International Economic Cooperation and Policy Coordination," *Staff Papers*, International Monetary Fund (Washington), Vol. 35 (June 1988), pp. 259–96.

International Monetary Fund, *IMF Survey* (March 9, 1987), p. 73.

Johnson, Manuel H., "Recent Economic Developments and Indicators of Monetary Policy," Address before the Money Marketeers of New York University, New York, March 15, 1988 (unpublished, Washington, Board of Governors of the Federal Reserve System).

Jurgensen, Philippe, *Report of the Working Group on Exchange Market Intervention* (Washington: U.S. Treasury, 1983).

Kenen, Peter B., "Exchange Rates and Policy Coordination," Brookings Discussion Papers No. 61, The Brookings Institution (Washington, October 1987).

Kydland, F., and E. Prescott, "Rules Rather than Discretion: The Inconsistency of Optimal Plans," *Journal of Political Economy* (Chicago), Vol. 85 (June 1977), pp. 473–91.

Lamfalussy, Alexandre, "Current Account Imbalances in the Industrial World: Why They Matter," in Volcker and others, *International Monetary Cooperation* (1987).

Lucas, Robert, "Econometric Policy Evaluation: A Critique," in Karl Brunner and Allan H. Meltzer, eds., *The Phillips Curve and Labor Markets*, Carnegie-Rochester Conference Series on Public Policy 1 (Amsterdam: North-Holland, 1976), pp. 19–46.

Masson, Paul R., Steven Symansky, Richard Haas, and Michael Dooley, "MULTIMOD: A Multi-Region Econometric Model," in International Monetary Fund, *Staff Studies for the World Economic Outlook* (Washington: International Monetary Fund, 1988).

McKibbin, Warwick J., and Jeffrey D. Sachs, "Coordination of Monetary and Fiscal Policies in the Industrial Countries," in Jacob A. Frenkel, ed., *International Aspects of Fiscal Policy* (Chicago: University of Chicago Press, 1988).

Mundell, Robert A., "The Monetary Dynamics of International Adjustment under Fixed and Flexible Exchange Rates," *Quarterly Journal of Economics* (New York), Vol. 74 (May 1960), pp. 227–57.

―――――, *The Dollar and the Policy Mix*, Essays in International Finance No. 85 (Princeton, New Jersey: Princeton University Press, May 1971).

Mussa, Michael, *The Role of Official Intervention*, Group of Thirty Occasional Paper No. 6 (New York, Group of Thirty, 1981).

Niehans, Jurg, "Generating International Disturbances," in Y. Suzuki and M. Okabe, eds., *Toward a World of Economic Stability: Optimal Monetary Framework and Policy* (Tokyo: University of Tokyo Press, 1987), pp. 181–218.

Oudiz, Gilles, and Jeffrey D. Sachs, "Macroeconomic Policy Coordination among the Industrial Economies," *Brookings Papers on Economic Activity*: 1 (1984), The Brookings Institution (Washington), pp. 1–75.

Poehl, Karl Otto, "Cooperation—A Keystone for the Stability of the International Monetary System," First Arthur Burns Memorial Lecture, at the American Council on Germany, New York, November 2, 1987.

Polak, Jacques J., *Coordination of National Economic Policies*, Group of Thirty, Occasional Paper No. 7 (New York, Group of Thirty, 1981).

———, "Economic Policy Objectives in the Major Industrial Countries and their Effects on Policymaking," in IMF and HWWA-Institut, *Economic Policy Coordination* (Washington: International Monetary Fund, 1988).

Putnam, Robert D., and Nicholas Bayne, *Hanging Together. The Seven-Power Summits* (Cambridge, Massachusetts: Harvard University Press, 1984).

Putnam, Robert D. and C. Randall Henning, "Bonn Summit of 1978: How Does International Economic Policy Coordination Actually Work?" Brookings Discussion Papers in International Economics No. 53 (Washington: The Brookings Institution, October 1986).

Rogoff, Kenneth, "Can International Monetary Policy Cooperation be Counterproductive?" *Journal of International Economics* (Amsterdam), Vol. 18 (May 1985), pp. 199–217.

Schultze, Charles, "Prepared Remarks: Macroeconomic Policy," in Martin Feldstein, ed., *International Economic Cooperation* (forthcoming, Chicago: University of Chicago Press, 1988).

Stein, Herbert, "International Coordination of Economic Policy," *The AEI Economist* (Washington: The American Enterprise Institute, August 1987).

Tanzi, Vito, "Fiscal Policy and International Coordination: Current and Future Issues," Conference on Fiscal Policy, Economic Adjustment, and Financial Markets, Boconni University, January 27–30, 1988.

Taylor, John, "An Econometric Evaluation of International Monetary Policy Rules: Fixed versus Flexible Exchange Rates" (mimeographed, Stanford University, October 1986).

Tobin, James, "Agenda for International Coordination of Macroeconomic Policies," in Volcker and others (1987), pp. 61–69.

Triffin, Robert, *Gold and the Dollar Crisis: The Future of Convertibility* (New Haven, Connecticut: Yale University Press, 1960).

U.S. Congress, *Report to the Congress of the Commission on the Role of Gold in the Domestic and International Monetary Systems* (Washington: Government Printing Office, March 1982).

Vaubel, Roland, "International Collusion or Competition for Macroeconomic Policy Coordination? A Restatement," *Recherches Economiques de Louvain* (Louvain), Vol. 51 (December 1985), pp. 223–40.

Volcker, Paul A., and others, *International Monetary Cooperation: Essays in Honor of Henry C. Wallich*, Essays in International Finance No. 169 (Princeton, New Jersey: Princeton University Press, December 1987).

Wallich, Henry C., "Institutional Cooperation in the World Economy," in Jacob A. Frenkel and Michael Mussa, eds., *The World Economic System: Performance and Prospects* (Dover, Massachusetts: Auburn House, 1984), pp. 85–99.

Williamson, John, *The Exchange Rate System*, Institute for International Economics, Policy Analyses in International Economics, No. 5 (1983; second edition, 1985).

——— and Marcus H. Miller, *Targets and Indicators: A Blueprint for the International Coordination of Economic Policy*, Institute for International Economics, Policy Analyses in International Economics No. 22 (September 1987).

Comment

Jürg Niehans

1

Frenkel, Goldstein, and Masson provide a broad and rich survey of the manifold aspects of policy coordination. It is a very valuable and well-balanced survey, full of important points which would warrant detailed discussion. At the policy or strategy level, on the other hand, the paper is inconclusive and eclectic—no doubt intentionally and with good reasons. It is evident that at the present time the International Monetary Fund has not made up its mind what sort of leadership, if any, it wants to provide in international policy coordination.

In the few minutes allotted to me I find it difficult to do the paper justice at the level of technical detail, even more so as I only received the paper in the week of the conference. I shall thus go in the opposite direction, sketching the broad outlines of what I think might be a feasible strategy. I shall not try to be original but synthetic, distilling from the paper what it suggests to me.

2

The authors argue that the need for policy coordination arises from externalities. I am sure we can all agree. However, the argument is much more fundamental than the jargon word "externalities" suggests. Whatever men do almost invariably affects others, and human society is largely the result of efforts to cope with this problem. From this fundamental point of view the case for some sort of coordination is overwhelming. It is the methods which the controversy is about.

3

In general, the methods of coordination, as suggested by Frenkel, Goldstein, and Masson, seem to be of two basic types. One type consists of discretionary measures, taken ad hoc in an ever-changing sequence in the light of current developments. The other type of coordination relies on minimum rules, intended to remain constant over time, within which everyone is free to do what he (or she) wants and the others have to accept it. Obvious examples of discretionary coordination are the army and the firm, while civil and criminal codes exemplify rules coordination. It should be noted that the distinction has nothing to do with the presence or absence of sanctions, with enforceability. Both the army and criminal law rely on sanctions, and for both methods of coordination enforcement begins with moral suasion, continues with retaliation and social pressure, and ends with courts of law.

I believe that this general taxonomy is relevant also for the international coordination of macroeconomic policies, where the European Recovery Program would exemplify the discretionary approach while the Bretton Woods System was essentially based on rules. I shall, on balance, make a case for rules coordination and against discretionary coordination. It will be seen that the argument does not run along the line of Friedman's "rule versus discretion" issue. In fact, I favor rules at the international level precisely to allow national policymakers to use discretion if they so wish.

4

Let me begin with the case for discretionary coordination. It is based on a general proposition: in any given model, the optimal outcome with discretionary coordination is at least as good as in the absence of coordination and in many cases it is better. As a consequence, the specialists on welfare theory, game theory, and, in particular, differential games are always likely to find that discretionary policy coordination is the source of potential gains, large or small.

5

On the other hand, there is also a case against discretionary coordination.
(1) First, if coordination is itself costly, it is no longer true that it cannot make matters worse; its costs may exceed its benefits. I do not believe, though, that this is a very weighty objection, since the costs of conferences, experts, and game theorists are probably not very large compared to the potential benefits they seem to promise.
(2) Second, and more importantly, the proposition that coordination cannot hurt is only valid within a given model. However, even the

best models that have been built include no more than tiny fragments of reality and most of them are far from reflecting even what is already known about international monetary dynamics. In this situation, it is quite likely that coordination efforts guided by those models will turn out to be entirely misguided in practice. In fact, the main source of disturbances is faulty economics. (Branson has alluded to this in his paper, and the unfortunate "locomotive theory" of the late 1970s is a telling example.) Economists' welfare functions are naive and summit economics tends to be obsolete. The more effective discretionary policy is, the more damage it is likely to do.

(3) Third, in general, human affairs discretionary coordination tends to be used where there is some sort of common executive. In fact, men have created or accepted executive governments precisely for the sake of discretionary coordination. In those areas, on the other hand, in which there is no common executive, mankind has usually found it wise to rely on rules.

(4) In the absence of a supernational government, discretionary coordination is, in fact, likely to be impossible. The more democratic a government is, the more difficult it will find it to suspend its democratic decision making for the sake of international coordination (as the authors emphasize). I see no way to "coordinate" the Swiss electorate or the U.S. House of Representatives. The idea of an international committee telling Congress and the Ways and Means Committee that they must raise taxes does not appeal to my sense of reality. Vibrant democracies cannot be coordinated.

(5) Discretionary coordination creates an inexhaustible source of policy conflicts. These conflicts will begin at the lowest technical levels, say with the construction of index numbers and the choice of indicators, and they will reach up to the highest level of summit decisions.

6

On balance I believe that the case for discretionary coordination is weak and the case against it quite strong.

Let me now state the case for rules, at first in general terms.

(1) Historical experience shows that the rules approach can be made to work (examples are provided by the gold standard, Bretton Woods and the European Monetary System.

(2) Rules can be introduced and experimented with in a piecemeal, pragmatic fashion, starting from the most elementary.

(3) Within the given rules, each government retains its freedom of action.

(4) This is the approach mankind has typically used to cope with

externalities in the absence of central planning by common executive government.

7

Of course, there is also a general case against the rules approach.
(1) Historical experience indicates that even the most simple rules are often violated. A telling example is the collapse of the Bretton Woods System because of the "benign neglect" by the United States. This objection is certainly relevant, but if simple rules are not implemented, discretionary coordination will fare even worse. And if the rules are not implemented, the world is still no worse off than if they had never been tried.
(2) Simple rules, moreover, may not be enough to avoid serious disturbances. This objection, too, has some force. In fact, expectations should not be too high and any perfectionism would be misplaced. It should nevertheless be possible to achieve a distinct progress. In fact, if the Phillips curve and its shifts had been understood in 1960 in the way they are understood today, the Bretton Woods System would probably still exist, performing most of the services we expect from coordination.

8

However, the case for or against the rules approach cannot really be conclusive in general terms. It has to be based on a specific set of rules. Ten years ago we would probably have been inclined to think that a monetary rule is enough, at least as a beginning. International disturbances seemed to be generated mostly by monetary policy. In the meantime we learned that shifts in fiscal policy may generate disturbances which are no less violent. In fact, they are more recalcitrant because purely monetary disturbances can ultimately be neutralized by prices, but fiscal disturbances may require huge international capital flows. (This is strongly confirmed by simulation studies, including those by Frenkel, Goldstein, and Masson.) In addition to a monetary rule we thus need a fiscal rule.

9

What should the monetary rule be? Historically, monetary rules used to relate to the price of some international asset like gold or foreign exchange. Eventually, the world may again return to such a system, and I would tend to regard a fixed rate system (with a rather wide "band") in some sense as ideal, as first best. For the time being, however, the western world is not ready for a fixed-rate system, simply because it has still not succeeded in putting its economies on a firm zero-inflation path.

To use monetary policy to stabilize real exchange rates, as envisaged by Williamson, would not only be unfeasible, but would be an almost sure-fire recipe for monetary instability (as we know at least since the discussion about the OPTICA proposal and as is confirmed by the simulations presented by Frenkel, Goldstein, and Masson).

For the present, it seems to me, we should be content with the most basic monetary rule, which is: "Conduct monetary policy in such a way that it creates neither long-run inflation nor long-run deflation." (Surprisingly, prices are hardly mentioned in the paper under discussion.) The case for such a rule would include the following points:
(1) It would eliminate one major source of international disturbances.
(2) It would require no sacrifice in long-run growth and employment.
(3) It would still leave central banks free to use discretionary measures over the short run and even to intervene in the foreign-exchange market.
(4) It is relatively easy in practice to implement this rule with the traditional means of monetary policy—we know how to control inflation, although the task is not completed.
(5) The rule should be acceptable over a wide spectrum of opinions about monetary policy, including those of monetarists, Keynesians, new classical macroeconomists and so on.

These points would have to be weighed against the following limitations of a zero-inflation rule:
(1) The rule does not guarantee stable exchange rates. However, if combined with an appropriate fiscal rule, the remaining disturbances are probably manageable. (An encouraging example is provided by the relative stability of the exchange rates between the Federal Republic of Germany, Switzerland, and Austria.)
(2) Zero inflation cannot be formulated as a binding commitment. This is indeed true, but it may be counted as a virtue rather than a vice. After all, we want to begin with pragmatic policy rules, not with international treaties and institutions.

10

The basic fiscal rule is more difficult to frame (as the authors make amply clear). Some propose to use fiscal policy to control interest differentials, which are in turn supposed to control capital flows and thus the trade balance. I believe this is based on faulty theory, reflecting a lack of understanding of capital flows. At the present time, I think it is best simply to postulate that fiscal policies, whatever they are, should be sustainable in the long run. A case can be made for such a fiscal rule.

(1) It would preclude large swings in desired foreign assets and thus the need for large capital flows in excess of sustainable levels.

(2) Such a rule would not preclude anticyclical policies from year to year.

(3) Finally, each government would remain free to choose between different patterns of taxes, expenditures, and debt.

The main argument against this fiscal rule is that it is not as specific as one would wish. This must be admitted, but the sustainability requirement would clearly exclude measures like the tax cut of 1981, which is precisely where the present problems began. Further precision could perhaps be added in the future.

In conclusion, I believe a feasible coordination strategy could be developed along the following lines:

(1) Limit policy coordination to the monetary rule of long-run price stability and to the fiscal rule of long-run sustainability.

(2) Use the means of international cooperation to hold countries to these rules.

(3) Revise and modify the rules in the light of experience.

This is close to the "minimalist" strategy sketched by Frenkel, Goldstein, and Masson (but their smoothing simulations fail to do it justice). I would expect it to produce a major step forward. If successful for five years, we would probably be close to the emergence of a new fixed-rate system grouped around the dollar.

Comment

John S. Flemming

The paper by Frenkel, Goldstein, and Masson is rich in insights and I found myself wanting to challenge statements on almost every page, but I restrict myself here to three principal themes.

The first relates to the essential issue of the externalities or public goods which lie at the heart of a case for explicit coordination. The nature of the market failures, which all can acknowledge in principle, is not clarified here. Markets can cope with the fact that there are fewer relative prices than goods, like tomatoes—why is the same not true of currencies?

Accepting the existence of spillovers, the authors recognize their asymmetry; large economies' policies have spillover effects on small economies whose own individual actions do not impinge significantly on large ones. Using the language of externalities, rather than public goods, the authors suggest that *internalizing* these effects requires only the getting together of the big *generators* of the external effects.

This is not true if the greater part of their spillover effects is, collectively, onto small countries, all of whom would have to be represented at a meeting where those effects were to be contained by a bargaining process. Of course there is a real problem of the costs of coordination in such a large group. The authors' solution is to choose a slightly larger group than otherwise and have it consider not only differences and imbalances within the group, but also indicators of the aggregated performance of the group.

It is certainly vital that attention not be restricted to indices like exchange rates and current account balances, which are entirely relative. They could appear to be satisfactory while group inflation and output performance were abysmal. Why, however, should one not have a relatively small group concern itself with aggregate indicators for a larger group?

The paper discusses a number of issues under the general heading of rules versus discretion. At this point in particular the authors' use of the word "coordination" to cover the whole spectrum of possible nonmarket interactions is unhelpful. Some of the less *dirigiste* structures would rely on indicators. It is suggested that rule-based reactions could not occur if there were multiple indicators. This seems to involve imposing unnecessarily tight restrictions on the admissible complexity of conditional or feedback rules.

The question whether a general preference for rules over discretion implies a *dirigiste* enforcement of coordination is an important one. Could one have rules of conduct, designed like good manners, to make for a smoother-running world economy?

For ten years international lawyers and maritime experts negotiated, under the auspices of the United Nations, a reformulation of the Law of the Sea. It was, after general agreement, to become mandatory if ratified by a certain number of states—a goal never achieved. I have had occasion to enquire whether this meant that all the effort had been wasted, and have been told that this was not so at all. The *model* will be extremely influential, and individual countries will be much more confident if their behavior is within the nonbinding rules rather than outside them. Arbitration in international disputes, and courts operating in grey areas of the conventional law will rely on its code, and so on. While there are not close analogues to all these features it is worth noting that rules can be useful even without formal enforcement machinery.

Finally I turn to the model simulations. I have great difficulty with the implications of the fact that, to meet the "Lucas critique" of policy simulation, and given the inadequate flexibility of alternative descriptive procedures, the model assumes both policy credibility and consistent expectations. Both of these are highly questionable as descriptions of the world.

Thus the simulation of alternative policies involves changing not only policy but the content of expectations; the starting point would have been different if policy had been credible, expectations rational, or (as we shall see) foresight perfect. I do not think that adding back the residuals from fitting a model with these features to the historical data period meets the bill. Consider, for instance, the simulation of smoother policies which are said not to produce a smoother outcome. It is quite possibile that the explanation lies entirely in the correlation between the policy effects and the historic residuals.

In the paper it is suggested that actual, discretionary policy must have been stabilizing although this involves a breach of the way in which credibility is assumed to operate. It is said that "the credibility of the government's policy stance" is assumed to be *complete*. I wonder how the modelers know, in the absence in some cases of unambiguous policy pronouncement, what the stance of policy was. What they must have done is to assume that agents knew from the start what (future) governments were going to do. Did this take the form of knowing their reaction functions? Or did agents know the contingencies to which the governments would react with their well-designed stabilization policies?

While the assumptions in this area are somewhat obscure, those in the capital market are very explicit: perfect markets and full compliance with arbitrage conditions. This is totally at variance with experience. While it can be argued that good models predicted that the U.S. dollar would fall from the beginning of 1985, as it did as its budget was brought under control, it is quite clear that interest differentials did not reflect this rational prospect as required by the arbitrage conditions (and welfare was probably raised by this breach).

I have already mentioned the simulation in which policy variables are smoothed by being replaced by their five-year moving averages. This is in an attempt to model the notion that good manners would involve "smooth" instrument trajectories. In a "new classical" world of flexible prices and clearing markets it is typically the *present value* of the path of future instrument values that is most important, at least for certain key instruments. This raises two issues which can be illustrated by reference to public expenditure.

Suppose expenditure has been growing and is expected to continue to do so, at 5 percent per annum. If I announce that from now on it is not to grow at all, the path of expenditure is "smooth" but its present value drops very sharply (at a 10 percent discount rate from twenty times the current level to ten times—present value is halved overnight). Perhaps we should interpret smoothness as applying to the growth rate, so that we should use the smoother sequence 5 percent, 4 percent, 3 percent, 2 percent, 1 percent, 0 percent—but this will have no significant effect on the drop in the present value (which now falls to twelve times the initial level of expenditure).

Thus smoothness is difficult to interpret, and even more difficult to achieve without unimaginable restrictions on governments' autonomy. These difficulties do not, of course, undermine the welfare economics argument (advanced by Robert Barro, among others) for ex ante smoothing of, for instance, tax rates—but the optimal rate in these cases jumps discretely on arrival of discrete quanta of "news."

The second point is that in a new classical model the smoothing of such policy instruments would have no effect on their present values and thus on behavior. The fact that it does in the simulation may be due, as mentioned above, to the correlation pattern with base-run residuals. Alternatively it highlights the deviation of the model from new classical assumptions despite those relating to capital market substitutability and arbitrage.

On the big issues, however, I do accept that interactions exist between national policies which are not fully traded. I do not, however, see any panaceas in either models or institutions, but I have some hope for the evolution of rules of national good housekeeping in forms which have desirable interactive properties and whose adoption will prove conducive to a smoother development of the world economy.

CHAPTER 5
Summary and Conclusions

Wilfried Guth

Economic Policy Objectives and Policymaking in the Major Industrial Countries

Jacques Polak's stimulating paper on this ambitious subject provided an ideal background for the discussion of the current issues on the national and international level.

Polak's knowledgeable analysis of the radical change in policy concepts over the past three decades and the associated change in the role of policy instruments found broad agreement, while his assessment of these developments attracted some qualifying comments. His thesis that there has been a clear retreat from activist demand management and ambitions of macroeconomic fine tuning was thoroughly confirmed in the course of the conference by participants who were or had been actively involved in policymaking. At the same time, some speakers insisted that, among the whole arsenal of economic policy tools, discretionary demand management cannot and should not be completely dismissed as an instrument in appropriate situations.

As to the underlying reasons for the pronounced shift among economic policy priorities and instruments in the late 1970s and the early 1980s, both Helmut Schlesinger and Martin Feldstein stressed the poor results and the adverse side effects of the previous activist government policies.

According to Schlesinger, the governments of the major industrial nations, regardless of their ideological background, had no choice but to concentrate on the fight against inflation and adopt more "conservative" structural policies in order to prevent further serious erosion of the free-market conditions in their economies. In his view, the industrial countries' impressive economic performance from the mid-1950s to the second half of the 1960s was in large measure attributable to the prevailing favorable supply-side conditions rather than to activist growth and employment policies. He recalled, inter alia, the very low level of commodity and energy prices and the beneficial effects of the rapidly expanding international trade and technology transfer.

In the discussion of present economic policy objectives and priorities, the question was repeatedly raised whether the emphasis on price stability was not receding somewhat in favor of growth as a primary goal. The calls for greater symmetry in the adjustment obligations within the European Monetary System (EMS) were mentioned as an indication of such a conceivable change in an environment of greatly reduced inflation and persistent high unemployment in many countries. On the other hand, there was a strong feeling that a relapse into post-Keynesian policy attitudes of the past was hardly in the offing and that the chastened view as to how growth could be promoted over the long term, which Polak mentioned in his paper, would continue to prevail among policymakers.

In this context, Schlesinger pointed out that economic growth was, after all, in his view not a final goal; instead he defined national prosperity, social peace, and the preservation of nature as primary concerns of the industrial nations.

As regards the role of policy instruments under the economic policy concepts of the 1980s, monetary policy has clearly assumed a major part in securing appropriate conditions for inflation-free long-term growth. In the discussion on the design of monetary policy, Feldstein expressed himself strongly in favor of targeting nominal GNP rather than monetary aggregates, as the GNP approach facilitated adjustment to unpredictable velocity changes. On the other hand, Jacob A. Frenkel mentioned the problem of large lags in statistical measurement and the usual necessity of substantial revisions as possible drawbacks to nominal income targeting and asked whether we were not potentially falling into a new trap of fine tuning as our notion of where the target should be may change over time. And Jacques Melitz suspected that nominal income targeting as opposed to money supply targeting might imply a greater risk of accommodative policies. Schlesinger, on his part, stressed that the Bundesbank has never treated its monetary targets as targets in their own right but has always regarded them literally as "intermediate targets." He was supported by Feldstein in advising pre-announced targets as a guide to the public's understanding of and confidence in monetary action.

Both Schlesinger and Feldstein rejected the idea of using nominal exchange rate targets as a guide for monetary policy. Feldstein pointed out that international trade and capital flows are affected by real magnitudes, that is, by real rather than nominal exchange rate changes, and he warned of the potential adverse effects on domestic economic targets of attempts to stabilize or otherwise influence (nominal) exchange rates through monetary policies. According to Schlesinger, the stabilization of nominal exchange rates was not a goal "in its own right" for the central banks of the major industrial countries, even though, more recently, they have tried to maintain orderly conditions in foreign exchange markets by coordinated interest rate policies and interventions. His argument that the major central banks' primary responsibility was the preservation of the domestic purchasing power of their currencies and that exchange rate targets could not provide a suitable nominal anchor for economic policy decisions in their countries was not challenged.

Turning to the other traditional instruments for demand management (besides monetary policy), the general demise of incomes policy because of its proven inflationary bias, as described by Polak, was not questioned or commented on at any length. In contrast, and not surprisingly, there was a great deal of discussion during the entire conference on the role of fiscal policy and the connected problem of the appropriate mix of monetary and fiscal policies. The fiscal rigidities resulting from the more critical view in the 1980s on government finance and the efficiency of the fiscal tool, which Polak so aptly traced in his paper, did not lead him or other members of our group to conclude that fiscal policy could be dismissed as an instrument for discretionary government action. On the contrary, since monetary policy was primarily responsible for medium-term price stability and its usability for other goals was correspondingly restricted, many speakers felt that fiscal policy had to play an instrumental role in influencing economic growth and promoting the necessary corrections of international payments imbalances.

In this context, Frenkel mentioned the growing recognition of and emphasis on fiscal interdependence, whereas some years ago the focus had clearly been on monetary interdependence through the exchange rate. He noted that still much of the analysis was in terms of the total size of budget deficits or current account deficits, and he suggested that more attention should be given to the components of these deficits or the quality of the underlying measures, which would also imply a distinction between government revenue and government spending.

This brings us to the role of structural policies. Polak's finding that such supply-side-oriented policies have moved to the foreground in today's macroeconomic policy concepts was evidenced by many contributions to the discussion throughout the conference. At the same time, his assessment that the results of the new policy stance have thus far generally been unimpressive, with the exception of the United Kingdom, was widely shared.

Is it lack of courage or concern for social peace which prevents politicians from taking more vigorous action in the fields of deregulation and privatization as well as in eliminating protection in the form of trade barriers and subsidies? This question was not fully answered. There was, however, a broad consensus that the possible role of international institutions or organizations in promoting structural adjustment in developed countries should not be overrated. Hans-Eckart Scharrer, who drew attention to the positive results of sectoral deregulation in a number of countries, pointed out that the benefits of supply-side-oriented policies were in fact being transmitted via the market mechanism, that is, through the competition among countries and regions for investments. By the same token, the project of a single European market based on the mutual recognition of national standards was welcomed by a good number of speakers as a means for speeding up the necessary improvement in supply-side conditions—not least in the Federal Republic of Germany, where progress on this score has clearly been disappointing so far.

Among the various instruments of microeconomic government policies, *structural* tax changes—as distinct from the traditional tax changes under the Keynesian fiscal policy concept—no doubt deserve attention, as the "competition" between tax reforms around the globe has clearly shown. Feldstein, therefore, found broad support when he stressed the important role of structural tax policies in the endeavor to improve resource allocation and long-term growth. Furthermore, he pointed out that in today's global environment of high capital mobility in which individual countries are largely unable to control their real interest rate, the demand for investment and the mix between consumption and investment can be influenced by targeted tax rules.

All in all, the need for determined efforts to improve supply-side conditions in industrial countries was uncontested and it was widely accepted that this was probably the only feasible approach at this moment to foster growth in Germany where the limit for further constructive action has been reached both in monetary and fiscal policy.

But as already indicated, some speakers (like William Branson and Wilhelm Nölling) clearly warned about the dangers of a distorted policy mix with an overemphasis on the supply side. And Heinrich Matthes reported on the concern of the EC Commission about Europe being caught in a "low-growth trap" and on the "two-handed strategy" it had designed to avoid this danger. He pointed out that the case for a strategy which attributed equal importance to demand and supply-side policies was more urgent today than ever; this is not only because of the aggravated center-periphery problem within the EMS but also in view of the 1992 exercise which will bring a big supply shock to the economy. Matthes believed that the full benefits of a single European market could only be reaped if the demand side was given serious reconsideration. According to Frenkel, structural policy and demand management via fiscal and monetary policies should be viewed as complementary rather than as subsidiary. He felt that structural policies should be seen as a means to provide the infrastructure and the credibility that are necessary for the effectiveness of conventional fiscal and monetary policies.

Capital Flows and Capital Market Innovations, and Impact on Economic Policies

These topics were the subject of a roundtable discussion chaired by Richard D. Erb, Deputy Managing Director of the Fund.[1] As it turned out, the Chairman's view that "the impact of economic policies on capital flows and capital market innovations" might perhaps have been a more appropriate title for their debate, was shared by the majority of the panelists.

According to Benedikt Fehr, international capital flows are generated in reaction to the more or less market-oriented domestic policies pursued in the major financial centers. If the volume or direction of such flows is considered to be disturbing, governments should, in his view, adjust their domestic policies rather than try to correct them at the international level through protectionist action or other dirigistic interventions aimed at influencing interest and exchange rates.

In his comments Horst Bockelmann pointed to our insufficient understanding of, and the failure thus far to master, the consequences of the evolving global financial market and the associated risk of instant transmission. He maintained that both economic policy coordination and national policymaking would have to be improved to cope with this situation, but was not certain that even then the manifold risks inherent in today's financial system could be effectively controlled.

Rolf Breuer commented on capital market innovations, which could be the reason for or the result of capital market imbalances (as is the case with swaps and futures). He pointed to the lack of transparency in this area, which complicated the task of policymakers and sug-

---

[1] Panelists: Horst Bockelmann, Head, Monetary and Economic Department, Bank for International Settlements; Rolf-E. Breuer, Member of the Board, Deutsche Bank AG, Frankfurt; Benedikt Fehr, Financial Journalist, *Frankfurter Allgemeine Zeitung*; Helen B. Junz, Deputy Director, Exchange and Trade Relations Department, International Monetary Fund; Heinrich Matthes, Deputy Director General, Commission of European Communities; Wilhelm Nölling, President Landeszentralbank; and Shijuro Ogata, Deputy Governor, Japan Development Bank.

gested that the supply of more extensive information on innovation-induced global capital flows would be a worthy matter for international cooperation.

Helen Junz remarked that, in the past, financial innovations had mainly been defensive action in an environment of instability. And she asked whether, in the current phase of genuine innovation, as capital restrictions are being lifted around the globe, we could expect innovations that would contribute to greater stability, for example, by supporting the debt strategy or by reducing transaction costs in the face of very high real interest rates. The answer would crucially depend on the further course of government policies.

Heinrich Matthes commented on the challenges facing the EMS in connection with the full capital liberalization that was envisaged. He recalled that the good performance of the exchange rate mechanism up to now had been warranted by the existence of interest rate differentials and by occasional realignments. And he stressed that financial liberalization would be incompatible with the EMS only if the authorities were to aim simultaneously at fewer exchange rate changes, smaller interest rate differentials, and divergent monetary policies. He concluded that the pressing task of closer policy coordination in the transition period to a single currency area could not be restricted to central banks but must be extended to the whole range of financial and economic policies with special emphasis on the supply side.

Wilhelm Nölling drew attention to the recent massive increase in the amount of trading and to the huge volumes of financial transactions that had clearly lost touch with real investment and production. Explicitly combining his question with a value judgment, he queried the advantages of and benefits from totally free financial markets and capital flows. He pointed to the adverse effects of high capital mobility on the effectiveness of monetary policies and on budgetary discipline. He doubted whether we had the necessary insight and appropriate instruments to control a crisis situation. Nölling suggested that we seriously try to get more information and pay attention to the findings of the Brady Report and its proposals.

In presenting the views of the Bank of Japan, Shijuro Ogata commented on the analytical problems in assessing monetary and financial developments as well as on the operational problems in the conduct of monetary policy in today's global financial system. Among the latter, he mentioned the difficult choice in central banks' day-to-day operations between responding to domestic stability needs and containing exchange rate changes, but also the impairment of the interest rate mechanism in the closely interlinked innovative markets.

This notwithstanding, he firmly believed that the trend toward liberalization, globalization, and innovation was irreversible. Since he considered capital flows to be a reflection of economic conditions and policies in the countries concerned, Ogata was strongly in favor of international macroeconomic policy coordination despite its undeniable deficiencies.

It is interesting and reassuring to note that none of the panelists nor any of the participants in the general discussion was in favor of reintroducing capital restrictions or throwing sand in the wheels in any other way. There was, however, general support for an enhanced and coordinated prudential supervision and for imposing sound rules of conduct so as to strengthen financial market structures.

In this context, the comments of Jürg Niehans on capital mobility deserve mention. He pointed out that the huge transaction volumes in today's international capital markets are a result of the highly perfected asset arbitrage. These arbitrage movements had hardly anything to do with actual international capital flows as measured in the financial statistics at an entirely different level. Such genuine capital flows took place between countries with inverse domestic savings/investment imbalances, that is, from countries with excess savings to those with excess investment. Niehans believed that the speed with which savings and investment in different countries reacted to disturbances was in actual fact much lower today than it was a hundred years ago, owing mainly to the longer gestation lags of investment. He pointed out that because of the low capital mobility very large changes in exchange rates and interest rates had been needed in order to achieve the international distribution of assets necessitated by the U.S. budget deficits that started in 1981. He concluded that we could only wish for a much higher capital mobility as this would help to reduce the adjustment problems generated by international disturbances.

International Adjustment and the Dollar: Policy Illusions and Economic Constraints

In his model-based comprehensive analysis of this topical issue William H. Branson arrived at the following main conclusions:
- A real depreciation of the dollar of about 15 percent, in effective terms (and from its level at the beginning of 1988), is needed to move the U.S. current account balance to equilibrium by the early 1990s.
- A real depreciation of the dollar is the very mechanism through which a shift in the fiscal mix between the United States and the rest

of the Group of Seven countries would restore international balance (whereas the view in official policy discussions seemed to be that fiscal contraction in the United States and a corresponding expansion in Europe and Japan could substitute for a further dollar depreciation).

- A preferable coordinated policy approach would be the combination of fiscal tightening in the United States and monetary (rather than fiscal) expansion abroad, as it would smooth the exchange rate path and reduce world real interest rates to the benefit of developing country debtors.

Branson's clear-cut presentation of a very complex issue provoked a differentiated and often controversial discussion.

The critical observations on some underlying assumptions in Branson's models (for example on elasticities) as well as his choice (and definition) of targets and variables are to a large extent covered in the contributions to this volume by Niels Thygesen, Alexander K. Swoboda, and Scharrer.

The considerations and conclusions in the general discussion that have a more direct bearing on the major countries' adjustment policies may be briefly summarized as follows:

It is extremely difficult if not impossible to determine reliably the *real* equilibrium exchange rate on which all models—and, of course, adjustment in reality—hinge. By the same token it is uncertain where we are on the adjustment path. From this, Feldstein concluded that the policymakers should not spend taxpayers' resources in trying to defend the current value of the dollar, whereas other speakers (Thygesen, Swoboda, Schlesinger, and Flemming, for example) felt that under the prevailing conditions there were valid reasons for the present Group of Seven policy stance on (nominal) exchange rates.

However, Branson's basic precept that fiscal policies aimed at external adjustment cannot substitute for (real) exchange rate changes was not seriously contested (unlike his projection of the dollar's movement over time in reaction to a U.S. budget cut). It was pointed out, though, that the central bank policy stance in the countries concerned played a decisive role for the relationship between fiscal policies and exchange rate changes.

Given the fact that there is a great amount of uncertainty about the "right" or sustainable dollar rate, participants felt that it should not be overlooked that conditional predictions of a further substantial fall of the dollar as given by Branson or other academics imply the danger of adversely affecting the confidence of the business community. The same is true with regard to potentially misleading statements from official parties on their exchange rate policy intentions. We should not forget that confidence is an essential ingredient of the willingness of industrialists to invest and thus of the chances for growth.

As to the scope of the international adjustment requirements, the view was widely shared that Branson's target of reducing the U.S. current account balance to zero by the early 1990s was unnecessarily ambitious and the medium-term adjustment constraints derived from his model were correspondingly overstated. Schlesinger saw no reason in this context why U.S. debt should not grow as long as it was kept in a sound relationship to GNP or exports. It might be useful for the United States itself and for the world if it were to remain a debtor country for a longer period. The near-term problem was how to establish a *sustainable* situation in a broad sense, that is including capital imports and exports, on the part of both the United States and the surplus countries.

In the discussion on policy options for promoting adjustment in the deficit and surplus countries, Branson's preference for a package with greater emphasis on fiscal contraction, that is, further progress in budget consolidation at the world level, found strong support in principle. On the other hand, Thygesen rightly pointed out that Branson's prescription for expansionary monetary policies abroad had already been followed in Japan and Germany and a further monetary expansion in these countries would be hazardous. Against this background, Morris Goldstein referred to a third possible package discussed in the Fund's *World Economic Outlook*—a combination of fiscal contraction in the United States with enhanced implementation of structural policies in the surplus countries aimed at increasing output. Doubtful as one may be about the progress we may reasonably expect in this area—even determined structural policies take time to become effective—one can only subscribe to the Fund's general formula, as stated by Frenkel, that what is needed is symmetry of action rather than symmetry of policy instruments.

What should be the role of trade policy in this context? In his comments on this question, Scharrer suggested that the downward adjustment of the dollar could be eased by the adoption of more liberal trade policies in Europe. His thesis was not generally endorsed, however. While everybody was clearly in favor of trade liberalization in its own right, some speakers warned about introducing this argument into the debate on macroeconomic adjustment and policy options to improve the U.S. current account deficit. The danger of a "symmetric argument" in support of protectionism in the United States was mentioned. In short, it was felt that the case for trade liberalization should be based on different grounds.

The controversial discussion on Branson's paper and on the Fund's

MULTIMOD presented by Goldstein, and extensively commented on by John Flemming on the following day, gave rise to some more general thoughts on the possibilities and limitations of econometric models as well as on their current role in forecasting and economic decision making. On the latter subject, the central bankers who participated in the conference reported that their banks had developed models of their own and encouraged the study of other models in order to gain a better understanding of this tool. The results of the models were used as background information and could help policymakers to clarify their minds, but did not serve as a basis for decision making.

Frenkel, one of the Fund experts working with such models, stressed that in his view their main role was to draw attention to the long-term implications of current developments and policy decisions. At the same time he admitted that experts had learned the hard way to be very modest about projections from mechanical models. It was therefore essential, to his mind, not to stick too narrowly to models but rather to rely on a continuous interaction between models and good judgment.

For the time being, the choice of appropriate (though necessarily imperfect) models will, no doubt, remain an essential issue in the international policy debate. The discussion of the Branson paper and the MULTIMOD presentation has clearly shown how difficult it will be to come to a common understanding on how economies work and which results the use of various instruments will have.

International Coordination of Economic Policies

The debate on this subject was based on two papers: Günter Großer's survey on the empirical evidence for the effects of policy coordination among the major industrial countries since the Rambouillet Summit meeting of 1975, and the conceptual paper of Frenkel, Goldstein, and Paul Robert Masson on the scope, methods, and effects of international policy coordination.

Großer aptly traced the changing course of international economic policy coordination since the mid-1970s and its underlying reasons and constraints. His methodological considerations indicated how difficult it is to clearly define and identify macroeconomic policy coordination and, even more, to evaluate its effects. These latter issues, which partly explain the diverging attitudes toward economic policy coordination, are further elaborated in Manuel Guitian's comments on Großer's paper.

The comprehensive survey by Frenkel, Goldstein, and Masson

SUMMARY AND CONCLUSIONS 211

served as a useful guide to an assessment of the potential risks and rewards of international economic policy coordination. The authors addressed the key issues of this highly complex undertaking in the field of political economy but refrained, understandably, from providing clear-cut answers on the policy or strategy level, as Jürg Niehans noted in his comment.

The discussion was greatly enriched by the contribution of firsthand information from participants who, like Toyoo Gyohten and Hans Tietmeyer, are or have been actively involved in international policy cooperation, and by their personal assessment of the further scope and direction of this process.

In view of the high degree of economic interdependence and, in particular, rapid world financial integration, it was generally felt that the question was not whether but how to cooperate. The versatile term "policy cooperation" was preferred by many speakers to the narrowly defined "coordination" featuring on the conference agenda, which could easily be associated with ambitious international demand management, along the lines of the Bonn Summit agreements in 1978.

Tietmeyer pointed out that cooperation among the major industrial nations had in recent years extended beyond mere coordination of macroeconomic policies to such issues as trade, development and debt, energy, and structural policy. And according to Gyohten the coordinated adjustment efforts of the Group of Five or the Group of Seven since the Plaza Accord of 1985 seemed to have moved recently to a third stage, in which the emphasis was on structural measures aimed at securing lasting adjustment (whereas the main thrust had initially been on the realignment of exchange rates and then on macroeconomic policy coordination geared to a shift in growth patterns). The practitioners' conception of a broad (and variable) scope of and for international cooperation was explicitly endorsed by various speakers from the academic world.

As far as the methods of international policy coordination are concerned, Niehans in his comments on the paper of Frenkel, Goldstein, and Masson examined the issue of rules versus discretion from a variety of aspects. On balance he opted for a limited number of simple rules on the international level that would allow national policymakers to use discretionary measures in the short run. His proposed macroeconomic coordination strategy relies on two basic (domestic) policy rules: the monetary rule of long-run price stability and the fiscal rule of long-run sustainability.

Not surprisingly, nobody had difficulties in accepting these basic long-term rules, but the question of how they should be implemented in the conduct of policy was raised in various respects. Tietmeyer stressed that rules needed to be sufficiently precise, that it mattered how they were defined and by whom. Branson pointed to the underlying analytical problem of the proposed fiscal rule by recalling the experience with the Reagan Administration's tax cuts in 1981, which would not have been prevented by this sustainability rule as they had been expected to lead to an increase in tax revenue. Alexander Swoboda, for his part, reflected on the advisability of some modest contingency rules for the discretionary part of Niehans' long-run scheme, possibly in the form of assignment rules à la Mundell-Fleming.

In connection with the discussion on rule-based versus discretionary forms of policy coordination, the classical issue of symmetry or burden-sharing was addressed by various speakers. It was pointed out, for example by Gyohten and Pieter Korteweg, that under the rules of Bretton Woods and the EMS the adjustment burden fell mainly on the deficit countries, whereas in the current discretionary coordination exercise among the Groups of Three, Five, or Seven, adjustment pressures seemed to be greater for the surplus countries, which are confronted with the threat of rising protectionism on their export markets and widespread international criticism.

This was seen in connection with the underlying structural asymmetry, that is, the great importance of the U.S. economy for the rest of the world on the one hand, and the small effects of economic performance and policies in the OECD partner countries on the United States and its external accounts on the other. As suggested by Großer, this issue of underlying asymmetry no doubt deserves consideration in the debate on the appropriate mixture of rules and discretion in international policy coordination and in the work of economists in this field.

Quite apart from the very modest measurable gains to be achieved by economic policy coordination, many speakers had their doubts about the current practice of the major industrial countries in this field. They expressed concern about a possible delay of urgent policy action and the creation of unjustified expectations among the general public in connection with summit meetings. It was feared that useful "competition of policies" could be crowded out by negotiated coordination. Renate Merklein pointed to the risk that short-term-oriented politicians might be induced to take joint decisions that would prove harmful in the longer term. She questioned, for instance, the wisdom of lowering the savings rates in the surplus countries in the current coordination exercise and recalled Gottfried Haberler's dictum that the world needs all the capital it can get.

Tietmeyer agreed that certain risks were involved in current international cooperation procedures, but at the same time he stressed the serious risks of noncooperation. The dialogue among the major countries on such issues as trade, agriculture, and the environment had helped to avoid bilateralism. Tietmeyer stressed that the Economic Summit was not a decision-making forum but could encourage new initiatives. In line with Shijuro Ogata, he felt that the yearly meetings provided the heads of state and government with a unique opportunity to focus their attention on problems in the international field that they did not normally deal with. The work on the decision-making level was carried out by the finance ministers and central bank governors of the five or seven major industrial countries, and the policies of the partner countries, for example in the fiscal field, had indeed been influenced by these international discussions. On the other hand, Tietmeyer did see room for improvement in cooperation procedures. To his mind, there should be less meetings, communiqués, and press conferences; it was the permanent work that was important.

The restriction of important decisions on international policy cooperation in the eighties to a small group of large industrial countries was mentioned with unease by several speakers. Polak raised the issue of the cost in terms of alternative solutions and expressed concern about the implications for the role of the IMF of the current, highly politicized, coordination by negotiation among half a dozen countries. He referred to the alternative approach of the Fund's country-by-country annual consultations, which covered all countries and, fundamentally, amounted to a judgment on whether economic policies were internationally satisfactory. Although there was also a political element in these consultations, they were at least based on the nonpolitical input of the Fund's staff. Polak felt that neither the international institutional approach nor the negotiations among a few major countries should be dispensed with entirely. But it was essential that a reasonable optimum be reached in the combination of the two endeavors. Failing serious efforts to this effect, there was a danger of the Fund's role being undermined.

Günter Grosche joined Polak in emphasizing that the Fund is called upon to help out in the cooperation among member states. He pointed out that the Fund was entrusted, in the framework of its surveillance task, with the promotion of a stable system of exchange rates based on sound monetary and financial rules, and that it advised its members accordingly. The implementation of such policy advice required leadership and public support. He expressed the hope that the forthcoming Annual Meeting in Berlin would raise public awareness of the Fund's role, not only in this issue, but also in international policy cooperation.

Conclusions

It is no easy undertaking to draw a few brief conclusions from the very rich and vivid discussion at our conference. All I will endeavor to do is to identify a few central points that seem of particular importance to me in the world of today.

- There was widespread, if not unanimous, agreement that the present situation of external and internal imbalances, particularly in the United States, has to be corrected and therefore does not provide a basis for any Bretton Woods-type or similar scheme of stabilizing real or nominal exchange rates. Such stabilization was not considered a primary goal of economic policy by any of the participants. This important conclusion of our conference was perhaps contrary to some expectations. On the other hand, most participants, in particular, central bankers and members of ministries of finance, expressed the view that it was essential to maintain orderly exchange markets and to stabilize the highly interdependent financial markets in general. Even those academics who favored a substantial further real depreciation of the dollar devoted a great deal of their thinking to the question how this correction could be smoothed or minimized. That is, of course, a much more limited endeavor than any Bretton Woods-type agreement.
- As to the policy instruments to be used to correct disequilibria and promote stable growth, there was widespread agreement that fiscal policy could not be dismissed, despite its rigidities. There was universal emphasis on the importance of supply-side policies, and the feeling prevailed that there was a clear need for courageous action in this field in a number of countries, in the Federal Republic of Germany in particular—but at the same time a certain amount of patience was required. In that sense the meeting differed in a very constructive way from some of the simplified discussions of the past on the responsibilities of surplus countries, in which it was said that these countries just had to grow faster by whatever means. It was generally accepted that there are no quick fixes in the present situation. That was not a spectacular conclusion, but an important one.
- On the highly topical subject of international policy cooperation and coordination, a very interesting result of our discussion was the clear dividing line drawn between the two terms. In sum,

there was great support for the concept of intensive cooperation and very little enthusiasm for coordination in the sense of macroeconomic fine-tuning, because it was generally felt that such coordination would not function well and was not even desirable. It was noteworthy in this context that all the government officials participating made it clear that their governments would not accept a system of quasi-automatic indicators obliging them to take specific macroeconomic action; the so-called objective indicators should be an analytical instrument and nothing more. Overambition in coordination could easily lead to disappointments and to the opposite of the desired results, namely, controversies between countries if the one tried to force the other into a position that was not in its "enlightened self-interest." Thus, a valuable result of this conference was that the seeming contradiction between prominent experts, like Feldstein, who were on record as being against international cooperation and all those in favor was resolved in a pragmatic and sensible way. I think none of the participants disagreed that our world today would not be manageable without great efforts in international cooperation, but it seems equally true that there is still great room for improvement in these endeavors. One could quote Goethe's Faust here: "Wer immer strebend sich bemüht, den können wir erlösen."

- In my interpretation of our discussion, the other seemingly great difference between proponents of discretionary policy coordination and those arguing for a rule-based approach also turned out not to be so fundamental. When Niehans described his "rules," which may also be regarded as policy goals—namely, monetary policy geared at price stability as the highest priority, avoiding inflation and deflation and fiscal policy following the same standard principles—the proponents of discretionary policies had no problems accepting that notion. As it turned out, the old slogan "stability begins at home" was not repudiated. There was general agreement that only governments that had achieved credibility on their home ground could engage in meaningful international cooperation.

At this point I wish to express my respect and admiration, and above all my gratitude, to all participants who through their astuteness, their vivid contributions, and, last but not least, their "discipline" made the conference such a pleasure to chair—and, I dare say, such a success. The organizers deserve great praise for assembling such an ideal mixture of professors, academics of the highest caliber, Fund officials, government officials, central bankers, journalists, and some free-lance people, if I may call them that, plus bankers like myself. Given this representation, we can claim in all modesty that we covered a very broad spectrum of today's thinking.

Needless to say, none of us entertained the illusion that we would arrive together at the clear-cut and perfect solutions to pending problems that had eluded others up to then; that was not the purpose or the ambition of the conference. But let me nevertheless express my belief that the conference made a valuable and constructive contribution to an important ongoing debate.

Appendix

NATIONAL ECONOMIC POLICIES AND THEIR IMPACT ON THE WORLD ECONOMY

Conference organized by the International Monetary Fund in co-sponsorship with the HWWA-Institut für Wirtschaftsforschung-Hamburg

May 5–7, 1988

Participants

Peter Bernholz	Institut für Sozialwissenschaften, University of Basel
Horst Bockelmann (Panelist)	Head, Monetary and Economic Department, Bank for International Settlements, Basel
William H. Branson (Author)	Woodrow Wilson School for International Affairs, Princeton University
Rolf-E. Breuer (Panelist)	Member of the Board, Deutsche Bank AG, Frankfurt
Marjorie Deane	*The Economist*, London
Richard D. Erb (Panel Chairman)	Deputy Managing Director, International Monetary Fund
Benedikt Fehr (Panelist)	*Frankfurter Allgemeine Zeitung*, Frankfurt
Martin Feldstein	Harvard University and President and Chief Executive Officer, National Bureau of Economic Research Inc., Cambridge, U.S.A.
John Flemming	Chief Economic Advisor to the Governor, Bank of England
Jacob A. Frenkel (Co-author)	Economic Counsellor and Director, Research Department, International Monetary Fund
Morris Goldstein (Co-author)	Deputy Director, Research Department, International Monetary Fund
Günter Grosche	Executive Director, International Monetary Fund
Günter Großer (Author)	Director, Department of World Business Trends, HWWA-Institut
Manuel Guitián (Discussant)	Deputy Director, European Department, International Monetary Fund
Wilfried Guth (Moderator)	Chairman, Supervisory Board, Deutsche Bank AG, Frankfurt

Toyoo Gyohten (Discussant)	Vice Minister of Finance, for International Affairs, Ministry of Finance, Tokyo
Rudolf Herlt	*Die Welt*, Hamburg
Andrew Hilton	President, Group for International Studies and Evaluation, U.K. Ltd.
Erik Hoffmeyer (Discussant)	Chairman, Board of Governors, Danmarks Nationalbank
Helen B. Junz (Panelist)	Deputy Director, Exchange and Trade Relations Department, International Monetary Fund
Pieter Korteweg	President of the Board of Management, Robeco Group, Rotterdam
Gisela Kurtz	Deutsche Bank AG, Frankfurt
Heinrich Matthes (Panelist)	Deputy Director General, Commission of the European Communities, Brussels
Jacques Melitz	National Institute of Statistics and Economic Studies, Paris
Renate Merklein	*Der Spiegel*, Hamburg
Jürg Niehans (Discussant)	Institute of Economics, University of Bern
Wilhelm Nölling (Panelist)	President, Landeszentralbank, Hamburg
Shijuro Ogata (Panelist)	Deputy Governor, Japan Development Bank, Tokyo
Jacques J. Polak (Author)	Director of Research (1958–80), Executive Director (1981–86), International Monetary Fund
Helmut Reincke	*Neue Zürcher Zeitung*, Zürich
Günter Rexrodt	Senator of Finance, Berlin
Hans-Eckart Scharrer (Discussant)	Director, Department of International Finance, Economic Relations Between Industrial Countries, HWWA-Institut
Karl Schiller	Professor of Economics (emer.), University of Hamburg, formerly Federal Minister of Finance and Economic Affairs
Helmut Schlesinger (Discussant)	Deputy Governor, Deutsche Bundesbank, Frankfurt
Hans-Jürgen Schmahl	Acting President, HWWA-Institut
Jürgen Schröder	Lehrstuhl für Volkswirtschaftslehre II, University of Mannheim
Alexander K. Swoboda (Discussant)	Graduate Institute of International Studies, Geneva

Hans Tietmeyer (Discussant)	State Secretary, Ministry of Finance, Bonn
Niels Thygesen (Discussant)	Institute of Economics, University of Copenhagen
Peter Torday	*Wall Street Journal, Europe*, London
Roland Vaubel	Lehrstuhl für Volkswirtschaftslehre III, University of Mannheim
Karl Wohlmut	University of Bremen, Institute of World Economics and International Management

Seminar Coordinators

Hellmut Hartmann	Chief Information Officer, Information Division, External Relations Department, International Monetary Fund
Otto G. Mayer	Chief, President's Office, General Coordination, HWWA-Institut
Hans-Gunter Schoop	Public Relations, HWWA-Institut